Rethinking Sexual Identity in Education

Rethinking Sexual Identity in Education

Susan Birden

ROWMAN & LITTLEFIELD PUBLISHERS, INC.
Lanham • Boulder • New York • Toronto • Oxford

ROWMAN & LITTLEFIELD PUBLISHERS, INC.

Published in the United States of America
by Rowman & Littlefield Publishers, Inc.
A wholly owned subsidiary of The Rowman & Littlefield Publishing Group, Inc.
4501 Forbes Boulevard, Suite 200, Lanham, Maryland 20706
www.rowmanlittlefield.com

PO Box 317, Oxford OX2 9RU, UK

British Library Cataloguing in Publication Information Available

Library of Congress Cataloging-in-Publication Data

Birden, Susan, 1955–
   Rethinking sexual identity in education / Susan Birden.
       p. cm. — (Curriculum, cultures, and (homo)sexualities)
   Includes bibliographical references and index.
   ISBN 0-7425-4294-7 (cloth : alk. paper) — ISBN 0-7425-4295-5 (pbk. : alk. paper)
   1. Homosexuality and education—United States. 2. Gender identity in
education—United States. 3. Education—Social aspects—United States. I. Title. II.
Series.
   LC192.6.B54 2005
   371.826'64—dc22
                              2004010039

Printed in the United States of America

♾™ The paper used in this publication meets the minimum requirements of
American National Standard for Information Sciences—Permanence of Paper for
Printed Library Materials, ANSI/NISO Z39.48-1992.

Contents

Preface

In S. E. Hinton's award-winning young adult novel, *The Outsiders*, we enter into the divided teenager world of 1960s Oklahoma. Here "greasers" and best buddies, Johnny Cade and Ponyboy Curtis—from poor or parentless families living on the east side of town, meet up with Cherry and Marcia whose "soc" (as in society and social) boyfriends are drunk and abusive. As the story unfolds, the two young women, who live in splendid west side homes along tree-lined Tulsa streets with parents who govern the community, first reject but then come to side with these "delinquents," as the lads "rumble" with their soc boyfriends angered about "messing with their women." When one of the boyfriends is killed in the melee, the lads hide out as comrades in arms and, in the process, confront the pervasiveness of class conflict, identity, and prejudice. Meanwhile, Cherry journeys into the outside, spying for the greasers and entering Ponyboy's world; the pair finds common ground in literature, pop music, and sunsets. But, she remains an outsider just as Ponyboy, reciting a Robert Frost poem, realizes life's temporality, the loss of boyhood innocence, and the collapse of his idyllic world by the weight of reality: "So Eden sank to grief. . . . Nothing gold can stay."

Susan Hinton, writing from the point-of-view of a male adolescent, was just a teenager when she began her novel in frustration over student conflicts at her Tulsa high school. In order to have credibility with readers of this tale about male bonding and violence, the publisher insisted on disguising her gender. Thus novel and novelist, fiction and reality, convey a theme of "those people who side with the out." This theme underlies *Rethinking Sexual Identity in Education*.

Like Hinton, Susan Birden employs biographical and autobiographical sources to explore an "Out-Siders' praxis" that can result in "radically different consequences" from those ordained by a conventional reading of identity—be it class, race, gender, or sexuality. It is the latter, however, that is the focus of Birden's book.

Rethinking Sexual Identity in Education examines six praxes of sexual identity, five of which have been used by "Out-Siders" to understand sexual diversity and to address soc's heteronormative environment, which, like Hinton's Tulsa, is girded by gender relations. The essentialist praxes of inclusion, coming out, and location, Birden argues, have more direct impact in "mitigating the effects of compulsory homosexuality" than the constructionist and postmodern praxes (refusal, performativity), which dominate academic discourse queering our conventional readings of sexuality. But, as with the greasers and socs, there has been little conversation between the activist and academic camps, resulting in lost opportunities for educating about sexual identity.

But, "What would happen if the real lives of lesbian and gay people were allowed to challenge the theories?" queries Birden. Answering this through the lens of pragmatism (just as Ponyboy and Cherry sought a pragmatic resolution to their rival groups' conflicts), *Rethinking Sexual Identity in Education* is a manual for educators that is as theoretically sound as it is strategically wise. Birden recognizes the pedagogical impact of settings that create or stimulate conversations across boundaries (theory/practice, gay/straight, introspection/action, liberal/conservative), which "forge new understandings among diverse people" generating personal insight, social justice, and community transformation.

Failing to engage in such border crossings—and to challenge not only the borderlines but the very concept of borders—is a failure to educate others and, more importantly, ourselves. As Ponyboy chided Cherry when she first rebuffed him at the drive-in: "It's okay. . . . We aren't in the same class. Just don't forget that some of us watch the sunset too." But let us not dally before "dawn goes down to day."

James T. Sears
Series Editor

Acknowledgments

I wish to thank series editor James T. Sears for both his support of this project and his scholarly trailblazing in the area of sexual identity and schooling. In addition, I appreciate the work of Jehanne Schweitzer and the editorial staff at Rowman & Littlefield for their expert editing and for guiding me through the production process with great kindness.

I am fortunate to have a community of friends and colleagues with whom I have discussed the ideas in this book. I particularly wish to thank Susan Laird, who made me believe that I had something worthwhile to say to the world and whose detailed critiques, provocative challenges, unstinting encouragement, and wise and witty commentary contributed greatly to this project. I also want to thank Joan K. Smith and Catherine Hobbs for their careful and thoughtful reading and helpful feedback on earlier drafts of this book, as well as Irene Karpiak and Connie Dillon for their receptivity and dialogue. Several friends have provided especially valuable personal support during the process of writing this book: Mary Ann Kavanaugh, Shirley Wunder, Alice Johnson, and Charlotte Smith. The shared meals and shared laughs revived me again and again.

I also want to thank my mother and late father, Myrtle and Lawrence Birden, who taught me to value learning. They created an environment that made my educational priorities their own, from spelling words and long division to music lessons and term papers. As a child I thought that was normal. As an educator I realize just how rare it was.

Most of all, I am deeply grateful to Colleen Kavanaugh, who has discussed the ideas in this book evening after evening, listened to my frustrations, celebrated my successes, and offered unflagging support and encouragement. Her friendship, perceptiveness, candor, and audacious spirit offer more than one could ask in intellectual and emotional companionship. This book is dedicated to her.

CHAPTER ONE

Compulsory Heterosexuality as Mis-education

Heterosexism: Alive and Well

The world is often a hostile place for gay and lesbian people. For every four teenagers who admit same-sex feelings to family members, one is forced out of the home or suffers physical abuse following the admission.[1] In urban areas of the country the problem has become so pronounced that those who self-identify as lesbian or gay constitute up to 40 percent of homeless teenagers.[2] The world of schooling—which requires the attendance of all youth and is charged with teaching, nurturing, developing minds and bodies, and serving as advocates for the young—has frequently proven itself to be even less hospitable than society at large. In fact, schools are primary sites for anti–lesbian and gay prejudice. An astounding 97 percent of youth surveyed report regularly hearing homophobic remarks from their peers.[3] Not only are homophobic remarks routine, but according to research conducted by the American Association of University Women, being called *lesbian* or *gay* is the most upsetting form of sexual harassment experienced by youth.[4] Over 90 percent of lesbian and gay teens have reported experiencing some type of verbal or physical abuse.[5]

While the pressures of coming into sexual identity are substantial for all adolescents, the foregoing examples demonstrate that the struggles for lesbian and gay teens are compounded by the psychological damage inflicted by years of bearing witness to, or experiencing, anti–lesbian and gay prejudice in countless forms. In the past several years lesbian and gay teens have become recognized as one of the nation's highest-risk groups. However, the risky behaviors that surface during the lesbians' and gays' teen years do not begin during adolescence. They are the product of a lifetime of learning in the hegemonic ideology of heterosexism.

In practice, heterosexist ideology is instilled through numerous mechanisms. Family members initiate children into heterosexist ideology almost from birth, teaching acceptable gendered conduct as well as uneasiness with cross-gendered behaviors. This education is reinforced and expanded by religious institutions, peer groups, and the media, where heterosexual love is presented as the only viable option while the value of nonheterosexual relationships is omitted entirely, denounced, or denigrated.

By the time children have reached first grade, they have already compiled a significant amount of data about what it means to be gay in a heterosexist society, even though much of what they have learned may well be incorrect, born of fear and prejudice rather than factual information.[6] Schools are in a unique position to correct much of this misinformation at an early age before it ripens into anti–lesbian and gay prejudice and violence. But public education in the United States has been placed in the unenviable position of serving the dichotomous and often mutually exclusive roles of preserving traditional values while promulgating desirable social evolution. The result has been that our nation's schools have repeatedly been used as a fierce battleground for divisive issues: coeducation, racial integration, sex education, immigrant education, and now issues surrounding sexual diversity.

When issues regarding lesbian and gay people surface in the context of schools, a host of players emerge who attempt to influence school policy by galvanizing public opinion and influencing legislative action. Often, however, sexual diversity issues never get as far as public debate. Schoolteachers and administrators routinely avoid such conflicts by conflating gay and lesbian identity with "talk about sex" and labeling both "age-inappropriate."[7]

Thus, while some school personnel, especially those in religious schools, may educate for compulsory heterosexuality through the curriculum proper, they more often become complicit without ever openly denigrating nonheterosexuals. Classroom silence about lesbian and gay identity speaks loudly, as does the mysterious deafness that school personnel often evidence in the presence of derogatory epithets. "Gay," "fag," and "homo" surface during a child's primary education. By the time he or she reaches high school, the child will hear such slurs over twenty-five times per day.[8] Misinformation propounded by the students themselves frequently goes uncorrected by teachers who are either afraid or unwilling to address students directly on issues of sexual identity. Research has revealed that a significant proportion of these missed educational opportunities is due not to animus against lesbian and gay people but to teachers' lack of knowledge and their feelings of ineffectiveness when addressing such highly charged issues.[9] Whether owing to ignorance, design, or benign neglect, these factors all contribute to a hidden curriculum of compulsory heterosexuality where every child is presumed heterosexual until proven otherwise.

I believe, as John Dewey states, "Schools are, indeed, one important method of the transmission which forms the disposition of the immature; but it is only one means, and, compared with other agencies, a relatively superficial means."[10] Certainly, schools are one "method of transmission" for heterosexist ideology, but as has been presented in the foregoing discussion, education for compulsory heterosexuality is not confined to the schoolhouse. Rather, it is provided across multiple configurations of education: schools intersecting with families, families overlapping with religious groups, religious groups influencing community groups.[11] On many issues these multiple configurations of education convey messages that are at odds with the values of another institution within a configuration or between configurations, creating educative and cognitive dissonance for the learners. However, when it comes to compulsory heterosexuality these multiple configurations— intersecting, overlapping, using varied styles and diverse "educators" in various formats—converge into amazing consonance.

The potency of the message of compulsory heterosexuality is not, of course, uniform within all populations. For instance, those who reside in the Midwest or the South, or who grew up in rural areas or in small towns, are more likely to harbor negative attitudes about lesbian and gay people than those who live in or were raised in other settings. Adult males tend to have more intense negative feelings than do females and are more concerned about gay males than they are about lesbianism. People with intense negative feelings toward lesbians and gays also tend to have more conservative religious ideology, more traditional attitudes about gender roles, and greater social prejudices as compared to those with less intense feelings toward lesbians and gays.[12] These findings are certainly subject to qualification and should not be used to generalize about specific individuals. For example, while males are generally more negative than females about homosexuality, men working as public school counselors express more positive feelings than do their female counterparts.[13] Nor do these generalizations suggest that New England, for instance, is without negative attitudes toward lesbian and gay people; rather, it suggests that, as a general rule, the intensity of negative emotions is not as great there as it is in the South. While intensity fluctuates, the consonance still remains throughout virtually all regions of the country and in all populations.

The consonance of the compulsory heterosexuality message has not been completely without challenge. In fact, the National Education Association (NEA) adopted a code of ethics in 1975 that specifically states how educators

> shall not on the basis of race, color, creed, sex, national origin, marital status, political or religious beliefs, family, social or cultural background, *or sexual orientation*, unfairly a) Exclude any student from participation in any program; b) Deny benefits to any student; c) Grant any advantage to any student.[14] [emphasis mine]

In 2000, the NEA emphasized this commitment to equality by adopting resolution B-9, "Racism, Sexism, and Sexual Orientation Discrimination," which specifically addresses the need for development of

> plans, activities, and programs for education employees, students, parents/guardians, and the community . . . to identify and eliminate discrimination and stereotyping in all educational settings.[15]

The resolution goes on to say that such plans, activities, and programs must

a. Increase respect, understanding, acceptance, and sensitivity toward individuals and groups in a diverse society composed of such groups as American Indians/Alaska Natives, Asians and Pacific Islanders, Blacks, Hispanics, women, gays and lesbians, and people with disabilities;
b. Eliminate discrimination and stereotyping in the curriculum, textbooks, resource and instructional materials, activities, etc.;
c. Foster the use of nondiscriminatory, nonracist, nonsexist, and nonstereotypical language, resources, practices, and activities;
d. Eliminate institutional discrimination;
e. Integrate an accurate portrayal of the roles and contributions of all groups throughout history across the curriculum, particularly groups who have been underrepresented historically;
f. Identify how prejudice, stereotyping, and discrimination have limited the roles and contributions of individuals and groups, and how these limitations have challenged and continue to challenge our society;
g. Eliminate subtle practices that favor the education of one student over another on the basis of race, ethnicity, gender, disability, or sexual orientation
h. Encourage all members of the educational community to examine assumptions and prejudices that might limit the opportunities and growth of students and education employees;
i. Offer positive and diverse role models in our society, including the recruitment, hiring, and promotion of diverse education employees in our public schools.[16]

Were educators and teacher educators seriously, vigorously, and creatively to address the words and spirit of this resolution, the consonance of compulsory heterosexuality in public education would be shaken to its core. The powerful words of this resolution premise the research that follows in this book.

Furthermore, the NEA has not been the only organization to call for dismantling anti–lesbian and gay prejudice in this nation's educational system. As detailed in the article "The Struggle over the Text: Compulsory Heterosexuality and Educational Policy," online organizations are educating citizens about how to promote educational policies and reforms that can foster the health and well-being of lesbian and gay students, pushing for the establishment of clubs in schools by making clever use of the Equal Access Act.[17] Further educational dissonance is promoted by chapters of PFLAG (Parents and Friends of Lesbians and Gays). PFLAG's mission is to support, educate, and advocate for sexually diverse students, teachers, and families. The group works both nationally and locally with the media, developing training materials that can be used in schools, after-school charter groups, and community groups to promote respect and celebration of diversity.

GLSEN (Gay, Lesbian and Straight Educational Network) has also developed a presence in many communities by assisting teens in setting up gay–straight alliances in schools (extracurricular groups in which students talk about issues related to sexual orientation), providing educational materials, and lobbying legislative bodies. In fact, GLSEN's sex-education book *Just the Facts about Sexual Orientation and Youth: A Primer for Principals, Educators and School Personnel* has been endorsed by the American Medical Association, the American Psychological Association, and the American Association of Pediatrics, among others.[18]

However, despite the recommendations and work of the NEA, GLSEN, PFLAG, and others, the educational dissonance created by these efforts has not yet reached a level where the consonance of compulsory heterosexuality has been significantly interrupted. School administrators still routinely oppose efforts to set up lesbian– and gay–straight alliances. Conservative Christian groups—such as Focus on the Family, the Eagle Forum, the Christian Coalition, and the militant American Family Association—expend enormous amounts of time, energy, and financial resources fighting the efforts of the NEA and lesbian–gay advocacy groups. In fact, many of the conservative groups have redoubled those efforts of late.

For almost a decade, Focus on the Family has devoted a great deal of effort and money to convert adult gays. They have counseled, advertised, and spent millions of dollars sending "ex-gays" around the nation to extol the healing power of this ministry. Yet, those efforts have not been going well of late. In 2000, John Paulk, who boasts of being straight for fourteen years, was photographed in a gay bar.[19] About the same time, another "ex-gay" spokesman, Wade Richards—who has been used in press conferences by the conservative group Americans for Truth about Homosexuality and who has been featured on ABC's *20/20*—came out to *Advocate* magazine as an "ex-ex-gay."[20] So when the seven hundred participants at a Christian conference convened on April 21, 2001, they decided, as had many other Christian groups, to unleash their formidable network of politicized Christians to fight homosexuality, starting in toddlerhood.[21] They also planned a protest at the national NEA convention for July 2001.[22]

Because the loudest conflicts in schools in the last few years have been over gay–straight student alliances, some groups, such as the American Family Association, have been working to persuade religious groups to commandeer teens to start "opposition groups" to the gay–straight alliances forming in high schools. These groups hope to make use of the Equal Access Act in the same ways that lesbian and gay advocacy groups have done. Further, with over eight hundred gay–straight student alliances now in existence and with five recent lawsuits all resolved in favor of those student groups, many of these conservative Christian groups are shifting their legal focus from after-school activities to in-school education.[23]

Thus, it would appear that while efforts are certainly taking place to change school climates, such efforts have not yet reached broadly or deeply enough to significantly disturb the consonance of compulsory heterosexuality in most of our nation's schools. Before a new consonance can be created in which the effects of compulsory heterosexuality are mitigated, there must be an amplified dissonance, for the hegemony of heterosexist ideology is still alive, well, and receiving active promotion.

Heterosexism, Theoretically

If the foregoing are examples of heterosexism in practice, what is heterosexism in theory? Heterosexism has been broadly defined as the belief that heterosexuality is inherently superior to nonheterosexuality in its various forms. This characterization, however, has been the subject of endless consideration in feminist, as well as lesbian and gay, theory. For instance, James T. Sears distinguishes between two manifestations of heterosexism: *cultural heterosexism*, which is the stigmatization, denial, or denigration of nonheterosexuality in cultural institutions ranging from the church to the courthouse; and *psycho-*

logical heterosexism, which is a person's internalization of this worldview that erupts into antigay prejudice.[24]

Many lesbian feminists have pointed to heterosexism not only as the *ism* from whence comes anti–lesbian and gay prejudice but also as the paradigmatic model for the oppression of women in a patriarchal society. Through her conceptualization of *compulsory heterosexuality*, Adrienne Rich effects recognition of heterosexuality as an institution that both forcibly and subliminally imposes heterosexual "preference" on women, ensuring males' rights of physical, economic, and emotional access to women. Rich discusses the practical means by which constraints and sanctions have historically enforced or ensured the coupling of women with men and have obstructed or penalized women's coupling or allying in independent groups with other women. She suggests that heterosexuality needs to be recognized as a political institution. Compulsory heterosexuality, thus conceived, is an ideology that suppresses homoerotic attraction, expression, and bonding, as well as gender expression that deviates from essentialized "feminine" and "masculine" social norms by means that range from literal physical enslavement to the disguise and distortion of possible options.[25]

What impresses one in Rich's analysis is the extent to which compulsory heterosexuality is not simply the maintenance of inequality and property possession but a pervasive cluster of forces, ranging from physical brutality to control of consciousness, which suggests that an enormous potential counterforce is having to be restrained. Some of the forms by which male power manifests itself are more easily recognizable as enforcing heterosexuality on women than are others. Yet, through these many venues, women have been convinced that marriage and sexual orientation toward men are inevitable, even when they are unsatisfying or oppressive. Chastity belts; clitoridectomies; rape; child marriage; pornography; sexual harassment; disqualification from professions; salary inequality; erasure of lesbian existence in art, literature, and film (except that as exotic and perverse); and the idealization of heterosexual romance and marriage are all part and parcel of the social and political institutionalization of compulsory heterosexuality. In other words, women's heterosexuality, compulsory heterosexuality, is not simply an issue of "preference" but a state that has also been imposed, managed, organized, propagandized, and maintained by force.[26]

Audre Lorde builds on the feminist analysis of heterosexism by maintaining that it is based not just on the dominant group's perception of its own dominance but its *right to dominance*.[27] This perceived right to dominance thinly veils the right to exert force when it is necessary to maintain one's superior status.

Marilyn Frye claims that it is cultural norming, associated with heterosexism, that requires that both man and woman "announce" their sex through style of gait, clothing, hair, style.[28] In a culture in which one is deemed sinful, sick, or disgusting if one is not heterosexual, it is very important to keep track of one's sexual feelings and the sexes of those who inspire them. Heterosexuality is announced by announcing one's sex. Frye argues that, in a culture in which being lesbian or gay is almost universally forbidden, it always behooves one to announce one's sex. It is, she suggests, a general and obvious principle of information theory that when it is very important that certain information *must* be conveyed, the most suitable strategy is redundancy, through as many media as possible. On the other end, when the receiver of information receives the same information over and over, conveyed by every medium one knows, another message comes through as well: this information about sex is very, very important. Despite the fact that both sexes continually announce their sex and receive information about sex, men and women are not, however, "equally or identically affected by announcing their sex. The male's announcement tends toward his protection or safety, and the female's announcement tends toward her victimization."[29]

Understanding heterosexism, according to Sarah Lucia Hoagland, involves analyzing not just women's victimization but also how women are defined in terms of men or not at all, how lesbians and gay men are treated— indeed scapegoated—as deviants, how choices of intimate partners for women and men are restricted or denied through taboos to maintain a certain social order.[30] Hoagland goes on to define a new term, *heterosexualism*, which represents an "entire way of life promoted and enforced by every formal and informal institution of the fathers' society, from religion to pornography to unpaid housework to medicine. Heterosexualism is a way of living that normalizes the dominance of one person and subordination of another."[31]

Another lesbian feminist, Janice Raymond, grants that heterosexism accepts the dominance–submission duality but has argued that the term *hetero-relations* better expresses the wide range of affective, social, political, and economic relations that are ordained between men and women by men. *Hetero-reality*, the worldview that woman exists always in relation to man, has consistently perceived women together as women alone. For Raymond, it is critical that one understand that the norms of hetero-reality have intended woman-for-man and not man-for-woman. Women are ordained for men in ways quite different from those in which men exist for women. Raymond calls on the biblical dictum that makes this difference quite clear. Simply put, woman is *ontologically* for man; that is, she is formed by him and cannot do without him. Her desire and destiny are consumed by his voracious appetite; her essence and existence always depend on relation to him. Man, however, is *accidentally* for woman. That is, man's desire and destiny, while including women, are not encompassed by relations with women. Instead, his destiny is that of world building in the company of his fellow men. Therefore, Raymond asserts that while heterosexism is problematic for women, the larger problem is that we live in a hetero-relational society where most of women's personal, social, political, professional, and economic relations are defined by the ideology that woman is for man. Hetero-relations give men constant access to women and have consistently transformed the worlds of women into hetero-reality.[32]

On a more philosophical level, Raymond argues that hetero-reality and hetero-relations are built on the myth of androgyny. Arguments supporting the primacy of hetero-relations are based on a cosmic male–female polarity in which the lost halves seek to be rejoined. All of life's relations are then imbued with an androgynous energy and an attraction that seeks to reunite the selves divided from each other, forever paired in cosmic complementarity. All of life becomes a metaphor for marriage. Every social relation demands its other half, whether in the bedroom or the boardroom. Ultimately, the power of hetero-relations derives from their idealization. Like the idealization of slavery, says Raymond, hetero-relations have become the dominant structure of a social system by their benign presentation. The more "domesticated" the ideal becomes, the more "benefits" it seems to offer women, and the more entrenched it is as a social system.[33]

Postmodern thinker Judith Butler has also reconceptualized heterosexism, naming the "heterosexual matrix" that which designates a grid of cultural intelligibility through which bodies, genders, and desires are naturalized. This definition draws on the normalizing function of heterosexuality—what Monique Wittig calls the "heterosexual contract"—as well as on Adrienne Rich's definition of "compulsory heterosexuality."[34] Butler claims that it becomes important to recognize that oppression works not merely through acts of overt prohibition but covertly, through the constitution of viable subjects and through the corollary constitution of a domain of unviable subjects ("unsubjects"). Compulsory heterosexuality sets itself up as the original, the true, the authentic; the norm that determines the real implies that being homosexual is always a kind of miming, a vain effort to participate in the plenitude of naturalized heterosexuality, which will always fail. Yet, the naturalistic effects of heterosexualized genders are produced through imitative strategies. What they imitate is a phantasmatic ideal of heterosexual identity, which is produced by the imitation as its effect. In this sense, the "reality" of heterosexual identities is performatively constituted through an imitation that sets itself up as the original and as the ground of all imitations. In other words, heterosexuality is always in the process of imitating and approximating its own phantasmatic idealization of itself—and *failing*. Precisely because it is bound to fail and yet endeavors to succeed, the project of heterosexual identity is propelled into an endless repetition of itself. In its efforts to naturalize itself as the original, heterosexuality must be understood as a compulsive and compulsory repetition that can only produce the *effect* of its own originality. In other words, compulsory heterosexual identities are theatrically produced effects that posture as grounds, origins, and normative measures of the real.[35]

Thus, heterosexism has been considered by most gay and queer theorists to be the ideology that sets the stage for anti–lesbian and gay prejudice by normalizing sexual complementarity, sharply dividing the world according to biological sex, and requiring continual announcements of that division. Lesbian feminists, however, have conceptualized heterosexism as a dual platform that relies not only on rigid sexual complementarity but also on the hegemonic group's perceived right to dominance, which acknowledges the pervasive sexism and, to a lesser extent, the imperialism inherent in this definition, as well as thinly veiled violence.

Definition of Terms

My own use of *heterosexism* relies on the dual platforms that are consistent with the definition set forth by lesbian feminism. This broader understanding of heterosexuality necessitates the recognition that while lesbian and gay people are scapegoated by heterosexism, they are affected differently because of the gender issues. This definition also makes it plain that heterosexual women, as well as lesbians, are adversely affected by heterosexism. Further, I will use *compulsory heterosexuality* to denote the mis-educative process by which heterosexism is reproduced. Thus, two of the effects of heterosexism for lesbian and gay people are entrenched sexism and anti–lesbian and gay prejudice.

I prefer the term *anti–lesbian and gay prejudice*, and I use it instead of the more commonly ascribed *homophobia*, unless the author I am discussing specifically chooses the word *homophobia*. There are several reasons for my aversion to the term *homophobia*. First, *homophobia* is a psychological term that means an unreasonable fear of, or antipathy toward, homosexuals and homosexuality. Properly derived from the Greek by exact analogy with other words, *homophobia* should mean "fear of what is similar," not "fear of homosexuality." The relation of these two terms is then based more on a superficial similarity to *homosexual*.

Further, as David Halperin has pointed out, the term *homosexual*, is a bastardized term using a Greek prefix and Latin root, which was coined by Charles Gilbert Chaddock in 1892 to denote the narrow issue of sexual object choice. *Sexual inversion* was the terminology most frequently used before Chaddock's coinage, which despite its own drawbacks did at least refer to a broad range of deviant gender behavior of which same-sex object choice was only an indistinct aspect.[36] While *homosexual*, which most obviously means "of one sex" or "of one kind," may be quite adequate in reference to a sexual act, it is, as John Boswell has discussed, more troublesome when applied to a "homosexual" person. Is this someone "of one sex"? By extension, one supposes, a "homosexual person" is one given to "homosexual acts." But, how many such acts must one indulge in before becoming "homosexual"? One? Ten? And what of the person who only dreams of committing the act but never realizes it? Is he or she "homosexual"? Teens, for instance, are frequently told that they are not necessarily "homosexual" even though they may have experimented with same-sex sexual activity; men in prison are not considered "homosexual," unless they identify themselves as such, even though there is rampant "homosexual" sex. Clearly, there is more to being a "homosexual" than performing "homosexual" sex.[37]

Even given the difficulties inherent in defining exactly who is and who isn't "homosexual," there is still a scholarly disinclination to employ the word *gay* or *lesbian* instead of *homosexual* because of the reluctance on the part of some academics to employ a popular neologism. Yet, John Boswell has established that *gay* probably antedates *homosexual* by several centuries and has generally been employed with far greater precision. Also, most males (and many females) use *gay* to describe themselves when they are conscious of erotic preference for their own gender. This obviates the most urgent defect of *homosexual*, by making the category one that is principally self-assigned.[38]

This terminology also has advantages beyond semantic precision. First, *homosexual* has come to be associated with males more than females. Second, when applied to men or women, the word *homosexual* implicitly suggests that the primary distinguishing characteristic of gay people is their sexuality. *Gay* or *lesbian*, for instance, allows the reader to draw her or his own conclusions about the relative importance of love, affection, devotion, romance, eroticism, or overt sexuality in the lives of persons so designated. Finally, it may be noted that gay and lesbian people tend to prefer these terms when applied to themselves, over the more pathologically oriented *homosexual*. Boswell contends that there can be no more justification for retaining a designation out of favor with gay and lesbian people than for continuing to use *Negro* when it has ceased to be acceptable to African Americans.[39]

Therefore, not only does *homophobia* point to the use of *homosexual*, but our understanding of homophobia has come to be viewed in a far less simplistic way than the terminology of "the unreasoning fear of homosexuals and homosexuality" indicates. Over the years, homophobia has been expanded to include disgust, anxiety, and anger.[40] James Sears points out that homophobia has also come to mean not just fear but hatred and revulsion by same-sex attraction in others, and often the desire to inflict punishment as retribution.[41]

These implications are not merely psychological but also political. Hence, Celia Kitzinger has suggested that we stop using *homophobia* altogether because it emerged from the academic discipline of psychology and not from a liberation movement. She questions characterizing heteropatriarchal fear of lesbians as irrational; then she challenges the nonpolitical orientation of *phobia*, noting that within psychology, the only alternative to *homophobia* is liberal humanism.[42]

Phobias within psychology are most often associated with trauma. It seems odd to label fear produced by psychological trauma, or *phobia*, as one would label a fear that has been carefully cultivated across multiple configurations of education, in this case *homophobia*. In fact, the "fear" of homosexuals is rather more like the "fear" we teach children for hot stoves or electricity—that is, an altogether reasonable fear, based on the repercussions faced by "homosexuals." Gary Kinsman argues that the concept of homophobia merely "individualizes and privatizes gay oppression and obscures the social relations that organize it."[43] Simon Watney also articulates this general distrust of "homophobia":

> The remarkable speed and ease with which the later concept of homophobia was taken up as an explanation of hostility towards homosexuality shows the measure of the force of the idea that sexuality is a system of innate drives rather than a range of historically and socially constructed alternatives.[44]

Thus, anti–lesbian and gay prejudice is more semantically correct, more descriptive, more historically accurate, and more acceptable to the persons it describes, while also acknowledging the social and political elements of compulsory heterosexuality involved in its development.

The Effects of Anti–Lesbian and Gay Prejudice

The dual platforms inherent in my use of the term *heterosexism* clearly suggest that not just the rigid gender complementarity, but also the thinly veiled violence inherent in its definition, begs investigation. The effects of sexism in institutions—from the family to the school to the church—have been the subjects of feminist research for decades, but the effects of anti–lesbian and gay prejudice have been interrogated far less frequently. How, then, does such prejudice play itself out in the various configurations of education?

The home, that environment praised almost universally by conservatives as the necessary ingredient for healthy, happy children, can erupt in violence when youth reveal their same-sex feelings. Teens are also still routinely subjected to so-called reparative or conversion therapy, an attempt to change the sexual orientation of lesbian and gay teens, even though such methods have been denounced by the American Psychiatric Association.[45] In addition to physical and psychological abuse, the Department of Health and Human Services has estimated that as many as 25 percent of youth are forced out of their families' homes when they reveal their sexuality, with even higher percentages in urban areas.[46] Lacking job skills, approximately half the gay and bisexual males forced out of their homes engage in prostitution to support themselves.[47]

Peers can be just as unwelcoming. In a survey of sexual attitudes conducted with over a thousand American teenagers, 32 percent of males and 16 percent of the females reported they would sever ties with same-sex friends if they learned that those friends were homosexual.[48] In a fourteen-city study of lesbian, gay, and bisexual youth, 80 percent reported verbal abuse, 44 percent reported threats of attack, 33 percent reported having objects thrown at them, and 30 percent reported being chased or followed.[49]

Schools are also a ripe environment for anti–lesbian and gay prejudice. Testimony from the National Gay and Lesbian Task Force has substantiated research by other organizations indicating that nearly half of gay males and nearly one-fifth of lesbians are harassed or attacked in high school or junior high school.[50] In a study of 4,159 Massachusetts high school students, over 31 percent of youth self-identifying as lesbian, gay, or bisexual were threatened or injured with a weapon at school in the past year, compared to less than 7 percent of their peers. The same study found that over 18 percent of the lesbian, gay, and bisexual students had been in a physical fight resulting in treatment by a doctor or a nurse, compared to 4 percent of their peers. Over 22 percent of lesbian, gay, bisexual, and transgender (LGBT) youth had skipped school in the past month because they felt unsafe on route to or at school, compared to just over 4 percent of their peers.[51]

The fear of being labeled lesbian or gay, or of facing those feelings in oneself, inhibits the development of close relationships with members of the same sex in all youth, not just gay and lesbian teens.[52] However, lesbian, gay, bisexual, transgender, and questioning (henceforth LGBTQ) teenagers are especially preoccupied with their social discomfort and are trying to figure out where they fit in. They frequently encounter difficulty concentrating in class, shun classroom participation, shy away from extracurricular activities, and even drop out of school altogether.[53] Qualitative studies of gay and lesbian youth have shown that one of the most difficult feelings with which they deal is the sense that they exist

> in a box, with no adults to talk to, no traditional support structures to lean on for help in sorting out their problems, and no young people like themselves with whom to socialize. In effect, these young homosexuals [perceive] themselves to be stranded in an environment that [shuns] their very existence.[54]

Psychological research indicates that internalizing such anti–lesbian and gay sentiments not only negatively affects the self-esteem of gay and lesbian adolescents but also increases the likelihood of self-destructive behavior. For many this means fending off accusations of being lesbian or gay by peers and school personnel via engagement in premature heterosexual involvement, which in turn leads to high percentages of teen pregnancy and sexually transmitted disease.[55] Most gay teens, and even more lesbian teens, use drugs (including crack and cocaine) and drink alcohol to excess.[56]

Even more frightening is the fact that suicide is now the leading cause of death among LGBT youth.[57] The Surgeon General's 1999 *Call to Action* reports that suicide in children ten to fourteen years of age has doubled over the last ten years; in the age group from fifteen to twenty-four, it is now the third leading cause of death. The U.S. Department of Health and Human Services indicates that as many as 30 percent of all successful teen suicide attempts are by lesbian and gay teens. Three-quarters of those LGBTQ youth who commit suicide do so soon after labeling themselves as homosexual. Studies on youth suicide consistently find that lesbian and gay youth are two to six times more likely to attempt suicide than other youth.[58] The same Massachusetts study quoted earlier states that 46 percent of youth identifying as lesbian, gay, or bisexual had attempted suicide in the past year, compared to less than 9 percent of their peers. Nearly 24 percent of those lesbian, gay, and bisexual suicide attempts required medical attention, compared with just over 3 percent of their peers.[59]

Mis-education in the Wake

John Dewey's thinking about education makes clear that the education for compulsory heterosexuality is not educative at all, but mis-educative. Dewey defines as mis-educative any experience that has the effect of arresting or distorting the growth of further experience. He includes experiences that engender callousness or promote lack of sensitivity and responsiveness because the possibilities of having a richer experience in the future are restricted.[60] Based on his definition, the experiences of lesbian and gay youth that involve abuse, harassment, extreme social discomfort, drug and alcohol abuse, premature sexual involvement, and of course suicide all arrest and distort the educative potential across the various configurations of education. However, it would appear that the anti–lesbian and gay prejudice evolving in others also serves to "engender callousness" and "promote lack of sensitivity and responsiveness," serving in Dewey's language to stunt the educative experience of non-LGBTQ youth as well.

Clearly, what is needed are teachers, counselors, and administrators who are prepared to mitigate the effects of anti–lesbian and gay prejudice for LGBTQ youth and their peers. This fact becomes more urgent given that the Institute of Mental Health has indicated that youths' problems are more often clearly evident at school than at home. In a national study, 76 percent of all completed teen suicides were preceded by a significant decline in academic performance the year prior to their deaths.[61] Yet, data suggest that the overwhelming majority of preservice teachers are more homophobic than the general population.[62] Further, colleges of education in many parts of the country—responsible for preparing teachers, counselors, and administrators—have considered questions of sexual diversity to be outside their purview, a matter better relegated to the realm of morality and personal opinion than curriculum.

As dire as the situation appears for LGBTQ students, they are not the only ones for whom compulsory heterosexuality is mis-educative. Curricula on the family are still standard fare in most elementary schools; the experience of being part of a family is specific and personal and yet one to which almost everyone can relate. While multicultural approaches to the variety of family constellations are employed in many school districts, most still do not embrace discussions of families with same-sex parents. Yet, for the six to fourteen million children in the United States who have been reared from their first years by a gay or lesbian parent, the mis-education of compulsory heterosexuality designates the families who love and support them as "age-inappropriate subject matter."[63] It is further estimated that one family in four includes a lesbian or gay member.[64] The educational system's function as a heteronormative community creates a profound cognitive dissonance for these children torn between their families and the need for acceptance by peers and teachers. The fact that so many early childhood educators and administrators have insisted on teaching about family in rigid, traditional models has posed confusing scenarios for young children to attempt to negotiate. In some cases, the same-sex parents may charge the child with silence about the home situation, fearing that school personnel will recriminate against the child. Even the most forthright and open lesbian and gay parents face "coming out" to their children's teachers with great anxiety.[65]

And the issues do not stop with students. While lesbians and gay men may be growing more visible in many walks of North American life, teachers who come out in school still risk harassment, dismissal, and physical violence.[66] Thirty-nine states still have no employment protection for lesbian and gay teachers, making coming out financially as well as psychically risky.[67] Regardless of merit, vast numbers of dedicated teachers do not even feel physically safe in school because of their sexual identity.

Personal accounts by closeted lesbian and gay teaching professionals indicate that most have a strong desire to come out, to live free of the paralyzing demands of hiding. There is almost a universal desire for authenticity. Even more tragically, these teachers believe, almost to a person, that when they are forced to hide their sexual identity, they become less available to their students owing to a fear of being "outed." Teachers who could provide a wealth of support and information to students who are questioning their own sexual identity are silenced in school systems that are sorely lacking reliable information and credible resources.

Unfortunately, the school system's complicity in mis-education by compulsory heterosexuality is frequently mirrored by higher education. Colleges and universities are seen as guardians of truth and sources of new knowledge, but all too often higher education, like its K-12 counterpart, preserves and even endorses the prejudices of its surrounding culture. Discrimination in hiring, tenure, and promotion of gay men and lesbians in academia is pervasive, even when subtle and covert.[68] Formal studies of lesbian and gay history and issues, like those of women and minority groups, are either tolerated around the edges or disallowed altogether.

There are many who believe that academe may be one of the most difficult places to be "out" as gay or lesbian, particularly in the more conservative regions of the country and in colleges associated with conservative religious organizations. Thus, while the presence of lesbians and gay men on college and university campuses has long been considerable, unmasking their presence has been much more arduous. Where equal access has been a critical issue for racial minorities and women, gay men have long been well represented in academia; and more lesbians have joined their ranks, as women have been allowed in colleges and universities. That said, however, the fact that gay men and lesbians are present on college campuses does not mean that most, or even a substantial number of them, feel free to be "out." The question, as John d'Emilio has pointed out, becomes not whether there are lesbians and gay men on campuses but whether they can be "out" and still remain there.[69]

As the research encapsulated here overwhelmingly confirms, most of North America's educational institutions, K-12 and university alike, attach a social stigma to the "out" or "outed" gay or lesbian person. The mis-education of compulsory heterosexuality, the entrenched heterosexist policies and anti–lesbian and gay practices in education, has reinforced a scenario in which being "out" as a student or teacher sets the stage for discrimination, harassment, and verbal and physical violence. "Out" all too often translates into "outsider."

"Out" on the Margins

Certainly gay and lesbian people are not the only people to have been marginalized by this country's educational system. Difference, whether based on race, sex, ethnicity, or ability, has often rendered a marginalized status. Thus, while I am in no way claiming that being marginalized because of sexual identity is worse than being marginalized based on race, for instance, it does present a distinctive hurdle, just as does the oppression facing African Americans, despite sharing some similarities to the oppression of Latino/a Americans. Yet, while all oppressions are unique in many respects, there are those forms that run parallel and those that intersect.

For instance, there are some clear links between historical representations and oppressions of Jewish people and that of lesbian and gay people. Heterosexism, a system of advantages bestowed on heterosexuals, and *Christianism*— a term used by Warren Blumenfield that assumes that everyone is, or should be, Christian—both exclude the needs, concerns, and life experiences of people who are not part of the hegemonic culture.[70] Both groups share religious condemnation. In addition, both heterosexism and *Christianism* are based on entrenched beliefs that lesbians, gays, and Jews have the opportunity and the obligation to change if they want to lead a moral life. Both homophobia and anti-Semitism propagate the fear that group members are recruiting children and are seeking the domination and destruction of "civilized" society.[71] Of course, it is also possible for most members of both groups to "pass" as part of the hegemonic group, a decision that in many cases is accompanied by shame and self-loathing.

Other researchers have pointed to the similarities between gays and lesbians and Asian Americans and Pacific Islanders, the latter of whom are routinely subjected to brutal beatings and oppressive exploitation as well as the eroticization of Asian Pacific women.[72] Reyes and Yep point to the cases in which American Asian and Pacific Islander men have been murdered or brutally beaten. Further, homosexuals and Asian Americans/Pacific Islanders are often multiply marginalized, challenging the process of community building based on narrow identity definitions, which creates the political dilemma of prioritizing oppressions.[73]

Even though anti–lesbian and gay prejudice resembles anti-Semitism and xenophobia, lesbian and gay issues are also distinct in many respects. For instance, unlike those subject to oppression based on race or ethnicity, lesbian and gay people are almost always minorities in their own birth families and, in fact, may keep their sexual identity hidden from family members even more than from friends, teachers, or colleagues.

Anti–lesbian and gay prejudice also shares many similarities with gender oppression, but they do not run in perfect tandem either. Feminist theory offers an enormous amount of scholarly work dismantling the "natural," "innate," and "universal" character of male dominance and heterosexism, which fuels lesbian and gay oppression just as it does gender oppression. Much of that theoretical work came directly out of the so-called Second Wave Women's Movement starting in the late 1960s, following Simone de Beauvoir's analysis of women in the role of the "Other."[74]

However, years before Beauvoir's analysis and that second wave of feminism, Virginia Woolf interrogated the notion of what it means to be an outsider. Her analysis, I believe, can shed some light on what it means for lesbians and gay men to be "outsiders" as a result of being "out." In the educational treatise *Three Guineas*,[75] while questioning what women might do to prevent war, Woolf created a wry and systematic deconstruction of several epistemological ideals by showing that the material facts of women's lives may well make it impossible, and perhaps even ethically undesirable, to see and understand the world as men do.

Woolf's outsiders were women, specifically the daughters of educated men. These outsiders grew up in the same households as their brothers, speaking the same language with the same accents, and learning the same rules of etiquette. Nevertheless, a huge gulf lay between the daughters and sons of educated men. Denied the opportunity to attend the prestigious public schools and great universities; denied the opportunity to travel alone at home and abroad; denied property, inheritance, and until recently the right to vote and to enter a few of the professions that "circled in the lower spheres," the daughters of educated men had received very different educations from that of their brothers. The daughters had been taught by very different teachers.

The sons walked the lawns of Eton and learned from the robed masters with titles before their names and letters after their names. The daughters had received an unpaid-for education from the "four great teachers": poverty, chastity, derision, and freedom from unreal loyalties.[76]

Woolf suggested, however, that if one were to judge an education not simply by its power to obtain appointments, to win honor, or to make money, that perhaps one might not judge the unpaid-for education so harshly. If in fact this unpaid-for education offered some ethical advantages that could not be obtained through a paid-for education, then women would be foolish to throw it away no matter what "bribe or decoration" was offered in exchange. Woolf proposed that one such ethical advantage of the unpaid-for education was that although the daughters and sons of educated men may look at the same things, they may see them differently.[77] That is, one's perspective on a situation will be influenced by where one is standing: the margins will promote very different perspectives from that of the center.

Further, Woolf suggested that receiving a university education and practicing the professions seemed to encourage a disposition to war. That is, by propagating and sustaining barriers of wealth and ceremony, and by emphasizing separations and distinctions from one another, these "poisoned vanities" make both the professions and the universities cities of strife, possessiveness, and competition where no one can work or talk freely for fear of "transgressing some chalk mark" or "displeasing some dignitary."[78] While readily acknowledging the important contribution made by education in people's lives and the great sacrifices to which people subject themselves to obtain an education, Woolf concluded that a professional education, far from teaching generosity and magnanimity, teaches people to jealously guard their knowledge and elite status. Historically, they have even banded together to keep other groups from receiving a professional education, through the use of subtle methods or, when necessary, by force.[79]

Woolf's answer to the regrettable situation was transformation of the university education. She envisioned learning that took advantage of the characteristics of poverty and youth by urging experimentation and adventure; by exploring the ways that body and mind can cooperate; by combining, rather than by segregating and specializing. Such an education, Woolf imagined, would produce whole persons who sought learning for its own sake, if every type of merit could participate in that educational process.[80]

Although Woolf ultimately abandoned her educational vision as impractical—since women, like men, wanted degrees and titles—she continued to urge reforming the professions through an Outsiders' Society, which practiced the professions experimentally, in the interests of research and for the love of the work itself. The values and conduct she established for the Outsiders' Society would change the professions for the better by ridding them of possessiveness, jealousy, pugnacity, and greed, while exposing instances of tyranny and abuse. By exercising free mind and will, a prospect made possible by earning personal income, women could protect culture and intellectual liberty by reading and writing their own thoughts, in their own words, in their own ways, swearing that once they had enough money to live, they would refuse to commit "adultery of the brain" any longer. Should they choose to take up this challenge, remembering the lessons of the four great teachers and using their education to reveal and ameliorate abuses and injustices, they would no longer be "outsiders," but "Outsiders." Woolf went on to suggest that a careful examination of the world would yield evidence that such Outsiders were already working in obscurity for the betterment of society.[81]

There are numerous comparisons that may be made between Woolf's outsiders and lesbians and gay men in the North American educational system. Certainly lesbians and gay men have some familiarity with the "four great teachers." The fact that hostility and violence, real and perceived, compromise gay and lesbian teens' ability to participate fully in classes and extracurricular activities; to form close friendships; and to find acceptance from peers, teachers, and administrators bears testimony to the poverty of their educations. When thirty-nine states deny employment protection on the basis of sexual orientation, schoolteachers and college faculty find themselves in a situation similar to Woolf's impoverished women, forced to depend on the beneficence of their patriarchal institutions.

Early in their lives, lesbian and gay people learn about chastity from their experiences in the hallways of schools and universities that punish, with taunting and harassment, even the hint of same-sex affection. Lesbian and gay parents who send their children into classrooms that are mis-educating for compulsory heterosexuality likewise feel this enforced chastity, as do lesbian and gay youth who are frequently denied information about lesbian and gay sexuality, even in health classes and seminars on sexually transmitted diseases. That there have existed many famous artists, literary figures, politicians, scientists, religious figures, and entrepreneurs who were gay or lesbian is a jealously guarded secret.

Students and teachers at all levels of the educational system are well acquainted with derision. In academic circles this derision is sometimes veiled as advice on "appropriate" topics for research. Themes involving sexual identity may be trivialized in bids for promotion and tenure as well as for publishable papers. Like Woolf's outsiders, academicians are often forced to commit "adultery of the brain" by researching not what interests them but what is deemed acceptable to the departments, colleges, and universities that hold the keys to their future employment and tenure. Even then, known lesbians and gay men, when allowed to remain employed, often tend, as did Woolf's female civil servants, "to be possessed of a certain leaden quality . . . circling in the lower spheres" of the profession.

Many lesbian and gay students and teachers believe that even when they are accepted on their campuses, it is provisional at best, being based on the school's grudging tolerance of "out" people or the lesbian or gay person's passing as heterosexual. Like Woolf's outsiders, many gays and lesbians feel not only disappointed by their institutions and administrators but often embittered. As Woolf suggested, the freedom from unreal loyalties often comes quite easily to outsiders.

Despite the marked similarities, however, potent differences exist between these two groups of outsiders. After all, Woolf's daughters of educated men weren't lesbian teachers, teenage boys being gay bashed, or same-sex parents sending their child into a first-grade classroom filled with children from "traditional" families. Woolf was writing about an easily identifiable, rather discrete group of people made up of one sex, one economic and social class, one race, and one religion. There was no question that the daughters of educated men would be recognized as outsiders. One of the most pressing questions that gays and lesbians face, however, is *whether* they will be identified as outsiders. That is, because we have been taught by heterosexist ideology to "give the benefit of the doubt"[82] to people regarding their sexual identity, remaining closeted is, for most lesbian and gay people, a very real possibility. In addition to the ease with which most people may remain closeted, the choice to identify as lesbian or gay is made even more difficult because it is tantamount to revoking heterosexual privilege[83] in favor of a stigmatized identity. Staying closeted, of course, does not come without a price. It opens the door for exposure, or threats of exposure, from others; it demands constantly shifting strategies for concealing the truth; and it is habitually accompanied by self-loathing because of dishonesty inherent in the decision. The lesbian or gay outsider, then, can be an outsider in insider's clothing. And herein lies the rub: to choose to be "out" opens one to potential harassment, discrimination, denigration, and violence; to choose to be closeted stunts the development of friendships, support networks, and emotional and mental development needed for healthy living. For the gay or lesbian student, teacher, or academician, life becomes a tight wire act: the illusion of safety on one side, the hope of authenticity on the other.

Given the differences in these two groups of outsiders, Woolf's call to action for the Outsiders' Society is instructive but intended for a particular audience. Therefore, while her suggestions remain useful for contemplating ethical conduct, the unique circumstances of lesbian and gay people in the current educational environment beg a solution that is fully cognizant of the multiple issues specifically related to sexual identity. Further, the exigencies of outsiders' teaching and learning in hostile environments, especially of those who have chosen authenticity over safety, demand a response from educators that is as philosophically sound and strategically crafted as that which was fashioned by Woolf for the daughters of educated men.

"Out" in Praxis

"Outsider" terminology has become part of the feminist lexicon in the past thirty years.[84] My own use of the term will apply to LGBTQ people in North American education, drawing and expanding on Woolf's characterizations. Hence, *outsider* will recognize marginalized status, and *Outsider* will refer to LGBTQ people who are working to expose and eradicate situations of tyranny and abuse. In addition, I will conceptualize *Out-Sider,* a term that will refer to those people who side with the "out": those teachers, administrators, counselors, therapists, coaches, teacher educators, researchers, students, friends, and family members who may be, but need not be, LGBTQ themselves and who are working to mitigate the effects of the mis-education by compulsory heterosexuality and disrupt the heterosexism that plagues our nation's configurations of education. Further, I am suggesting that this educational approach be not just a schooling practice but also a life practice. I am suggesting a need for a praxis that Out-Siders can learn and teach as curriculum: an *Out-Siders' Praxis.*

Praxis, in its simplest construal, means "theory plus action." It was first conceptualized by Aristotle, who drew distinctions between *theoria* (from which the word *theory* is derived), meaning speculation, contemplation, or "a spectator above"; and *techne,* meaning craft, skill, art. *Theoria* was at the top of the hierarchy of knowledge; *techne* was at the bottom. *Phronesis,* which is most commonly translated into English as *practical wisdom,* was knowledge born of a combination of *theoria* and *techne.*

Theoria, theoretical knowledge, was concerned with "ends" considered to be timeless, immutable truths. In this sense, *theoria* retains a sense of dispassionately observing a spectacle. *Theoria* encompasses philosophy and mathematics as well as the natural sciences. The knowledge of *techne,* as Janet Atwill has pointed out, is never static or normative.[85] Because it is intimately concerned with the production of art, there are no well-defined boundaries between the subject and knowledge. *Techne* marks a domain of human intervention and invention that is defined against forces of necessity, spontaneity, experience, chance, compulsion, and force. It is often associated with transgressing existing boundaries in ways that redefine relations of power and efforts to rectify transgressions.[86]

Thus, *phronesis* is concerned with action and human behavior, subsuming ethics and politics. The knowledge of *phronesis*, practical knowledge, is never concerned with what is necessary, but what is best. It assumes not only intellectual insight to make the right choices but in-depth acquaintance with the various practical considerations needed to proceed skillfully, creatively, in a timely manner to intervene in the practical problems of human beings. The solutions provided through practical wisdom are thus always time- and location-dependent, suggesting that *praxis*, the practice that derives from practical wisdom, not only becomes inseparable from the subject who creates and enables it but also redefines the subject through its practice.[87]

Aristotle clearly stated that practical wisdom was not about knowing the right thing but about doing the right thing.[88] Lesbian feminist Charlotte Bunch states that the integration of theory and action, each continually challenging and shaping the other, gives one a framework for understanding situations, sorting options, and preventing the "any action/no action" bind. Separated by thousands of years, Aristotle and Bunch are, for all intents and purposes, saying the same thing: *praxis* is fundamentally pragmatic.

Pragmatism has been no more succinctly defined than in William James's famous question "What difference would it practically make to anyone if *this* notion rather than *that* notion were true?"[89] A pragmatic approach is undertaken not merely to attempt to formulate some new "truth" but to obtain some valued result—or in Deweyan terms, an "end in view"—that *ought* to exist. Once the appropriate "end in view" has been decided through practical reasoning, the pragmatic viewpoint dictates that attaining that goal becomes a moral imperative, disclosing the utter dependence of theory and practice on each other.[90] Simply stated, a pragmatic approach brings our reason, passion, and imagination to bear on a situation to solve problems. It is then practical reasoning that connects the actual to the possible.[91]

Praxis is also dependent on a community. Aristotle argued that because knowledge of an ordinary experience could appear to be different from the perspective of various observers or participants, practical wisdom is dependent on comprehending as many viewpoints as possible. While Aristotle's perspective champions the value of collective decision making, it further implies that praxis must always be founded on community norms, which shape the limits of acceptable behaviors and judgments.

This understanding of community involvement in praxis is also borne out in Dewey's notion of "social intelligence," which rejected the prevailing idea of mind as a purely "individual affair." Dewey insisted that understanding reality depended on the various standpoints used to gather perspectives, holding that finite creatures can grow wiser only if they share perspectives. Dialogues across differences are essential for those who desire to grow.[92] Praxis, then, is a considered yet active, inventive yet interventive way of life undertaken by individuals within a reflective community. As such, praxis is always inherently political because our actions always affect other people.

In addition, practical wisdom was held in classical thought to be a necessary condition for true goodness, or *arête*. That goodness has a requisite intellectual element seems somewhat out of sync with our modern notions of virtue, but *arête* incorporates not just good intentions or desires but the entire gamut of attributes needed by an individual for achieving appropriate ends or goodness: theory, skill, and an understanding of how to achieve one's desires. This viewpoint is also critical to the problem solving of the pragmatists and neopragmatists. Richard Rorty suggests that the practical reasoning coming from moral wisdom is the attempt to modify our beliefs, desires, and activities in ways that will bring us, or our society, greater happiness than that we have now.[93]

There is yet another key element in the pragmatist conception of praxis that derives from practical wisdom. Dewey believed that emotions were an important part of practical reasoning. He argued that imagination was integral to intelligent thought since it opened the door for new possibilities through creativity. According to Dewey, when a person engages in creative inquiry, such inquiry bestows value on a thing, person, or situation.[94] Dewey wrote:

> The reasonable act and the generous act lie close together. A person entirely lacking in sympathetic response might have a keen calculating intellect, but he would have no spontaneous sense of the claims of others for satisfaction of their desires. A person of narrow sympathy is of necessity a person of confined outlook upon the scene of human good. The only truly general thought is the generous thought.[95]

In Deweyan thought, interpersonal understanding is always a possibility; but without sympathy—or in his words, generosity—there is always a danger of misunderstanding. With generosity, however, the recognition of others' needs, desires, and hopes can propel us beyond the bounds of ourselves. By engaging the perspectives of others, we can reason with passion and imagination to envision new possibilities and hope for things we had never before even dreamed existed.[96] To be wise, to exhibit moral reasoning, one has to see the possible in the actual. To grow, to exhibit practical reasoning, one must work for making the possible probable.[97]

Only this complex yet hopeful understanding of praxis will circumscribe the fundamental norms for a community of Out-Siders. Out-Siders will share an educational commitment to generous dialogue across difference and to the abatement of heterosexism and anti–lesbian and gay prejudice, representing a retreat from compulsory heterosexuality. The *Out-Siders' Praxis* will be the theory and action of a pragmatic collective that concerns itself with ethically responding to the exigencies of daily life for LGBTQ outsiders who have made the difficult and continuous decision to honor authenticity over safety. Further, just as Woolf suggested that a careful view of the world would reveal Outsiders already at work for the betterment of society, so do I suggest that Out-Siders have already found opportunities to work toward eradicating the effects of mis-education at the hands of compulsory heterosexuality.

Notes

1. G. Remafadi, "Homosexual Youth: A Challenge to Contemporary Society," *Journal of the American Medical Association* 258 (1987): 222–25.

2. National Network of Runaway and Youth Services, *To Whom Do They Belong? Runaway, Homeless and Other Youth in High-Risk Situations in the 1990's* (Washington, D.C.: National Network, 1991), quoted in http://pflag.org/schools/schoolsfacts.htm.

3. Massachusetts Governor's Commission on Gay and Lesbian Youth, *Making Schools Safe for Gay and Lesbian Youth* (1993), at http://pflag.org/schools/schoolsfacts.htm.

4. Quoted in PFLAG's *Focus on Safe Schools*, at http://pflag.org/schools/schoolsfacts.htm.

5. Virginia Uribe and Karen M. Harbeck, "Addressing the Needs of Lesbian, Gay, and Bisexual Youth: The Origins of PROJECT 10 and School-Based Intervention," in *Coming Out of the Classroom Closet: Gay and Lesbian Students, Teachers and Curricula*, ed. Karen M. Harbeck (New York: Harrington Park Press, 1991), 17.

6. See interview with teachers and children in the documentary film *It's Elementary: Talking about Gay Issues in Schools*, by Debra Chasnoff and Helen Cohen, for Women's Educational Media (1996). Also see qualitative interviews conducted by Virginia Casper and Steven B. Schultz in "What Do Children Know?" in *Gay Parents/Straight Schools: Building Communication and Trust* (New York: Teachers College, Columbia University, 1999).

7. Casper and Schultz, "What Do Children Know?" 38–44.

8. Kelley Carter, "Gay Slurs Abound," *Des Moines Register*, March 7, 1997, 1.

9. See James T. Sears, "Educators, Homosexuality, and Homosexual Students: Are Personal Feelings Related to Professional Beliefs?" in *Coming Out of the Classroom Closet: Gay and Lesbian Students, Teachers, and Curricula*, ed. Karen M. Harbeck (New York: Harrington Park Press, 1991), 29–74.

10. John Dewey, *Democracy and Education* (New York: Free Press, 1916), 4.

11. According to Lawrence Cremin, relationships among the institutions that constitute a configuration of education may be political, pedagogical, or personal, all with overlapping lines of support and control. Lawrence A. Cremin, *Public Education* (New York: Basic Books, 1976), 30–31; quoted in "Exhibits and Publications: A Tribute to Lawrence A. Cremin," Milbankweb, at http://lweb.tc.columbia.edu/exhibits/cremin_quotes/publiced1.html.

12. James T. Sears, "Thinking Critically/Intervening Effectively," in *Overcoming Heterosexism and Homophobia: Strategies That Work,* ed. James T. Sears and Walter L. Williams (New York: Columbia University Press, 1997), 21.

13. Sears, "Thinking Critically/Intervening Effectively," 22.

14. National Education Association, "Code of Ethics of the Education Profession," principle 1.6, at www.nea.org/aboutnea/code.html.

15. National Education Association, "NEA 2000–2001 Resolutions," B-9, at www.nea .org/resolutions/00/00b-9.html.

16. National Education Association, "NEA 2000–2001 Resolutions," B-9, at www.nea .org/resolutions/00/00b-9.html.

17. See Susan Birden, Linda L. Gaither, and Susan Laird, "The Struggle over the Text: Compulsory Heterosexuality and Educational Policy," *Educational Policy* 14, no. 5 (November 2000): 638–63.

18. Birden, Gaither, and Laird, "The Struggle over the Text," 642–43.

19. Sharon Lerner, "Christian Conservatives Take Their Antigay Campaign to the Schools," at http://traversearea.com/GLSEN/ARTICLES/art63.htm.

20. Human Rights Campaign, "New 'Ex-Gay' Defector Reveals Cracks in the 'Ex-Gay' Ministries," at http://traversearea.com/GLSEN/articles/art17.htm.

21. Lerner, "Christian Conservatives."

22. Lerner, "Christian Conservatives."

23. Lerner, "Christian Conservatives."

24. James T. Sears, "Thinking Critically/Intervening Effectively about Heterosexism and Homophobia: A Twenty-Five-Year Research Perspective," in *Overcoming Heterosexism and Homophobia: Strategies That Work* (New York: Columbia University Press, 1997), 16.

25. See Adrienne Rich, "Compulsory Heterosexuality and Lesbian Existence," in *Blood, Bread, and Poetry* (New York: W.W. Norton, 1986), 23–75.

26. Rich, "Compulsory Heterosexuality and Lesbian Existence," 23–75.

27. Audre Lorde, *Sister Outsider* (Freedom, Calif.: Crossing Press, 1988), 45.

28. Marilyn Frye, *The Politics of Reality: Essays in Feminist Theory* (Freedom, Calif.: Crossing Press, 1983), 23.

29. Frye, *The Politics of Reality,* 17–38.

30. Sarah Lucia Hoagland, *Lesbian Ethics* (Palo Alto, Calif.: Institute of Lesbian Studies, 1988), 28.

31. Hoagland adds that heterosexualism has been so normalized in Anglo-European culture that we cease to perceive the dominance–subordination relationship to be problematic or wrong as long as it is exercised benevolently: "the 'loving' relationship between men and women, the 'protective' relationship between imperialist and the colonized, the 'peace-keeping' relationship between democracy (u.s. capitalism) and threats to democracy." Hoagland, *Lesbian Ethics,* 7–8.

32. Janice Raymond, *A Passion for Friends: Toward a Philosophy of Female Affection* (Boston: Beacon Press, 1986), 3–14.

33. Raymond, *A Passion for Friends,* 3–14.

34. Judith Butler, *Gender Trouble: Feminism and the Subversion of Identity* (New York: Routledge, 1990), 151n6.

35. Judith Butler, "Imitation and Gender Insubordination," in *Inside/Out: Lesbian Theories, Gay Theories,* ed. Diana Fuss (New York: Routledge, 1991), 20–21.

36. David M. Halperin, "Sex before Sexuality: Pederasty, Politics, and Power in Classical Athens," in *Hidden from History*, ed. M. Duberman, M. Vicinus, and G. Chauncey Jr. (New York: Penguin Group, 1989), 38.

37. John Boswell, *Christianity, Social Tolerance, and Homosexuality* (Chicago: University of Chicago Press, 1980), 41–46.

38. Boswell, *Christianity, Social Tolerance, and Homosexuality*, 41–46.

39. Boswell, *Christianity, Social Tolerance, and Homosexuality*, 45.

40. A. MacDonald, "Homophobia: Its Roots and Meanings," *Homosexual Counseling Journal* 3, no. 1 (1976): 23–33; quoted in Sears, "Educators, Homosexuality, and Homosexual Students," 38.

41. Sears, "Thinking Critically," 17–18.

42. Celia Kitzinger, "Heteropatriarchal Language: The Case against Homophobia," *Gossip* 5:15–20; noted in Hoagland, *Lesbian Ethics*, 28n.

43. Gary Kinsman, *The Regulation of Desire: Sexuality in Canada* (New York: Black Rose Books, 1987), 29; quoted in Diana Fuss, *Essentially Speaking: Feminism, Nature and Difference* (New York: Routledge, 1989), 109.

44. Simon Watney, "The Ideology of GLF," in *Homosexuality, Power and Politics* (London: Allison and Busby, 1980), 68; quoted in Fuss, *Essentially Speaking*, 109.

45. See "COPP Position Statement on Therapies Focused on Attempts to Change Sexual Orientation (Reparative or Conversion Therapies)," at http://navigation.helper .realnames.com/framer/1/112/default.asp?realname=American+Psychiatric+Association &url=http%3A%2F%2Fwww%2Epsych%2Eorg&frameid=1&providerid=112&uid=300 04965.

46. G. Remafadi, "Homosexual Youth," 222–25; National Network of Runaway and Youth Services, *To Whom Do They Belong?* at http://pflag.org/schools/schoolsfacts.htm.

47. Hilda F. Besner and Charlotte I. Spungin, *Gay and Lesbian Students: Understanding Their Needs* (Philadelphia: Taylor and Francis, 1995), 48.

48. Coles and Stokes survey, quoted in Besner and Spungin, *Gay and Lesbian Students*, 29. Also, in a national survey conducted by the American Association of University Women, U.S. youth in grades eight through eleven described their being called *lesbian* or *gay* as the most deeply upsetting form of sexual harassment (Louis Harris and associates, *Hostile Hallways: The AAUW Survey on Sexual Harassment in America's Schools*, [Washington, D.C.: American Association of University Women Educational Foundation, 1993]).

49. A. R. D'Augelli and S. L. Hershberger, "Lesbian, Gay and Bisexual Youth in Community Settings: Personal Challenges and Mental Health Problems," *American Journal of Community Psychology* 21 (1993): 421.

50. Karen M. Harbeck, ed., *Coming Out of the Classroom Closet: Gay and Lesbian Students, Teachers, and Curricula* (New York: Harrington Park Press, 1992), 17.

51. Massachusetts Department of Education, *Massachusetts Youth Risk Behavior Survey* (1997).

52. See discussion on the impact of homophobia in Besner and Spungin, *Gay and Lesbian Students*, 47–50. Janice Raymond has made it clear in her discussion of friendship and ideology of hetero-reality that same-sex relationships in men have received far more approbation than have women's relationships in *A Passion for Friends: Toward a Philosophy of Female Affection* (Boston: Beacon Press, 1986), 6–10.

53. Besner and Spungin, *Gay and Lesbian Students*, 48; Harbeck, *Coming Out of the Classroom Closet*, 14.

54. Harbeck, *Coming Out of the Classroom Closet*, 19.

55. Besner and Spungin, *Gay and Lesbian Students*, 48.

56. U.S. Surgeon General, *The Surgeon General's Call to Action, 1999*, at www .surgeongeneral.gov/library/calltoaction/fact3.htm.

57. Massachusetts Department of Education, *Massachusetts Youth Risk Behavior Survey* (1997).

58. U.S. Department of Health and Human Services, *Report of the Secretary's Task Force on Youth Suicide* (1989).

59. Massachusetts Department of Education, *Massachusetts Youth Risk Behavior Survey* (1997).

60. John Dewey, *Experience and Education* (New York: Touchstone, 1997; original, 1938), 27.

61. Quoted in the National Education Association's Health Information Network, at www.neahin.org/mentalhealth/suicide.html.

62. James T. Sears, "Educators, Homosexuality, and Homosexual Students," 38–55.

63. These numbers are from C. J. Patterson's studies in 1992 and 1995. However, because of the sharp increase in lesbians who are becoming pregnant through artificial insemination and the percentage of adoptions by same-sex households now able to adopt children, this figure may well be too low. Casper and Schultz, "What Do Children Know?" 4.

64. PFLAG, "Policy Statements," at http://navigation.helper.realnames.com/framer/ 1/112/default.asp?realname=PFLAG&url=http%3A%2F%2Fwww%2Epflag%2Eorg%2F &frameid=1&providerid=112&uid=30017580.

65. See Casper and Schultz, "What Do Children Know?"

66. See Rita M. Kissen, *The Last Closet: The Real Lives of Lesbian and Gay Teachers* (Portsmouth, N.H.: Heinemann, 1996); Madiha Didi Khayatt, *Lesbian Teachers: An Invisible Presence* (Albany: State University of New York Press, 1992); Dan Woog, *School's Out: The Impact of Gay and Lesbian Issues on America's Schools* (Los Angeles: Alyson Publications, 1995); Kevin Jennings, ed., *One Teacher in Ten: Gay and Lesbian Educators Tell Their Stories* (Los Angeles: Alyson Books, 1994).

67. Lambda Legal, at www.lambdalegal.org/cgi-bin/pages/issues/record?record=18.

68. John D'Emilio, "The Issue of Sexual Preference on College Campuses: Retrospect and Prospect," in *Educating Men and Women Together: Coeducation in a Changing World* (Urbana: University of Illinois Press, 1987.)

69. D'Emilio, "The Issue of Sexual Preference."

70. Warren J. Blumenfield, "Homophobia and Anti-semitism: Making the Links," in Sears and Williams, *Overcoming Heterosexism and Homophobia*, 131.

71. Blumenfield, "Homophobia and Anti-semitism," 131–38.

72. Eric Estuar Reyes and Gust A. Yep, "Challenging Complexities: Strategizing with Asian Americans in Southern California Against (Heterosex)Isms," in Sears and Williams, *Overcoming Heterosexism and Homophobia*, 91.

73. Reyes and Yep, "Challenging Complexities," 91.

74. See Simone de Beauvoir, *The Second Sex* (Paris: Librairie Gallimard, 1949; New York: Vintage Books, 1989).

75. Virginia Woolf, *Three Guineas* (San Diego, Calif.: Harcourt Brace Jovanovich, 1938).

76. Woolf, *Three Guineas*, 78.

77. Woolf, *Three Guineas*, 8–10.

78. Woolf, *Three Guineas*, 17–21.

79. Woolf, *Three Guineas*, 17–21.

80. Woolf, *Three Guineas*, 33–35.

81. Woolf, *Three Guineas*, 99.

82. See Marilyn Frye's discussion about this in "On Being White: Thinking toward a Feminist Understanding of Race and Race Supremacy," in *The Politics of Reality: Essays in Feminist Theory* (Freedom, Calif.: Crossing Press, 1983), 114–15.

83. Heterosexual privilege is that sanction of opposite sex coupling that has been institutionalized in most organizations. For instance, states license marriages, provide tax forms that include the right to claim an unemployed spouse as a dependent and permit spouses to collect social security after the death of the spouse. Churches and synagogues have sacramentalized marriage. Community organizations provide spousal memberships and discounts. Businesses provide health and life insurance for spouses. Heterosexual privilege is the absence of many constraints faced by same-sex couples: mortgage companies that will not finance a home; insurance companies that will not write home insurance; being refused ordination in a church based on sexual orientation; being denied the right to marry; having legislation that prohibits consensual sexual relations; being subject to gay bashing; not being allowed to invite your partner to events that range from school proms to office parties to university picnics. Heterosexual privilege protects the emotional, economic, and physical security of heterosexuals in ways that are routinely denied to their lesbian and gay peers and colleagues. Barbara Smith has claimed that heterosexual privilege has been very difficult for women of color to renounce so that they may claim lesbian identity: "Heterosexual privilege is usually the only privilege that Black women have. None of us have racial or sexual privilege, almost none of us have class privilege, maintaining 'straightness' is our last resort." Barbara Smith, "Toward a Black Feminist Criticism," in *All the Women Are White, All the Blacks Are Men, But Some of Us Are Brave*, ed. Gloria T. Hull, Patricia Bell Scott, and Barbara Smith (New York: Feminist Press, 1982), 171.

84. For instance, Nadya Aisenberg and Mona Harrington talk about being outsiders in the academy, in *Women of Academe: Outsiders in the Sacred Grove* (Amherst: University of Massachusetts Press, 1988). Black lesbian feminist Audre Lorde refers to herself as Sister Outsider in her collection of essays by the same name. In "The Eye of the Outsider," Adrienne Rich examines a condition that most people spend great energy trying to deny or evade through whatever kinds of assimilation or protective coloration they can manage, in *Blood, Bread, and Poetry: Selected Prose* (New York: W. W. Norton, 1986); she also claims that lesbian identity is essential outsiderhood. Patricia Hill Collins uses the concept of "outsiders within" to talk about the particular perspective of black women's location in the domestic labor market in *Black Feminist Thought: Knowledge, Consciousness, and the Politics of Empowerment* (New York: Routledge, 1991).

85. Many thanks to Catherine Hobbs for directing me to Janet Atwill's insightful discussion of *techne* in *Rhetoric Reclaimed: Aristotle and the Liberal Arts Tradition* (Ithaca, N.Y.: Cornell University Press, 1998).

86. Atwill, *Rhetoric Reclaimed*, 6–7, 48.

87. See Aristotle, *The Nicomachean Ethics*, book 6; and Atwill, *Rhetoric Reclaimed*, 54, 170–71.

88. Aristotle, *The Nicomachean Ethics*, trans. Sir David Ross (Oxford: Oxford University Press, 1998), 1143b18–b35.

89. William James, *Pragmatism* (New York: Dover Publications, 1995; original, 1907), 18.

90. Jim Garrison, *Dewey and Eros: Wisdom and Desire in the Art of Teaching* (New York: Teachers College Press, 1997), 22.

91. Garrison, *Dewey and Eros*, 22.

92. Garrison, *Dewey and Eros*, 13–15.

93. Richard Rorty, "World Well Lost," in *Consequences of Pragmatism* (Minneapolis: University of Minnesota Press, 1982), 16.

94. Garrison, *Dewey and Eros*, 27.

95. John Dewey, *Ethics*, in *The Later Works, 1925–1953*, ed. J. A. Boydston (Carbondale: Southern Illinois University Press, 1985; original, 1932), 270; quoted in Garrison, *Dewey and Eros*, 36.

96. Dewey, *Ethics*, 38.

97. Dewey, *Ethics*, 77.

CHAPTER TWO

—

The *Praxes in re Sexual Identity*

In chapter 1, I suggest that Out-Siders have already been at work theorizing about, and acting against, heterosexism and the effects of compulsory heterosexuality. In this chapter I explore the ways in which various concepts of sexual identity have influenced activism. Further, theorists' understandings of sexual identity have influenced not only which particular aspects of heterosexism and compulsory heterosexuality have been specifically targeted but also the ways that education has been employed as a corrective. Accordingly, I argue that the ways in which theorists have ignored, embraced, evaded, or rejected sexual identity become central to the constitution of radically different praxes, with radically different consequences for lesbian, gay, bisexual, and transgender people.

Identity—whether based on race, gender, ethnicity, ability, or sexuality —has emerged during the last half-century as one of the most difficult problems for contemporary theory and politics. The concept of identity has been brought under philosophical scrutiny, as identity politics has fallen in and out of favor. Sexual identity, however, has proven especially divisive, fraught with questions and rhetoric about choice and destiny, nature and nurture, essentialism and social construction, morality and legislation.

At a practical level, sexual identity is a core concern for lesbian and gay outsiders since the decision about whether, when, to whom, or with whom to identify as lesbian or gay often has far-ranging social and political implications. At the philosophical level, it is one of the major issues of the day. Luce

31

Irigaray has this to say about the philosophical importance of sexual difference:

> Sexual difference is one of the major philosophical issues, if not the issue, of our age. According to Heidegger, each age has one issue to think through, and one only. Sexual difference is probably the issue in our time which could be our "salvation" if we thought it through.
>
> But, whether I turn to philosophy, to science, or to religion, I find this underlying issue still cries out in vain for our attention.[1]

It is no surprise, then, that sexual identity has become one of the most problematic topics for those engaged in research on lesbian and gay issues. In fact, Eve Kosofsky Sedgwick believes that many of the major modes of thought and knowledge in Western culture as a whole are structured and fractured by what she calls the "chronic, now endemic crisis of homo/heterosexual definition."[2]

Theory and action have been brought to bear on questions of sexual identity in an almost unlimited number of ways. There are, however, sufficient substantive similarities in the approaches to allow for grouping. Therefore, I will name and categorize these principal ways of thinking about sexual identity as the *Praxes in re Sexual Identity*, that is the praxes that have been developed with regard to sexual identity. The *Praxes in re Sexual Identity* then comprise these six major groupings: *Praxis of the Closet, Praxis of Inclusion, Praxis of Coming Out, Praxis of Location, Praxis of Refusal,* and *Praxis of Performativity.*

The fact that approaches to the question of sexual identity may be grouped for analysis is not to say that the borders of the categories neatly circumscribe the ideas contained therein, nor does it indicate univocality. Even though the categories facilitate analysis of the key principles that inhere in each, the theorists differ from one another in many respects. Furthermore, not always is there a one-to-one relation between theorist and praxis. For instance, Adrienne Rich's early works are written from the *Praxis of Coming Out;* yet, she was also one of the major theorists to conceptualize the key components in the *Praxis of Location.*

The *Praxes in re Sexual Identity* may be best conceptualized on a continuum. At one extreme is essentialist thought; at the other extreme is social constructionism. The praxes that derive from essentialist thought constitute the Realist Sexual Taxonomy; the praxes at the opposite end of the spectrum, social constructionism, derive from the Nominalist Sexual Taxonomy. (I discuss these Sexual Taxonomies, which I theorized elsewhere, in some detail as

I review the individual praxes.) The praxes that lie in the middle of the continuum borrow from essentialism and social constructionism. Therefore, the Realist Sexual Taxonomy includes the *Praxes of the Closet* and *Inclusion*, whereas the Nominalist Sexual Taxonomy comprises the *Praxes of Refusal* and *Performativity*. In the middle of the continuum are the *Praxes of Coming Out* and *Location*, both of which are part of the Pragmatist Sexual Taxonomy.

In the analysis that follows, I discuss the key premises in each of the *Praxes in re Sexual Identity*. In addition, I identify the theorists who have made significant contributions to the praxis, cite the major Outsiders and Out-Siders who have worked within the praxis, and examine the ways in the praxis has influenced education.

Praxis of the Closet

None of the *Praxes in re Sexual Identity* presents itself uniformly, but the *Praxis of the Closet* has been elaborated with especially astonishing diversity. It is unified, however, by the fact that the Western philosophical thought that informs the *Praxis of the Closet* has directly contributed to keeping lesbians and gays in the closet, by denigrating, demonizing, or trivializing nonheterosexuality; or has done so indirectly, by ignoring sexual identity. The North American educational paradigms built on that philosophical thought have remained true to form. I need to emphasize that I am certainly not suggesting that all those who write, or have written, within the *Praxis of the Closet* are closeted lesbians or gays themselves; rather, the philosophers who have contributed to the *Praxis of the Closet* have failed to address sexual identity in ways that support coming out.

While the *Praxis of the Closet* may have little to contribute to the understanding of sexual identity per se, it is a rich philosophical and educational resource to which the other *Praxes in re Sexual Identity* are deeply indebted. In fact, as I demonstrate, the practitioners and theorists working within the other five *Praxes in re Sexual Identity* traipse nimbly, routinely, and fruitfully in and out of the *Praxis of the Closet*, appropriating ideas that they then reconceptualize in service of new understandings of sexual identity. Within the *Praxis of the Closet*, therefore, educators and philosophers of education have taken three distinct approaches to lesbian and gay issues. Some ignore homosexuality, whereas others condemn it. Some philosophers of education never discuss homosexuality but conceptualize freedom and education in such revolutionary ways that they shine light on how these same notions might be applied to issues of sexual identity. Still other philosophers go so far as to say that heterosexism needs to be theorized, but they do not actually take that step themselves. Consequently, while theorists of the other praxes may find the theories informing the *Praxis of the Closet* problematic because of their treatment of nonheterosexuality, they have routinely found certain aspects of the theory in the *Praxis of the Closet* to be useful in their own thinking.

My concern in the following sections is not to delineate every philosophical perspective that comes from the Closet, for such would be an impossible task, constituting an effective review of philosophical thought over the last two thousand years. Rather, I recognize four major pedagogical approaches that instantiate the responses to sexual identity framed above: liberal education, religious instruction, critical pedagogy, and feminist pedagogy. These pedagogies have formed U.S. educational practices, past and present, contributing to the traditions that have promoted heterosexism, anti–lesbian and gay prejudice, and the mis-education of compulsory heterosexuality.

Liberal Education and Religious Instruction

Many contemporary educators and philosophers deem politics, perhaps especially sexual politics, to be subversive of "pure" education—that is, education undertaken for the sake of learning alone. However, politics and education have been intertwined in philosophical thought since the time of Socrates, Plato, and Aristotle. When Socrates recommended an education consisting of gymnastics for the body, music for the soul, dialectics for the mind, philosophy, number and calculation, geometry, and astronomy,[3] he was recommending it not for the masses but for the leaders of the state. The people charged with decision making for society as a whole were to be society's intellectual leaders as well. Similarly, Aristotle believed that the wisdom of *phronesis* was attainable only by free male citizens of the *polis*. Women, slaves, children, and the masses, according to Aristotle, had neither the freedom to make unimpeded choices about conduct nor the intellectual insight and education necessary for wisdom.[4] Consequently, this education that developed both mind and body, which has been the intellectual foundation of Western education, was designed and reserved for an elite male group of the leisure class.[5]

By the time of the fifth to tenth centuries, the curriculum of liberal arts education had solidified into the following: grammar, rhetoric, logic, arithmetic, geometry, music, and astronomy. The purpose of this liberal arts curriculum was to transmit literacy, numeracy, and cultural tradition.[6] By this time in history the education of the mind and body recommended by the Greeks had been reduced to education for the mind alone. When there is no place for the body in education, there is certainly no place for sexuality. Liberal curriculum was aimed then at inculcating a set of cultural values through texts and traditions believed to exemplify those values, to transmit that which society believes to be the fabric and framework of its culture—a culture characterized by heterosexism and compulsory heterosexuality. Consequently, a liberal education is not based on any unified philosophical system but a program containing books, methodologies, curricula, departmental divisions, funding programs, and methods for evaluating competence.[7] The product of liberal education is a kind of normative subject whose values conform to those protected by the liberal arts tradition, a tradition explicitly heterosexist.[8]

Liberal political thought—and the democratic form of government it spawned, to which the *Praxis of Inclusion* is deeply and directly indebted and committed—posed significant problems for liberal education. Liberal politics holds a conception of human nature that locates the measure of humanity in the capacity for rationality.[9] As democratic society acknowledged more and more groups to be capable of exercising rational thought, such groups were admitted to citizenship. Just as the Greeks believed that rulers needed education, so did democratic governments understand the necessity for educating those citizens who would participate in decision making by voting. Educational programs were established that would prepare these additional groups in basic education for citizenship. Therefore, liberal political thought promoted—in modern Western civilization—public schooling, coeducational colleges, Native American boarding schools, the Tuskegee Institute, the black colleges for DuBois's Talented Tenth, and immigrant education—all aimed at including more people in education for citizenship.

The curriculum proper of liberal education largely ignored homosexuality.[10] However, that does not mean that homosexuality was ignored entirely, for Western theology and philosophy were intertwined. Centers of learning where one might pursue a liberal education during the Christian era were associated first with Europe's monasteries and later with church-affiliated universities in Europe and North America. Religious instruction could and did address questions of homosexuality, uniformly condemning it as sinful.

In the United States, however, the overt interweaving of religious instruction and liberal education began to unravel in the mid-nineteenth century for two reasons: first, the rise of public education and public institutions of higher learning; and, second, the secularization of philosophy in areas of ethics, aesthetics, education, and law. As liberal education increasingly became divorced from religious instruction, discussion of moral questions associated with specific religious views became less prevalent in the curriculum proper. That is not to say that the stigmatization of homosexuality did not continue in the hidden curriculum, for it certainly did. However, because secular educational philosophy focused on the curriculum proper, sexual identity was dismissed as a topic for educational consideration, as was religion.

Whereas contemporary educational philosophers in the liberal tradition ignore homosexuality, conservative religious institutions and their affiliated educational institutions continue the tradition of religious instruction, actively denigrating and repressing nonheterosexual sexuality. Conservative religious instruction in churches and church-affiliated schools and colleges bases its condemnation of lesbian and gay sexuality on literal interpretive methods applied to the Bible.[11] Further, just because this religious instruction is not based in secular educational philosophy does not mean that its precepts are not widely influential in secular culture. In fact, the condemnation and denigration of nonheterosexuality by conservative religious groups is pervasive across many configurations of education, from churches and religious families to church-affiliated schools, and through not only conservative political organizations in public schools and universities but popular culture as well. Not only do these conservative religious–political groups work to repress nonheterosexual identities via political means, they also work to convert lesbians and gays through spiritual means supplemented with "reparative" counseling techniques and conversion therapies.[12] Further, these same groups have organized strong political opposition to sex education at the local and national levels. These groups protest that the majority of sex education programs in the country teach children how to have sex without getting pregnant, thereby promoting contraceptives, masturbation, and homosexuality.[13] Lack of evidence aside, these religious conservatives have an effective, if philosophically and ethically flawed, praxis from which they are working that is widely influential.

Critical Pedagogy

Liberal politics is based on the premise that coercive institutions are justified insofar as they promote liberty. Anarchists, however, reject this central task of government, believing that coercive institutions should be replaced by voluntary contractual agreements. Influenced by Pierre-Joseph Proudhon, anarchist Emma Goldman embraced sexual knowledge, pleasure, and freedom for girls and women as well as for boys and men.[14] Even though Goldman challenged society's coercive institutions, she did not challenge heterosexism.

Marxist thought, which envisioned the revolutionary change that would overthrow a capitalist society, has been exceedingly influential in the *Praxes of Coming Out, Location,* and *Refusal.* These praxes borrowed freely from Marx's conceptualization about developing critical consciousness, wherein oppressed groups come to see the world from the perspective of their own interests, not from the viewpoint of the oppressor class. Emancipatory praxis is therefore dependent on being able to educate those people that need liberation. Marxists did not address religious instruction, but they did find liberal education to be an ineffective mechanism for providing education for freedom since liberal education is based on preserving traditions and creating normative subjects based on dominant ideology. Therefore, emancipatory praxis demanded new, creative approaches to education that would be widely available to the working classes. It was in fulfillment of this educational need that consciousness-raising groups became a predominant and effective means of educating for revolution. By sharing perspectives, people would learn to look critically on society's dominant ideology and, in so doing, creatively engage in thought that could transform the material world.[15]

The educational foundations of emancipatory praxis never became as important in the United States as liberal education, but such education became highly influential in the women's movement, which I discuss in the next section.[16] However, critical pedagogy has become more widely acknowledged in educational circles in the United States in the last thirty years because of the influence of critical pedagogues Antonio Gramsci and Paulo Freire. It was Gramsci who argued that because the education of different classes is historically linked to the needs of each particular class, the so-called democratic access of education to all classes equally is deceptive because education does not, and cannot, transcend class.[17]

Paulo Freire's work was designed to help those underclasses in South America with whom he worked realize that they were fighting not just for the freedom from hunger but for the freedom to create and construct, to wonder and venture. Freire argued that, when separated from inquiry, individuals cannot be truly human; so, to be free, people must reject what Freire called a "banking" education in which students only receive, file, and store the deposits made by educators. True knowledge emerges only through invention and reinvention, through restless, impatient, continuing, hopeful, critical inquiry with other people.[18]

Like their liberal counterparts, the critical pedagogues never addressed sexual identity directly. However, critical pedagogy's concern with developing critical thinkers and focusing on personal historicity as the starting point for education became quite influential on the women's movement and, consequently, on lesbian feminism. The critical pedagogues' opposition to creating the normative subjects of liberal education did shine some light into the Closet by making inquiry about many oppressed groups, including lesbians and gays, conceivable.

Feminist Pedagogy

Despite the ways that liberal politics and emancipatory praxis participated in the progress of political and educational thought, feminists charged that while men have slowly enlarged the dialogue of humanity to include nonhegemonic classes or races, these political stances consistently failed to open that dialogue to women. In challenging this political and educational thought, feminists reintroduced the body into politics, specifically the female body.

Refusing to subsume women's experience under the category of *human experience*, feminists' deconstructive analyses demonstrated that *human experience* has been a synonym for *male experience*. Western culture has associated rationality with humanity and thus rationality with masculinity, all while considering emotionality to be feminine; therefore, traditional epistemology has created a scenario in which women have been viewed as less rational, and hence less human, than men. Feminists have shown the many ways that women have been left outside the dialogue of humanity in both theory and practice.

Feminist theory has also brought significant changes to education through insightful critiques and through certain reforms of education institutions, policies, and practices. Feminist pedagogy sought to connect learning to women's lived experiences, drawing not only on liberal politics' commitment to educational and political inclusion but also on emancipatory praxis's commitment to learning in consciousness-raising groups. These pedagogical commitments began to be played out in both formal and informal environments, such as women's studies courses in colleges and universities and, for example, courses on body education designed and taught by the Boston Women's Health Book Collective. Key to feminist educational practice was value for the words and experiences of women.

Feminist educational philosopher Lorraine Code made significant contributions to our understanding about the ways in which "malestream" epistemology has ignored women and issues traditionally associated with them.[19] Jane Roland Martin identifies an "epistemological inequality" between men and women in the liberal curriculum,[20] leading her to ask two fundamental, and fundamentally disruptive, questions: What is the place of women in education? and What happens to educational thought when women are brought into it? She writes:

> These theorists analyze the concept of education, discuss the nature and structure of liberal education, construct theories of teaching and learning, set forth criteria of excellence, and debate educational aims and methods without attending to the difference of sex.[21]

Martin has argued that since philosophers do not construct theories of education in a vacuum, education as preparation for carrying out societal roles means tying those proposals to their vision of a good society. Insofar as the society that the philosopher pictures is peopled by both sexes, we cannot evaluate the liberal educational ideal it holds up for males unless we know its expectations for females. In fact, Martin argues, we will not even know the correct questions to ask. Thus, when history neglects past philosophical conversations about women's education, it follows that the tasks, functions, institutions, and traits of character that philosophy, as part of our culture, has associated with women are likewise neglected.[22]

Moreover, Martin's research demonstrates that an additive approach to liberal education—merely adding women's issues to the ones currently studied, for instance—obscures the fact that when women's issues are taken seriously and read *within* theory, the entire meaning of the reading changes. She further suggests that being blind to gender is not the solution:

> So long as sex and gender are fundamental aspects of our personal experience, so long as they are deeply rooted features of our society, educational theory— and educational practice too—must be gender-sensitive.[23]

Consequently, Martin suggests that we must constantly be aware of the workings of sex and gender because in this historical and cultural moment, they at times paradoxically make a big difference even when, at other times, they make no difference at all. Finally, she states, "One of the unanticipated rewards of bringing women into the educational realm is that the study of the education of the 'other' half of the population enables us to see all of education differently."[24]

Indeed, several feminist educational philosophers have furthered educational thought about the politics of feminist pedagogy. For instance, Ann Diller, Barbara Houston, Kathryn Pauly Morgan, and Maryann Ayim provide insightful analyses of sexist education and suggest ways that traditional genderized liberal education should be reconstructed.[25] Feminist pedagogy, therefore, stands in a peculiar position of liminality—halfway in the *Praxis of the Closet* and halfway out. Feminist educators and philosophers may not have theorized issues of sexual identity, but they have been profoundly aware of the ways in which heterosexism and compulsory heterosexuality have circumscribed gender roles. They may not have written explicitly about overcoming anti–lesbian and gay prejudice, but many, if not most, have been advocates of those who have undertaken such work. They may not have taught classes on lesbian and gay issues, but many of these women provided safe classroom environments for lesbians and gay males to come out. Feminist theory laid the groundwork that made much of the theory and practice in the other five *Praxes in re Sexual Identity* possible. Therefore, while feminist pedagogy still technically lies within the Closet, it certainly has flung wide the door, allowing its inhabitants to see differently, to ask questions that were easily translatable into the language of sexual identity, and to comprehend the violence of heterosexism as it affects straight women as well as lesbians and gay men.

Conclusions of the Closet

I emphasized earlier that because a theory or practice is contained within the *Praxis of the Closet*, that does not mean that its theorists and practitioners are closeted lesbians or gays themselves. However, this is not to say that since questions about sexual identity have not been asked by practitioners of the *Praxis of the Closet*, that lesbian and gay outsiders have not worked therein. In fact, many closeted lesbians and gay men have given their lives to the visions offered by these various forms of praxis that have denied questions of sexual identity. Some of those lesbian and gay outsiders have worked toward educational goals with no intention of ever being out of the closet. However, in working for change for other gay and lesbian outsiders, some have claimed that they could be more effective inside the closet since they could then avoid having a social stigma attached to their work.

In reality, few gay and lesbian outsiders have ever worked on behalf of lesbian and gay people from the closet, since laboring on such a stigmatized issue usually raises the specter, the question, of whether the advocate is himself or herself one of the stigmatized group.[26] Moreover, their failure to make the particulars of sexual identity part of the decision-making process, as particulars of class or sex have been included, means that lesbian and gay people working within these praxes have functioned not as Outsiders but as outsiders. Even Virginia Woolf's own Outsiders' Society serves as an example of the *Praxis of the Closet*. Concerned as she was for the outsiders who were the daughters of educated men, she did not question outright the ways in which her Outsiders' Society might respond to sexual identity.

Praxis of Inclusion

The theoretical approach of the *Praxis of Inclusion* is indebted to both liberal education and liberal politics. In addition, the *Praxis of Inclusion* draws on the work of a long line of liberal feminists, from Wollstonecraft[27] to Stanton and Anthony[28] to Friedan,[29] who sought to accord to women the rights that had been reserved for male heads of households. The *Praxis of Inclusion* is also indebted to a more contemporary version of liberalism—reformed liberal thought, which has been strongly influenced by Hans-Georg Gadamer and Hannah Arendt. Theorists in the *Praxis of Inclusion* have steered clear of critical pedagogy and, with the exception of Martha Nussbaum, feminist pedagogy and religious instruction as well.

The liberal proviso that "right" takes priority over the "good" complicates the construction of the just society, for it challenges a society to create political, economic, and social institutions that maximize individual freedom without jeopardizing the community's welfare. When it comes to state interventions in the private sphere, those working within the *Praxis of Inclusion* generally agree that the less we see of government in our bedrooms, nurseries, or kitchens, the better.[30]

By privileging "right" over "good," Out-Siders working within the *Praxis of Inclusion* have challenged heterosexism by claiming that whatever one's belief might be about the propriety of nonheterosexual persons and their relationships, a democratic society demands that nonheterosexuals be afforded basic legal/political rights and protections. Therefore, Out-Siders working for lesbian and gay inclusion have been concerned primarily with, first, fighting legislative and policy initiatives that impeach the natural rights of lesbian and gay outsiders and, second, working to promulgate corrective legislation. Simply put, Out-Siders seek to accord to LGBTQ outsiders the rights and privileges previously reserved for heterosexuals.

Most Out-Siders grounded in the *Praxis of Inclusion,* then, support the right of lesbians and gay men to be protected against violence; to have consensual adult sexual relations without criminal penalty; to be free from discrimination in housing, employment, and education; to serve in the military; to marry or have the legal and social benefits of marriage; and to adopt children or to retain custody of children.[31] Using the *Praxis of Inclusion*'s commitment to individualism, Out-Siders have asserted the primacy of freedom and political dialogue, arguing that legal and political standing should be granted to nonheterosexual people on the basis of a shared humanity: the ability to reason and to participate in public life.

In no other *Praxis in re Sexual Identity* have non-LGBTQ Out-Siders worked as prominently as in the *Praxis of Inclusion*. This fact has been partly due to its theoretical base in liberal politics. Most Out-Sider groups actively working for lesbian and gay inclusion tend to be theoretically grounded in liberal politics—groups such as PFLAG, LAMBDA Legal, and the Boston Women's Health Book Collective. However, many people who support gay-friendly initiatives base their thinking not on liberal thought but on the findings of psychological and scientific research that have made their way into popular culture. Many of those findings maintain that homosexuality is not a choice or preference but an innate orientation. The claim is that homosexuality simply *is*, much as left-handedness simply *is*. While the individuals who adhere to this line of thought may not be consciously grounding their opinions in theory, this realist position has a long history in Western philosophical thought and is thoroughly compatible with the *Praxis of Inclusion*.

As I have theorized elsewhere,[32] the Realist Sexual Taxonomy posits that homosexual, heterosexual, and bisexual categories exist because people are naturally differentiated by choice of sex partner, even though not all societies allow expression of all varieties of erotic disposition. According to realists, homosexuality has always existed in a relatively stable percentage of persons across cultures and ages—whether through nature or nurture, and regardless of the societal, religious, or civil sanctions against it. Because these categories underlie human sexual experience, even when obscured by social constraints or particular circumstances, realists maintain that attempts to convert, punish, or deny full rights of citizenship to homosexuals merely subvert, rather than change, reality.

Lesbian and gay Outsiders working with non-LGBTQ Out-Siders have made significant strides via the *Praxis of Inclusion* in a wide range of configurations of education. The National Education Association's safe-school project has influenced public school policies in some areas. As a result of the work of LAMBDA Legal, PFLAG, and GLSEN among others, many school and college administrators are beginning to take seriously the need to protect lesbian and gay students against violence.[33] School officials in many areas are also beginning to evidence less resistance to gay–straight student alliances, following the resolution of five lawsuits in favor of the complainants.[34] Other Out-Sider groups, such as the Boston Women's Health Book Collective and the American Nurses' Association, have influenced health education and practice in community clinics, health care facilities, and school-based sex education courses.[35]

Out-Siders working within the *Praxis of Inclusion* have made many strides in legislation and policy initiatives across many configurations of education; however, many lesbians and gays who support this praxis are often criticized by the more radical groups who claim that the liberal position of "I am exactly like you except for the person I love" denies the very real differences that come from living a marginalized existence. It is also safe to say that the *Praxis of Inclusion* has been supported by gay–straight alliances, liberal political supporters, and the medical/scientific community far more vigorously than by contemporary theorists.

Nevertheless, the *Praxis of Inclusion* is well represented by Out-Sider theorists Susan Moller Okin[36] and Saul M. Olyan[37] as well as one of its most prominent, prolific, and vocal advocates, Martha Nussbaum.[38] Proffering the classical notions of "world citizen," Nussbaum has suggested that the "cultivation of humanity" is a worthy ideal for our contemporary society. She suggests that three capacities are essential to the cultivation of humanity: the capacity for critical examination of oneself and one's tradition; the ability to see oneself not simply as a citizen of some local region or group but as a human being bound to all other human beings by ties of recognition and concern; and the ability to think what it might be like to be in the shoes of a person different from oneself.[39] Given these considerations, Nussbaum charges that it is the responsibility of a citizen of the world to become acquainted with the issues related to sexual difference. We need knowledge if we are to think well about such a crucial area of human life, she says. Further, Nussbaum maintains that respect, tolerance, and friendship are all appropriate aims for a liberal democracy founded on mutual respect and toleration among citizens who differ deeply about basic goals and aspirations.[40]

A curriculum that remains silent about homosexuality is defective, according to Nussbaum, because it contains unjustifiable gaps in scholarship. Curricular silence also implies that certain people are not worthy of study. To say that about one's fellow citizen, she contends, whether implicitly or explicitly, is objectionable. Therefore, the need to study sexuality should be motivated, at least in part, by a wish to correct that bad situation. To do less, Nussbaum suggests, is a refusal of reason itself. Further, she claims that those who have studied sexuality, historically and cross-culturally, are more likely than those who have not to question many of the demeaning and misleading stereotypes frequently associated with homosexuality in our society. Those who are aware of the differences manifested by history are somewhat more likely than others to be tolerant of the differences they see around them.[41]

Nussbaum has been a vocal advocate of sexuality studies in undergraduate curricula. She worked on Brown University's Educational Policy Committee and was instrumental in developing inquiries about the university's curricular treatment of homosexuality. As a result of these studies, an interdisciplinary faculty determined to bring high-level scholarship on sexuality studies to the campus. They coordinated a conference in 1987, Homosexuality in History and Culture, the first major academic conference of its kind. Two years later Brown adopted a nondiscrimination statement that includes sexual orientation. By 1994 many departments in the university offered courses that included discussion of sexual orientation. Brown is now one of the few universities that offers an undergraduate concentration in the study of sexuality.[42]

Theorists within the *Praxis of Inclusion* have routinely ignored the influence of religious instruction regarding questions of sexual identity. However, Nussbaum and Saul Olyan contravened that proscriptive stance by coordinating a conference in 1995 that invited papers developing distinct and conflicting positions on sexual orientation and its public policy dimensions situated within major religious traditions: Judaism, Roman Catholicism, mainline Protestantism, and African American churches. Those papers have been compiled in *Sexual Orientation and Human Rights in American Religious Discourse.*[43]

Finally, Nussbaum's latest book, *Sex and Social Justice*, examines the arguments for and against feminism and liberalism and how both have affected U.S. women, as well as women in more repressive countries. In the work, Nussbaum also defends her commitment to lesbian and gay rights. She summarizes several legal cases and argues convincingly for values of equal liberty and equality under the law. Recognizing that rational argument alone will not resolve all the controversies, since resistance to full equality for gays and lesbians has deep psychological roots, she pleads for civil public dialogue in an atmosphere of generosity and understanding.[44]

Martha Nussbaum's theoretical premises have not gone without challenge. Jane Roland Martin has claimed that despite her deep admiration for Nussbaum's work, she is puzzled that it draws overwhelmingly from male philosophers when many feminist essays on women's education might have shed valuable light on the subject. Further, Martin charges that Nussbaum's constitution of "cultivating humanity" does not question how extending the capacities of logical analysis and reasoning to women can be effected without forcing women to live out their lives as walking contradictions. Despite Nussbaum's declaration of cultivating the whole human being for the functions of citizenship and life generally, it is telling, according to Martin, that such cultivation only takes place within the "mind."[45]

Desiring students of liberal education to be intelligent participants in debates about the world's pressing problems says nothing about their learning to participate in activities that might actually solve problems. Martin continues by arguing:

> I do not myself see how a liberal education conceived of as cultivation for *the whole human being* can be realized by an academy that remains in thrall to the education-gender system that now prevails. I do not see how an idea of liberal education as cultivation for *the functions of life generally* can be put into practice if that system is not dismantled. Nussbaum's discussion illustrates the problem. She ignores the cultivation of human beings for living in families—in

contrast to debating their structure; for regulating sexuality—as well as talking about it; for improving children's lives in addition to pondering this topic. . . . what good is it to teach young people to debate the structure of families and the future of children intelligently without also cultivating their abilities to participate wisely and well in these practices?[46] [emphasis in original]

Thus, according to Martin, even though Nussbaum's reformed liberal paradigm is intended to overcome the weaknesses of liberal politics, she takes for granted many of its principles. Consequently, Nussbaum's well-intentioned reform addresses many symptoms without ever getting to the root of the problem.[47]

Praxis of Coming Out

The *Praxis of Inclusion* and the *Praxis of Coming Out* are based on an insider–outsider duality. However, where the *Praxis of Inclusion* depends on gradualism, the *Praxis of Coming Out* is committed to radical, revolutionary change. Where the *Praxis of Inclusion* is based on principles, abstractions, broad scales, and liberal theory, the *Praxis of Coming Out* is based on experiential knowledge, group identification, and consciousness raising, revealing its roots in emancipatory praxis. The theorists within this praxis have been quite critical of liberal education and have challenged its exclusion of the body and sexuality. Religious instruction has not been routinely explored within this praxis, except for Mary Daly's vigorous critique of the Christian church's part in promoting sexism and heterosexism in *Beyond God the Father*.[48]

Although the major unifying tenet of this praxis has been its commitment to coming out, Out-Siders in the *Praxis of Coming Out* were eager to walk back into the Closet long enough to appropriate consciousness raising associated with emancipatory praxis as a potent educational tool. Out-Siders in the *Praxis of Coming Out* believed, as did Out-Siders in the *Praxis of Inclusion*, that legal and political inequalities that were part of heterosexist ideology must be challenged. However, in conformance with the notions of class consciousness, the *Praxis of Coming Out* advocated turning identity groups into political collectives. Further, Out-Siders working in the *Praxis of Coming Out* have not focused exclusively on legal and policy initiatives. They have challenged heterosexist ideology's perceived superiority and its right to dominance, which has been perpetuated through restrictions, socialization, gender roles, and force. In addition, it was within the *Praxis of Coming Out* that Adrienne Rich first conceptualized "compulsory heterosexuality," a term so self-evident to many lesbian and gay outsiders that it quickly became a bat-tle cry within the movement as a whole.

While lesbian feminism was developing within the women's movement, the gay activist movement was organizing in major urban centers. The dif-ferences in these two arms of the *Praxis of Coming Out* are reflected in the different ways that sexuality has been viewed within the two groups. Les-bianism was politicized within feminism, creating a culture that clearly de-lineated norms of acceptability; gay activism was associated with sexual ad-venture and exploration, stretching the boundaries of the acceptable. Much of the sentiment of gay activism mirrors this statement by Dennis Altman: "Now the version of liberation that I hold is precisely one that would make the homo/hetero distinction irrelevant; for that to happen, however, we shall all have to recognize our bisexual potential."[49] Thus, from its inception, gay activism tended to embrace diverse forms of sexuality, whereas even bisexu-ality in lesbian feminism contravened the norms of the movement.[50]

Gay male scholars in the *Praxis of Coming Out* tended to focus on re-claiming gay history for the liberal curriculum and for "outing" gay male lit-erary and historic figures. Initially, there was an intense interest by many scholars in classical Greek sexuality. Yale historian John Boswell wrote two landmark tomes on homosexuality and same-sex unions in premodern Eu-rope that received particular acclaim for the depth and breadth of his re-search.[51] Other historians were interested in exploring how homosexuality has been regarded in non-European cultures.[52] Edwin Haeberle investigated the relationship between the work of the sexologists in Germany and the Nazi war crimes committed against this stigmatized group.[53] John d'Emilio re-searched the establishment of gay communities in urban centers in the United States.[54]

Despite the prolific historical and anthropological research about homo-sexuality conducted by gay male scholars, theory development by gay males in the *Praxis of Coming Out* lagged far behind that of lesbian feminism. The most critical theoretical contribution of gay males to this praxis was the simple—and completely radical—emphasis on coming out as the central po-litical act of resistance to lesbian and gay oppression.[55]

The configurations of education were influenced in three ways by gay male activism. First, organizations such as GLSEN and the Lesbian and Gay Caucus in the National Education Association focused on providing safe op-portunities for coming out in schools. Second, colleges and universities were pressed into allowing lesbian and gay alliances on their campuses. Third, the historical research that "outed" many literary and historical figures has be-come public knowledge through media attention and through a few publications that give short biographical sketches of these men and women, with the former constituting the majority.

Lesbian feminist scholars, like their male counterparts, also worked to recover a little-known history for the liberal curriculum. The lesbian historical project was complicated by having to confront not only the silence surrounding homosexuality but also the dearth of historical documents about women in general. Lillian Faderman captured the need for a lesbian tradition in the poignant account of her own experience:

> In 1956, as a teenager, I began to consider myself a lesbian. Almost as soon as I claimed that identity, being already enamored of books, of course I looked around for literary representations that would help explain me to myself. I did not have far to look, because the pulp book racks at the local drugstore exhibited a dizzying array of titles like *Odd Girl, Twisted Sisters, Twilight Lovers, We Walk in Shadows*, and *Whisper Their Love*. I was fascinated by their lurid covers and astonishingly graphic sexual scenes, I was depressed by their pathos and bathos, and—intellectual snob that I was at the age of sixteen—I was bored by their heavy-handed prose, stock characters, and predictability.
>
> I wanted real "literature," the kind I read in my English classes, to comment on the lifestyle I had just recently discovered with such enthusiasm, to reveal me to myself, to acknowledge the lesbian to the world. Naturally, my high school English teachers never gave me a hint about where to look for such literature. As an undergraduate in college I was an English literature major, but the only time I learned about a lesbian book was in an Abnormal Psych class, where *The Well of Loneliness* was mentioned. As a graduate student, although I read Emily Dickinson, Sara Orne Jewett, Willa Cather, Virginia Woolf, Carson McCullers, Elizabeth Bishop, and even Sappho, I never had a professor who mentioned the word "lesbian" or acknowledged that love between women had ever been a subject of literary focus. In 1967 I received a Ph.D. in English literature without the slightest notion that lesbian literature had rich history and that many of the writers I admired—in fact almost all of those few women writers who were studied in graduate school—had contributed to that history.[56]

Faderman used that Ph.D. to uncover unacknowledged traditions, exploring how the work of the sexologists had changed female "romantic friendships," previously encouraged, into dangerous and deviant "sexual inversions."[57] Martha Vicinus sought to understand the intense friendships in girls' boarding schools; and groups such as the San Francisco Gay and Lesbian History Project revealed surprising information about scores of women over the last century who posed as men to access male privileges and rights.[58] Janice Raymond uncovered traditions of women's exclusive friendships with one another among nuns in the late Middle Ages and the Chinese marriage resisters in Kwangtung.

However, lesbian feminists, drawing on their rich feminist backgrounds, were intent on demonstrating the ways in which history, philosophy, medicine, and a host of other subjects had perpetuated huge gaps in scholarship by silencing, denigrating, hiding, and trivializing the contributions of women. These women charged that mainstream (malestream) thinking had created universal categories based on stereotypical masculine characteristics, then found women lacking by comparison. Demonstrating how our understanding of women, femininity, gender roles, and the family were all designed to prop up a patriarchal system based on male rights and privilege, Out-Siders recognized that sex was not simply a biological category but a socially constructed one. Adrienne Rich claims that once we understand the variety and intensity of societal forces to which women are subjected, one cannot any longer see women's "choice" of men as sexual partners as natural, normal, or biological. She forced recognition that sexuality, like motherhood, had become institutionalized. Rich also conceptualized the term *lesbian continuum*, perhaps one of her most controversial terms, by which she means the range of woman-identified experience in each woman's life and throughout history, not simply that a woman has had or desired genital sexual experience with another woman. She expanded the definition of *lesbian continuum* to include the sharing of a rich inner life, the bonding against male tyranny, the giving and receiving of practical and political support.[59]

Mary Daly's theoretical works, *Beyond God the Father* and *Gyn/Ecology*, are two of the most important contributions to theory in the *Praxis of Coming Out*. Daly delves into the *Praxis of the Closet* to borrow from two key existential theologians, Paul Tillich and Martin Buber. Rejecting the idea of God as a fixed male Being, she suggests that God must be viewed instead as the "Verb of Verbs." Daly sees the women's movement as a spiritual revolution. Women's rejection of their status as "Other," Daly contends, would prove redemptive for self and society. Daly believes that by rebelling against their status as "objects," women can force a radical new awareness on society and grow in their own consciousness. This new consciousness would be grounded in a fundamental refusal to objectify either self or others.[60]

In *Gyn/Ecology*, Daly's Amazon voyage, she examines the tortures of witch-hunts, clitoridectomies, foot binding, suttee, and modern gynecology. Since reality is constructed through language, *Gyn/Ecology* was her deconstruction of patriarchal definitions. By forcing new awareness through puns and neologisms, by inverting and reclaiming words used pejoratively about women, Daly reconstructs the language of these ideas into positive prototypes for the woman-identified woman in a community of cosmic sisterhood.[61]

Daly may be the preeminent lesbian feminist theorist of the *Praxis of Coming Out*, but she had plenty of worthy company. Adrienne Rich forced feminist recognition of motherhood as not just a biological necessity but as an institution that has been deployed for a patriarchal culture. Janice Raymond demonstrated the fallacy of traditional (male) wisdom that has assumed that women's lives and loves must always be directed toward men by discovering and theorizing about the primacy of women's friendships and "gyn/affection" as a principle force for women's affecting, moving, stirring, and arousing one another to full power.[62] Sarah Lucia Hoagland theorized a lesbian ethics,[63] and Luce Irigaray brought her psychoanalytic background to bear on questions of sexual difference.[64]

Lesbian feminists advocate alternative cultural arrangements, woman-defined ethics, and woman-directed energy to provide theoretical models for changing society and self. Developing a culture of resistance, they hoped to help the oppressed survive and fight back against the stereotypes taught by the hegemonic ruling class. This lesbian feminist purpose, theoretical and practical, entered the configurations of education in two distinct ways. First, these theorists were not simply preeminent lesbian feminists but preeminent *feminists*. Accordingly, much of their work was used routinely in women's studies courses. Second, academic feminism in this era was steadfast in its dedication to connecting to the community and to helping women, whether straight or lesbian, struggle against heterosexism. As a result, there were not clear-cut distinctions between scholars and activists. In fact, such distinctions would have been antithetical to women's studies and feminism.

Although Charlotte Bunch expresses concern that so much of the activism in the gay and lesbian movement was without a theoretical foundation,[65] in no other *Praxis in re Sexual Identity* have the efforts of the LGBTQ community and LGBTQ theorists been so thoroughly intertwined. The emancipatory focus of this praxis emphasizes education and scholars' working with the masses; so, theoretical and historical literature were written with activist audiences in mind.

As I have indicated, lesbian feminists and gay male activists and scholars share similar political goals and oftentimes members. But, those early days in the *Praxis of Coming Out* evidenced a great deal of animus, as well as profound disinterest, between lesbian feminists and gay male activists. Marilyn Frye[66] assesses the situation this way:

> Many gay men and some lesbians and feminists assume that it is reasonable to expect lesbian and feminist support for, or participation in, gay political and cultural organizations and projects, and many people think it is reasonable to

expect that gay men will understand and support feminist and lesbian causes. But both of these expectations are, in general, conspicuously not satisfied.

With few exceptions, lesbians—and in particular, feminist lesbians—have not seen gay rights as a compelling cause nor found association with gay organizations rewarding enough to hold more than temporary interest. With perhaps even fewer exceptions, gay men do not find feminist or lesbian concerns to be close enough to their own to compel either supportive political action or serious and attentive thought. Gay political and cultural organizations which ostensibly welcome and act in behalf of both gay men and gay women generally have few if any lesbian members, and lesbian and feminist political and cultural organizations, whether or not they seek or accept male membership, have little if any gay male support.[67]

Frye continues by asserting the feminist commitment to gay rights but makes it clear that in a culture that is hostile to women the principles and values of a male-supremacist society are inherent in gay male groups. Among the most fundamental of those male-supremacist principles and values are the following:

1. The presumption of male citizenship.
2. Worship of the penis.
3. Male homoeroticism, or man-loving.
4. Contempt for women, or woman-hating.
5. Compulsory male heterosexuality.
6. The presumption of general phallic access.[68]

Predictably, some lesbians discussed and practiced separatism in many forms. In fact, the insistence within this praxis on group identity and experience often created an uneasy alliance with non-LGBTQ Out-Siders. Since sexual identity is seen as "the difference that makes all the difference," Outsider activists sought to revalue and fight the stereotypes and gender complementarity of compulsory heterosexuality that constrict lesbian and gay identity and behavior. The Outsiders were often quite wary of heterosexual partnerships that might compromise the creation of an authentic lesbian and gay culture. Much of the volatility of these separatist positions has abated over time because lesbians and gays have needed each other's support, as well as heterosexuals' support, on political issues.

The *Praxis of Coming Out* is situated within the Pragmatist Sexual Taxonomy. This taxonomy draws from realist and nominalist thought by asserting that some sexual categories do exist but that we have been societally conditioned into behaviors that are not necessarily biological in origin.

Where the approach of the realists and the nominalists is first and foremost one of truth seeking, however, the pragmatists' primary concern is for transforming existing practice. The Pragmatist Sexual Taxonomy therefore stresses collective social action as an effective approach for changing oppressive circumstances into more desirable situations that allow freedom for individual development.[69]

Outsiders in the *Praxis of Coming Out* have been fundamentally committed to consciously recognizing themselves as a group in opposition to the hegemony of compulsory heterosexuality. Coming out as lesbian, gay, bisexual, or transgender evidences a choice for claiming, naming, and identifying oneself instead of allowing others to theorize, medicalize, characterize, or demonize one's existence. Adrienne Rich put it like this:

> Whatever is unnamed, undepicted in images, whatever is omitted from biography, censored in collections of letters, whatever is misnamed as something else, made difficult-to-come-by, whatever is buried in the memory by the collapse of meaning under an inadequate or lying language—this will become, not merely unspoken, but *unspeakable*.[70] [emphasis in original]

Speaking the unspeakable has been a primary theme for the *Praxis of Coming Out*.

Thus, while much of the societal reform on LGBTQ issues has been accomplished through the *Praxis of Coming Out*, its commitment to identity politics has drawn much criticism from theorists and activists alike. For instance, Audre Lorde finds that despite the important, useful, and thought-provoking ideas in *Gyn/Ecology*, Daly does not read, or read well, the works of women of color. Lorde points out that all of the mythical goddess images that Daly researched were white, thereby dismissing the many black foremothers. When non-European women were utilized as subjects, it was to discuss African genital mutilation, foot binding, and suttee. Consequently, Lorde believes that Daly's misuse of non-European women in the book served racist purposes. Finally, Lorde says:

> The oppression of women knows no ethnic nor racial boundaries, true, but that does not mean it is identical within those differences. Nor do the reservoirs of our ancient power know these boundaries. To deal with one without even alluding to the other is to distort our commonality as well as our difference.

Lorraine Code, too, expresses concern about the implications of identity politics. Feminism is, she claims, based on a paradox that we must claim and refuse the identity of "woman." Insufficiently nuanced affirmations and assignments of

identity with the essentialist, stereotyped implications they carry have been instrumental in marginalizing "minority" or "Other" women in the name of their
differences from a newly installed feminist norm. The "second wave's" early co-
optation of the experiences of black, working-class, and lesbian women in the
hegemonic theoretical discourses of white middle-class heterosexual feminism is
just one example of the problems inherent in identity claims, according to
Code. Even particularized, carefully specified identities tend to solidify—that is,
to acquire a nostalgic appeal in their capacity to offer a "home," a resting place,
an illusory coherence and stability.[71]

Martha Nussbaum has been critical of identity politics as well. She
charges that identity politics' commitment to a primary affiliative group does
not recognize human diversity and cultural complexity. As a result, Nussbaum argues that a new antihumanist view often emerges that celebrates difference in an uncritical way and denies the very possibility of common interests and understandings, even of dialogue and debate, that take one
outside one's own group. She finds that an especially damaging consequence
of identity politics in the academy is the belief that only a member of a particular oppressed group can write well, or even read well, about that group's
experience.[72]

Further, social constructionist Judith Butler claims that terms of identity
have made promises that are impossible to keep as a consequence of the set
of exclusions that bound the subjects whose identities they are supposed to
represent. According to Butler, identity claims hold out promises of unity,
solidarity, and universality. One can then understand, she argues, the resentment and rancor against identity. They are signs of dissension and dissatis-
faction that follow identity politics' failure to deliver. She underscores the
claim that identity as a rallying point will inevitably lead to disappointment.[73]

Thus, despite the legal, political, and social gains accomplished under the
Praxis of Coming Out, it presents a troubled theoretical position for Out-
Siders who were drawn to this praxis to find people like themselves but who
found that promoting unity meant ignoring complex identities and hence
diversity.

Praxis of Location

The *Praxis of Location* arose from the theoretical failure of the *Praxis of Coming Out* to manage composite identities. Within feminism as a whole, the use
of generalities enabled the formation of analyses, alliances, public discourses,
and mass actions that produced liberating social change. But the generalities

that informed these analyses were based on oppositional categories that are formed against the oppressive group. Those oppositional categories become problematic when composite identities are recognized.

Even though the *Praxis of Location* came into being because of weaknesses in the *Praxis of Coming Out*, many of its goals remained the same. That is, as with the *Praxis of Coming Out*, Out-Siders in the *Praxis of Location* sought to disrupt heterosexist ideology politically, legally, and socially. They challenged liberal education relentlessly but ignored religious instruction. Out-Siders in the *Praxis of Location* have been grounded in feminist pedagogy, working to disrupt heteronormative gender roles.

However, Out-Siders in the *Praxis of Location* also realized that gender roles are not simply heterosexist but are fashioned on white paradigms. In the *Praxis of Location* sexism, homophobia, and racism are inseparable.[74] Further, within the *Praxis of Location* mere tolerance of difference is replaced with a view of difference that, in the words of Audre Lorde, is

> seen as a fund of necessary polarities between which our creativity can spark like a dialectic. Only then does the necessity for interdependency become un-threatening. Only within that interdependency of different strengths, acknowl-edged and equal, can the power to seek new ways of being in the world gener-ate, as well as the courage and sustenance to act where there are no charters.[75]

In *Sister Outsider*, Lorde theorizes that complex social and epistemological experiences produced by the intersections of gender, race, class, and sexual identities create a composite identity that does not fit cleanly within a single category, such as "woman," "black," or "lesbian," and may in fact lead to exclusion in any one of the three single categories. She argues convincingly that the black lesbian feminist, for instance, is always *all* of these identities. Composite identity cannot be taken apart and analyzed in terms of its separate elements. Further, to protest one domination and leave other entrenched oppressions intact is inherently violent and silencing.[76]

Marilyn Frye writes convincingly about how heterosexual women and lesbians have been differently excluded and silenced.[77] She sees them differently located in oppression. But she also aptly understands that one could be located as an oppressed white lesbian and still act as an oppressor: "White feminists come to renewed and earnest thought about racism not entirely spontaneously. We are pressed by women of color."[78]

Whiteness, Frye goes on to say, is pretty obviously a social or political construct of some sort, a construct that is not just used but *wielded*. Whites exercise a power of defining who is white and who is not, and they guard that power jealously. Members may bend the rules of membership anytime, if necessary to assert the member's exclusive authority to decide who is a member. An insidious expression of this authority emerges when members of the "superior" group grant membership to others based on the "benefit of the doubt."[79] The parallel here with presumptive heterosexuality is striking, with the heterosexual assumption being that everyone is heterosexual until the question is forced, blatantly or explicitly.

The tendency of "whites" and "heterosexuals" to be generously inclusive, according to Frye, is parallel to the false universalizations for which feminists have criticized men who write, speak, and think as though whatever is true for them is true of everybody. For the most part, the people in these dominant groups do not even think about modifying nouns in those ways. "We don't think of ourselves as *white*, we are just *people*." It is therefore an important breakthrough for a member of a dominant group to come to know that she or he is a member of *a group*—that is, only *part* of humanity.[80]

Adrienne Rich says that the implications of white identity are mystified by the presumption that white people are at the center of the universe. According to Rich, to participate in a "politics of location" is to understand that one is viewed, treated, and comes to know one's Self based on many factors—including color, sex, age, and class—and on the places those parts of identity have taken one's Self, including those from which those identities have meant exclusion.[81]

Therefore, it is in the *Praxis of Location* that the circumscribing nature of locatedness comes to the fore. Recognizing complex identity means understanding that the oppressed in one situation can be the oppressor in another. Lived experience as a member of a dominant group circumscribes one's perceptions, which are often thoughtlessly white, heterosexual, or middle class. Such thoughtless existence promotes an arrogance that assumes that one's perceptions arise from the center. Yet, the white eye does not see from the center any more than does the male eye or the heterosexual eye, even if one believes it to be so.[82] The *Praxis of Location* recognizes that no collective movement can speak for anyone all the way through and that no liberation can come as a single individual.

Recognizing locatedness circumvents what Patricia Hill Collins has called the "additive models of oppression . . . firmly rooted in the either/or dichotomous thinking of Eurocentric, masculinist thought."[83] The emphasis on quantification and categorization occurs with the belief that the either/or categories must be ranked: one must be privileged, the other denigrated. Therefore, Collins argues that additive models of oppression must be replaced with interlocking ones that recognize the significance of race, class, gender, age, sexual orientation, religion, and ethnicity. Such a conceptual move characterizes oppression in a more generalized "matrix of domination" in which the overarching relationship is one of domination and the types of activism it generates.[84]

The *Praxis of Location*, like the *Praxis of Coming Out*, is part of the Pragmatist Sexual Taxonomy. However, in rejecting a theoretical foundation that is based on oppositional binaries and acknowledging that locatedness has been instrumental in shaping complex identities, the *Praxis of Location* moves further away from essentialism and more solidly into social constructionism. Recognizing the ineffectiveness of identity politics' oppositional categories, Out-Siders working within the *Praxis of Location* recognize that since the oppositional categories of identity politics are inadequate to serve a complex identity, coalitions must be fostered.

Therefore, the *Praxis of Location* enters into the configurations of education in several of the same ways that the *Praxis of Coming Out* has done. By the mid-1980s many women's studies and gender studies courses were significant arenas for exploring similarity and difference within locatedness. Black-women's studies courses were added to women's studies curricula, and existing courses were redesigned so that gender could be explored in a way that was sensitive to multicultural perspectives. There also emerged gay- and lesbian-themed courses in some universities[85] and even in some men's studies courses.[86]

James Sears is an Out-Sider educational theorist and researcher whose work in the academy has been influential in teacher education. His research has been informed by a multicultural approach to overcoming heterosexism and homophobia as well as by the recognition of his own locatedness as a gay man from the conservative Southern region of the United States.[87] Premised on understanding the location of gay and lesbian school students and the preservice teachers with whom he works, his teaching and research advocates sweeping social change through teaching methods and curricula.

There have been far fewer critiques of the *Praxis of Location* than perhaps any of the other *Praxes in re Sexual Identity*. Nonetheless, even when the category of *women* or *lesbians* or *gays* is defined relationally, it has met with criticism from extreme social constructionists who believe that such located identities still fail to address the linguistic constraints within which we are all defined. They believe that agency, claimed in both the *Praxes of Coming Out* and *Location*, is illusory and fails to grasp the significance of power relations. Judith Butler, for example, says:

> How will we know the difference between the power we promote and the power we oppose? Is it, one might rejoin, a matter of "knowing"? For one is, as it were, in power even as one opposes it, formed by it as one reworks it, and it

is this simultaneity that is at once the condition of our partiality, the measure of our political unknowingness, and also the condition of action itself. The incalculable effects of action are as much a part of their subversive promise as those that we plan in advance.

The effects of performatives, understood as discursive productions, do not conclude at the terminus of a given statement or utterance, the passing of legislation, the announcement of a birth. The reach of their significability cannot be controlled by the one who utters or writes, since such productions are not owned by the one who utters them. They continue to signify in spite of their authors, and sometimes against their authors' most precious intentions.[88]

It is the difference *within* homosexuality that Butler claims has been undertheorized. It is the "relation of being implicated in that which one opposes"[89] that has yet to be understood in its complexity.

Praxis of Refusal

The *Praxis of Refusal* is situated solidly within the Nominalist Sexual Taxonomy. Nominalists believe that all humans are capable of erotic and sexual interaction with either sex, but social pressure, legal sanctions, religious beliefs, and historical or personal circumstances determine the actual expression of each person's sexual feelings. Categories such as *homosexual* are merely arbitrary conventions applied to a sexual reality that is at bottom undifferentiated.[90]

Therefore, the *Praxis of Refusal* constitutes a turning point in the way Out-Siders see their work in addressing heterosexism, anti–lesbian and gay prejudice, and compulsory heterosexuality. While these Out-Siders still participate in protests and marches supporting legal and policy protections for lesbian and gay people, Out-Siders in the *Praxis of Refusal* see themselves in supporting roles for activism, not as the leading players. Activism in the *Praxis of Refusal* becomes secondary to what is perceived as most important: subverting any notion of "natural" or "normal" genders or sexuality; exposing the multivocal nature of power relations; and analyzing the ways in which discourse and tradition have combined to create the human subject. There has been little attention to education of any sort in this praxis, except for the postmodern feminists who have used feminist pedagogical methods and translated postmodern thought into useful material for women's studies classrooms.

Adherents to the *Praxis of Refusal* are many: Jeffrey Weeks, David Halperin, Carroll Smith-Rosenberg, Robert Padgug, Helene Cixous, and Jana Sawicki, to name but a few. All of these thinkers, however, owe much to the historical–philosophical works of Michel Foucault, who shaped so much of postmodern philosophical thought with his genealogical method, by means of which he detailed the creation and sexualization of the modern subject.[91]

Foucault's early works were influenced by Marx, the existential philosophers, and Nietzsche. However, it was to Martin Heidegger that Foucault was most indebted, for Heidegger conceptualized humans as embedded in concrete situations of action. He held that there is no pregiven essence of human beings. Humans are rather self-interpreting, becoming what they make of themselves in the course of their daily lives. Heidegger's influence is seen in Foucault's methodological choices throughout his life.

The *archaeological method*, as developed by Foucault, warrants brief mention here because it set the stage for the *genealogical approach* he used in his sexuality studies. Archaeology, in the Foucauldian sense, is a critical inquiry directed at disciplines and institutions in the human sciences. The archaeological method seeks to elucidate ways in which discourse and expert opinion come to constitute what we perceive as a learned practice and how that practice, in turn, infiltrates and shapes human behavior. The starting point for the archaeologist's research is anything within the discipline that is considered natural, obvious, or incontrovertible, not to assess its "truth" nor to offer an alternative theory, but to expose the circumstances within which it was manufactured in "discursive formations." Attentive to confusion, accidents, aberrations, and insurrections, the archaeologist first seeks out discourse that has been disqualified, labeled insufficient, or located low in the hierarchy of knowledge and then includes these discourses in the discipline's history. The result is a "diversifying effect" that shows the discipline to be far more randomly constructed and personality dependent than the discipline's scientific posturing presents.[92]

The genealogical method takes a similar approach but applies it to the construction of the subject instead of a discipline. Foucault's essay "Nietzsche, Genealogy, History" articulates his conception of his genealogical method: "Genealogy is gray, meticulous, and patiently documentary. It operates on a field of entangled and confused parchments, on documents that have been scratched over and recopied many times."[93] That which appears to be predetermined and inevitable is countered by a genealogical view that reveals morals, ideals, and concepts to be, not discovered truths, but products of conglomerations of blind forces. Where unification is purported, or where a coherent identity is indicated, genealogy reveals a pastiche of details: accidents, petty malice, suppressed deviations, complete reversals, errors, and false appraisals, "the hazardous play of dominations."[94] This pastiche is what gives birth to the practices and ideas that come to have value for human subjects. Reason itself, Foucault insisted, is not an extrahistorical absolute but a term that functions as an accolade:

> Examining the history of reason, [the genealogist] learns that it was born in an altogether 'reasonable' fashion—from chance; devotion to truth and the precision of scientific methods arose from the passion of scholars, their reciprocal hatred, their fanatical and unending discussions, and their spirit of competition—the personal conflicts that slowly forged the weapons of reason.[95]

Discourse provides the context for such maneuvers to congeal into learned procedures, "regimes of truth." Foucault, then, endorses an "effective history," devoid of constants, affirming knowledge as particular and perspectival, constituting not truth but truths, truths without epistemological foundations.

In his two major genealogical works, *Discipline and Punish* and *The History of Sexuality: An Introduction* (volume 1 of 3), Foucault's conceptions of truth, knowledge, power relations, and the construction of the subject are raised most definitively. *Discipline and Punish* details how lawful punishment has changed from the violent, retributive justice of a monarch to a supposedly more humane system of disciplinary techniques that operates through internalization of norms. Through methods such as normalizing judgment, hierarchical observation, and examination, self-controlling habits are instilled in the individual. Thus, while the individual is becoming more useful, he is simultaneously becoming a more docile body. That is, the bodily energies are habituated to external regulation, subjection, as well as self-improvement. Because disciplinary techniques work most effectively when the individual is complicit in the process, the individual must perceive the norms as integral to his or her self-image.[96]

It is not to be supposed that Foucault conceives of the power that produces these docile bodies to be conspiratorial. On the contrary, Foucault's conception of power, unlike that of the *Praxes of Coming Out* and *Location*, is impersonal, an intense web of power relationships, a network of practices, institutions, and technologies in which actions bear on actions, rather than dominant groups wielding power over subordinate groups. However, since there can be no individual interactions outside of power relations, there can be no prediscursive subject, for the subject is constructed and subjected within power relations.

In *The History of Sexuality: An Introduction*, Foucault took this notion of subjectification even further by examining the role played by norm-based sexuality, which has come to be regarded as truth about our "natural" sexual natures. Foucault's premise is that power has not operated primarily by repressing sexuality but by creating a proliferation of discourses that determine the modern forms sexuality has taken. Through intervention into family life by religious, medical, psychiatric, and governmental experts, discourse actualized the dualities of healthy and ill, normal and perverse, and legal and criminal. These terms become an effective means of social control through marginalizing and medicalizing "deviancy." Hence, after manufacturing truth about sexuality, we then appropriate the results as knowledge about ourselves and despise in ourselves thoughts that contravene those "natural" selves. Since the learned discourses have created and regulated sexuality, it is senseless to speak of a prediscursive "natural" sexuality, because any claim for an objective nature, or essence, is accessible only through representation and interpretation in discourse. One of the most significant philosophical consequences of his genealogical work is this: if a subject cannot be prediscursive, then truth must be historical and perspectival.

In his last two volumes of *The History of Sexuality*, Foucault shifted his attention from power and knowledge to ethics, which for Foucault meant the kind of relationship you ought to have with yourself: how the individual constitutes himself or herself as a moral agent. He was particularly interested in aesthetics—that is, creating one's self as a work of art, rather than conforming to some moral code. These two volumes, entitled *The Care of the Self* and *The Use of Pleasure*, explore Greek and Roman sexuality and ethics. Foucault stated clearly, however, that his interest was not in imitating these models, for they too are historically and culturally specific, but in studying them as one way in which individuals conceived of positive, enabling subjectification. Exploring ancient practices of the self suggested to Foucault that contemporary mechanisms of subjectification are culturally specific, creating a gap into which differing conceptions of self-constitution might enter in the future. His construction of ethics, in this sense, is tied closely to his notion of freedom, which is not an act of emancipation, or the arrival at an end state called "freedom," but a practice, an incessant process through which power relations are repeatedly subverted.[97]

Foucault's examination of the social regulation of sexuality; the forms of control; the patterns of domination, subordination, and resistance that shape the sexual; and the problematization and subversion of those relations form the basis of Foucault's politics of refusal. Because agency is subverted under the proliferation of discourses to which the individual is subjected, he or she must first come to recognition about the extent to which the "self" has been subjected, then refuse the identity ascribed to the self by "acting out" in local, discrete micropractices. Finally, he or she must re-create the self through positive, enabling subjectification.

Foucault was very critical of the identity politics embodied in the gay rights movement. He believed it was dangerous to base a political self-classification on a normalized binary category that depends on the maintenance of deviancy for definition. In many instances those relying on Foucauldian ideas for further research have built on this criticism, often indicting any practice of identity politics. I believe, however, that such blanket assertions are contrary to Foucault's intention.

For instance, in a series of interviews conducted in 1981 and 1982, Foucault addressed the issue of a gay identity politics straightforwardly. Taken together, they serve as an excellent explication of his concerns and commendations. Foucault clearly stated that we should distrust the tendency to relate homosexuality to the problem of "Who am I?" The problem is not to discover in that definition the truth of one's sex but to use that sexuality to arrive at a multiplicity of relationships. The point is to work at *becoming* homosexuals and not be fixed into just recognizing that we are.[98] That is, identifying oneself as homosexual does not mean assuming a predefined identity but creating a way to have life and relationships through homosexuality.

Asked if homosexuals should be encouraged to think of themselves as a class in a way that, say, unskilled laborers are encouraged, he replied:

> I would say that homosexual consciousness certainly goes beyond one's individual experience and includes an awareness of being a member of a particular social group. This is an undeniable fact that dates back to ancient times. . . . More recently certain homosexuals have, following the political model, developed or tried to create a certain class consciousness. My impression is that this hasn't really been a success, whatever the political consequences it may have had, because homosexuals do not constitute a social class.[99]

I take this to mean that coming to homosexual consciousness is not an individual affair but that it includes identifying as a member of a homosexual social group. But Foucault believed that attempting to force a political class-consciousness on this social group by using a (Marxist) political model had been unsuccessful.

Perhaps Foucault's clearest statements on identity politics came in a 1982 interview for the *Advocate*. Here he says that the world regards sexuality as the secret of the creative cultural life. He sees it as a process of having to create a new cultural life underneath the ground of our sexual choices. The interviewer asked Foucault whether one of the effects of trying to uncover the secret has meant that the gay movement has remained at the level of demanding civil or human rights around sexuality, which ultimately means only demanding sexual tolerance. Foucault's answer is instructive:

> Yes, but this aspect must be supported. It is important, first, to have the possibility—and the right—to choose your own sexuality. Human rights regarding sexuality are important and are still not respected in many places. We shouldn't consider that such problems are solved now. . . . Still, I think we have to go a step further. I think that one of the factors of this stabilization will be the creation of new forms of life, relationships, friendships in society, art, culture, and so on through our sexual, ethical, and political choices. Not only do we have to defend ourselves, not only affirm ourselves, as an identity but as a creative force.[100]

Foucault's response clearly indicates that identity is key and must be espoused to work for civil rights and freedom of sexual choice. What he cautioned against was not the use of identity politics per se but coming to believe either that attaining those rights and freedoms is the only goal or that one really resides within a fixed ontology; rather, by working to create and define themselves, homosexuals can create and define culture.

The *Praxis of Refusal* is grounded, first, in this notion of refusing the ways in which we have been subjugated and subjectified; and, second, in an ethical and aesthetic re-creation of the self. As Foucault made clear, however, such re-creation does not come without a price. The price for an ethical self is consciously and carefully choosing that to which one will be subjected in the process of aesthetic re-creation.

Foucault's insights into the creation of the subject have been instrumental in understanding the socially constructed and historically contingent nature of persons and disciplines. It would be hard to overestimate the influence of his work on studies of sexual identity. Yet, Foucault's only palpable impact on the configurations of education has been in the academy. There, however, he has been studied in a variety of departments, including history, philosophy, and courses in lesbian and gay studies and queer theory.

Feminist theorists believe that engaging Foucault could produce insightful critiques of mainstream theory and feminism itself, even though feminists as a whole agree that his rhetoric is masculinist; his perspective, androcentric; and his vision, pessimistic. Yet, feminists have found useful to many of their projects his critical stance toward mainstream philosophy, concepts of historical and perspectival truths, notions of a subject created within power relations, focus on sexuality as a key arena of political struggle, and genealogy's unearthing of submerged and marginalized voices.

Jana Sawicki, who has written extensively on forging a bridge between feminism and Foucault, values his analytic of power relations because it supports the politics of personal relations and accounts for individual and group participation in reproducing systems of domination, even while resisting others. She suggests that Foucault's primary contribution to feminist theory consists in bringing awareness about the deep irregularities and broad, impersonal forces that make us what we are.[101]

Foucault's work has been difficult to appropriate for education, in part, because he said little about it explicitly, except in *Discipline and Punish*, where he indicts education in a scathing comparison between schools and penitentiaries. As a result, most of what can be said about Foucault and education must be constructed from related analyses of his work. However, some philosophers of education have begun to use Foucauldian analytics to engage questions about the complex power relations that pervade educational institutions and the professional discourse regarding the effects of educational reform. Others, such as John Covaleskie, are concerned with how the educator fits in the web of power relations, in terms of interacting with students and in the ways educators themselves are held in the sway of powerful forces such as curriculum, evaluation, and assessment.[102] James D. Marshall has suggested that Foucault's suspension of normative notions of legitimacy and illegitimacy can assist educators in understanding the host of processes in which we engage to "shape up" children, processes that the liberal framework would not normally identify as being contrary to the interests of the child and, therefore, not instances of the use of power.[103] These, and other publications from feminist scholars and educational philosophers have suggested the value of appropriating a Foucauldian critique for education in local and discrete contexts, holding out the potential for radical global change.

Most of the other theorists in the *Praxis of Refusal* have had even narrower educational impact than Foucault since they have mostly been relegated to lesbian and gay studies and queer theory, or in the case of Cixous, Sawicki, and some of the other Foucauldian feminist critics, women's studies courses. While the *Praxes of Refusal* and *Performativity* have not affected the configurations of education broadly, they have affected feminist thought about identity profoundly.

Praxis of Performativity

Building on Foucauldian themes, as well as the work of Lacan and Derrida, the *Praxis of Performativity* is an even more extreme version of the Nominalist Sexual Taxonomy than is the *Praxis of Refusal*. Where the *Praxis of Refusal* questions the extent to which agency is possible, it nevertheless suggests that subjects, by understanding and refusing their acculturated subjectification, may reconstitute themselves as works of art through ethical experimentation and inquiry. Part of the process of refusal incorporates what Foucault calls "hyper- and pessimistic activism."[104] The *Praxis of Performativity*, however, is primarily concerned with linguistics, not activism. That is, Out-Siders in the *Praxis of Performativity* see their work to be through literary and psychoanalytic interpretation that "queers the discourse," decentering normative, naturalized, and prescriptive gender roles and identities present in liberal education. The theorists in the *Praxis of Performativity* have critiqued not only liberal education but critical and feminist pedagogy as well. Like most of the other theorists in the *Praxes in re Sexual Identity*, they have ignored religious instruction.

The *Praxis of Performativity* is far less concerned with the historical situatedness of lesbian and gay subjects than has been the *Praxis of Refusal* and far more concerned with present linguistic practice. There is within the *Praxis of Performativity* the desire to denaturalize the heterosexist present and to disrupt what Eve Kosofsky Sedgwick has called "the conceptual anonymity of the master canon."[105]

Through critical inquiry, adherents to the *Praxis of Performativity* propose that many of the major modes of thought and knowledge in twentieth-century Western culture as a whole are structured—and fractured—by a chronic crisis of homo/heterosexual definition, indicatively male, dating from the end of the nineteenth century. The *Performative* analysis begins with two inherent contradictions in Western thought. There is the contradiction between seeing homo/heterosexual definition on the one hand as an issue of active importance primarily for a small, distinct, relatively fixed homosexual minority; and on the other hand as an issue of continuing determinative importance in the lives of people across a spectrum of sexualities. The second is the contradiction between seeing same-sex object choice on the one hand as a matter of liminality or transitivity between genders and on the other hand as reflecting an impulse of separatism within each gender.[106] An assumption underlying Sedgwick's *Epistemology of the Closet* is that the relations of the closet, the relations of the known and unknown, the explicit and the inexplicit around homo/heterosexual definition have the potential for being peculiarly revealing about speech acts more generally. What counts as a speech act, according to Sedgwick, is problematized on a perfectly routine basis. "Closetedness" itself is a performance initiated as such by the speech act of a silence that accrues particularity. The speech acts of coming out, in turn, comprise specific performances.[107]

In addition, Sedgwick reminds readers that knowledge, in Foucauldian thought, is not itself power but a magnetic field around which power works. Ignorance and opacity collude and compete with knowledge in mobilizing the flows of energy, desire, goods, meanings, and persons. Thinking from this perspective means that it is the interlocutor who has, or pretends to have, the less broadly knowledgeable understanding of interpretive practice that will define the terms of exchange.

For instance, because men have superior extralinguistic resources and privileged discourse positions, they are often less likely to treat perspectives different from their own as mutually available for communication. Thus, their attitudes are more likely to leave a lasting imprint on the common se-mantic stock than are women's. Such ignorances can be, and are, harnessed, licensed, and regulated on a mass scale for striking reinforcements, perhaps especially around sexuality. For example, the laws that govern rape privilege men and ignorance inasmuch as it matters not at all what the raped woman perceives or wants just so long as the man raping her can claim not to have noticed that she wanted to stop. There was likewise an ingenious orchestra-tion of ignorance around homo/heterosexual definition in the U.S. Justice Department's 1986 ruling that said an employer may freely fire persons with AIDS so long as the employer can claim ignorance of the medical fact that there is no known health danger in the workplace from the disease.[108] These ignorances, argues Sedgwick, correspond to particular knowledges and circu-late as part of particular regimes of truth.

Thus, the speech acts of the closet and of coming out circle around the knowledges and ignorances of Western definitional contradictions and frac-tures. In the next analytical move in the *Praxis of Performativity*, Sedgwick demonstrates that categories presented in a culture as symmetrical binary oppositions—heterosexual/homosexual, in this case—subsist in a more un-settled and dynamic relation than is normally supposed. That is, the term B is not symmetrical with, but subordinated to, term A; further, term A actu-ally depends for its meaning on the simultaneous subsumption and exclusion of B. This dependence indicates that the supposed marginal category of the dyad is irresolvably unstable, since term B is at once internal and external to term A.[109]

The genital activity of one person can be differentiated from that of an-other along many dimensions: preference for certain acts, certain zones or sensations, certain physical types, certain frequency, certain symbolic invest-ments, certain relations of age or power, certain species, certain number of participants, and so forth. The *Praxis of Performativity* problematizes the fact that precisely one, the gender of the object choice, emerged at the turn of the century and has remained *the* dimension denoted by the now ubiquitous category of "sexual orientation." This development would not have been foreseen by the *fin de siècle* itself, where a rich "stew" of male proclivities seemed to have as indicative a relation as did homosexuality to the whole problematic of sexual "perversion."[110]

Judith Butler takes the instability of the homo/heterosexual dyad as her point of departure, premising her analysis on Foucault's notion that regulatory power produces the subjects it controls and that power is not only imposed externally but works as the regulatory and normative means by which subjects are formed. Her analysis, which is heavily influenced by the psychoanalytic works of Kristeva and Lacan and political anarchism, takes "sex" to be an ideal regulatory construct that is materialized over time.

One of the significant "discoveries" in second-wave feminist theory was the separation of biological sex and gender. Butler's analysis, however, re-conflates the two by claiming that because the category of "sex" is, from the start, normative and hence a regulatory ideal, it produces the bodies that it governs; that is, the regulatory force is made clear as a kind of productive power to produce, demarcate, circulate, and differentiate the bodies it controls. Thus, "sex" is an ideal whose materialization is compelled, and this materialization takes place (or fails to take place) through certain highly regulated practices.[111] Hence, because "sex" is not an essence, gender cannot be the expression of an essence or the externalization of an objective ideal. The various acts of gender create the idea of gender; without those acts, or performances, there would be no gender at all.[112]

Gender is then a construction that conceals its genesis. The construction "compels" our belief in its necessity and naturalness. Therefore, as in other ritual social dramas, the action of gender requires a performance that is repeated. This stylized repetition is at once a reenactment and a reexperiencing of a set of meanings already socially established. The appearance of substance is a constructed identity, a performative accomplishment that the social audience and the actors themselves come to believe and to perform.[113]

Thus, Butler is much opposed to identity categories, such as *lesbian* or *gay*, which she views as invariable stumbling blocks.[114] While she indicates that she does not "legislate" against the use of the term "lesbian," she questions what it means to avow a category that can only maintain its specificity and adherence by performing a prior set of disavowals. She asks, "Is lesbianism constituted in part from the very heterosexual matrix that it seeks to displace?"

To *be* a lesbian is not a performance from which one can take a radical distance, for it is psychically entrenched. The "I" does not play the lesbian as a role. Rather, it is through the repeated play of this sexuality that the "I" is insistently reconstituted as a lesbian "I." Further, it is paradoxically the repetition of that play that establishes the instability of the category that it constitutes. "For if the 'I' is a site of repetition, that is, if the 'I' only achieves the semblance of identity through a certain repetition of itself, then the 'I' is always displaced by the very repetition that sustains it."[115]

This performance of acts, the repetition of performance, means that the naturalistic effects of heterosexualized genders are produced through imitative strategies. The "reality" of heterosexual identities is performatively constituted through an imitation that sets itself up as the origin and ground of all imitations. Indeed, in its efforts to naturalize itself as the original, heterosexuality must be understood as a compulsive and compulsory repetition that can only produce the *effect* of its own originality. In other words, those compulsory heterosexual identities are theatrically produced effects that posture as grounds, origins, the normative measure of the real.[116]

Therefore, for Butler, the parodic replication and resignification of heterosexual constructs within nonheterosexual frames brings into relief the utterly constructed status of the so-called original, indicating that heterosexuality only constitutes itself as the original through a convincing act of repetition.[117] Further, if repetition is the way in which power works to construct the illusion of a seamless heterosexual identity and if heterosexuality is compelled to repeat itself to establish the illusion of its own uniformity and identity, then this is an identity permanently at risk. There can be no volitional subject behind the mime who decides, as it were, which gender it will be today. On the contrary, the very possibility of becoming a viable subject requires that a certain gender mime be already underway.[118]

Thus, if gender is "drag," an imitation that regularly produces the ideal it attempts to approximate, then gender is a performance that produces the illusion of an inner sex or essence or psychic core. The gender becomes naturalized through being constructed as an inner psychic or physical necessity. Although compulsory heterosexuality often presumes that there is first a sex that is expressed through a gender and then through a sexuality, Butler suggests it is necessary to fully invert and displace that operation of thought. It may be that the very categories of sex, of sexual identity, of gender are produced or maintained in the effects of this compulsory performance, effects that are disingenuously renamed as causes, origins. How then to expose the causal lines retrospectively and engage gender as an inevitable fabrication as nothing more than the effects of drag? Perhaps, she suggests, this will be a matter of working sexuality against identity, even against gender, and of letting that which cannot fully appear in any performance persist in its disruptive promise.[119]

Like Foucault, Butler has been critical of the essentialism in lesbian and gay politics, making her work feared and hated by those working within in the *Praxes of Inclusion, Coming Out,* and *Location.* Quotations like the following tend to send chills down the spines of radical lesbian feminists:

> If "women" within political discourse can never fully describe that which it names, that is neither because the category simply refers without describing nor because "women" are the lost referent, that which "does not exist," but because the term marks a dense intersection of social relations that cannot be summarized through the terms of identity. The term will gain and lose its stability to the extent that it remains differentiated and that differentiation serves political goals. To the degree that that differentiation produces the effect of a radical essentialism of gender, the term will work to sever its constitutive connections with other discursive sites of political investment and undercut its own capacity to compel and produce the constituency it names. The constitutive instability of the term, its incapacity ever fully to describe what it names, is produced precisely by what is excluded in order for the determination to take place.[120]

As was the case with Foucault, Butler's criticisms of identity have often been taken to constitute an intellectual legislation against use of such identities for any reason. Butler is quite clear, however, that such blanket assertions are not what she has in mind. She argues that identities must be critiqued and subjected to interrogation about the constitutive and exclusionary relations of power that have created them. There must be a self-critical dimension within activism that serves as a persistent reminder of the exclusionary force of one of activism's claims to identity:

> As much as identity terms must be used, as much as "outness" is to be affirmed, these same notions must become subject to a critique of the exclusionary operation so their own production: For whom is outness a historically available and affordable option? Is there an unmarked class character to the demand for universal "outness"? Who is represented by *which* use of the term, and who is excluded? For whom does the term present an impossible conflict between racial, ethnic, or religious affiliation and sexual politics? What kinds of policies are enabled by what kinds of usages, and which are backgrounded or erased from view?[121]

Butler goes on to say that "this is not an argument *against* using identity categories, but it is a reminder of the risk that attends every such use"[122] and that "it remains politically necessary to lay claim to 'women,' 'queer,' 'gay,' and 'lesbian,' precisely because of the way these terms, as it were, lay their claim on us prior to our full knowing."[123]

Even though the focus on disruptive language within the *Praxis of Performativity* holds enormous potential for education, the difficulty of the language and concepts has made them difficult for many educators to appropriate. Nevertheless, it has profoundly affected discourse on identity, even though it has been completely relegated to academic circles.

A few educational theorists are experimenting with the notions of the *Praxis of Performativity*. For instance, educational philosopher Cris Mayo has used the ideas premised in the *Praxis of Performativity*'s notions of contingent identity in her sex education research, where schools play a role in demarcating proper from improper identity and inscribe boundaries around particular identities and activities. Mayo suggests that contingent identities may be useful in negotiating the complications of local, versus global, meanings in young people's understandings of sexual feelings and experiences. Mayo believes that a genealogical approach can be useful to students who are negotiating their own identities because they can be encouraged to examine power relations, uses, and disjunctures of identity.[124]

Mayo cites the complications of local meanings in young people's understandings of their sexual feelings and experiences by counseling that what an outside person might view as a sexual relationship might not be viewed by the participants as such. For example, the fact that

> young boys masturbate together is not often considered to be an expression of their homosexual desires, but rather a group form of competition or amusement. . . . For some, engagement in these activities will figure as founding moments in their development of a gay identity, for others memories of these experiences may either fade or be denied because they do not form a founding or even important moment in their definition of sexuality.[125]

Mayo suggests that because of the interplay between identity and experience, those experiences not viewed by the participants as crucial are not found in memory in the same way as if they are viewed as crucial. She goes on to suggest that such contingent identities could be useful in sex education courses where abstinence is portrayed as the only recourse for adolescents and where female victimization is still a common theme that obscures female sexual desire and encourages girls to see marriage as a haven from this victimization. Mayo believes that the categories and foundations of identity that education provide constrain not only students' range of identity possibilities but may also hamper their ability to engage with others, either those who do not conform to identity standards or those who inhabit other identity categories.[126]

Adherents to other praxes have soundly criticized the ways in which the *Praxis of Performativity* has been wielded in essentialist–social constructionist

debates. However, there is also concern about the effects of such extreme social constructionism among those who would count themselves in the ranks
of the *Praxis of Performativity*. For instance, Harriet Malinowitz has wondered
what happens when familiar tags such as *lesbian* and *gay* are completely abandoned. After all, membership in these categories has at various points
throughout the twentieth century meant risking police raids; imprisonment;
street violence; incarceration in mental institutions; expulsion from jobs,
families, and religious institutions; loss of child custody; dishonorable dis-
charge from the military; McCarthyite inquisitions; disqualification from employment in education or government; and general social pariahhood.[127]
What happens if these categories are simply dissolved? Is calling oneself a
lesbian merely a totalizing and ultimately meaningless fiction? How can categories be destabilized without also abandoning the claim to material and
social entitlement and a repudiation of marginalization and prejudice?

Even the avowedly postmodern Margrit Shildrick has noted that regardless
of the permeability of boundaries, the act of "coming out," of identification, is
invested with enormous significance for lesbians and gay males. Whatever the
intellectual objections to the concept of identity may be, individuals still want
to experience those moments of mutual acknowledgment.[128]

The concern of many lesbians and gay men, as well as straight feminists,
is heard in the following question posed by Carole Vance, another social constructionist, at an international gay studies conference:

> To the extent that social construction theory grants that sexual acts, identities,
> and even desire are mediated by cultural and historical factors, the object of
> study—sexuality—becomes evanescent and threatens to disappear. If sexuality
> is constructed differently at each time and place, can we use the term in a com-
> paratively meaningful way? More to the point in lesbian and gay history, have
> constructionists undermined their own categories? Is there an "it" to study?[129]

Jeffrey Weeks's work has been shaped by a rejection of essentialist arguments, yet he has written that "despite the trouble, a politics of collective
identity appears necessary."[130] Why? Because Weeks is concerned about the
fact that social constructionism has no political belonging. "It does not carry
with it an obvious programme. On the contrary, it can be, and has been, used
recently as much by sexual conservatives as by sexual progressives."[131] Eve
Kosofsky Sedgwick echoes Weeks's concern:

> In particular, my fear is that there currently exists no framework in which to
> ask about the origins or development of individual gay identity that is not al-
> ready structured by an implicit, trans-individual Western project or fantasy or

eradicating that identity. It seems ominously symptomatic that, under the dire homophobic pressure of the last few years, and in the name of Christianity, the subtle constructivist argument that sexual aim is, at least for many people, not a hard-wired biological given but, rather a social fact deeply embedded in the cultural and linguistic forms of many, many decades is being degraded to the blithe ukase that people are 'free at any moment to' (i.e., must immediately) "choose" to adhere to a particular sexual identity (say, at a random hazard, the heterosexual) rather than to its other.[132]

Nussbaum and David Glidden have been far less charitable. Criticizing queer theory as faddish and chic, Glidden has argued that queer theorists promote eye-catching topics at the expense of substance and depth. In this way, he contends, scholars are cutting themselves off from the urgent concerns of a community that is debating issues of nondiscrimination and equality. Entirely lost is the idea of identity as something that unites us with others with whom we might make common cause.[133]

Nussbaum vehemently criticizes Judith Butler, claiming that her lack of hope for meaningful large-scale social change has meant that she can only envision transgressing the structures of power through parody, symbolic verbal politics, the subversive use of words. Nussbaum continues:

> In its small way, of course, this is a hopeful politics. It instructs people that they can, right now, without compromising their security, do something bold. But the boldness is entirely gestural, and insofar as Butler's ideal suggests that these symbolic gestures really are political change, it offers only a false hope. Hungry women are not fed by this, battered women are not sheltered by it, raped women do not find justice in it, gays and lesbians do not achieve legal protections through it.
>
> Finally there is despair at the heart of the cheerful Butlerian enterprise. The big hope, the hope for a world of real justice, where laws and institutions protect the equality and the dignity of all citizens, has been banished, even perhaps mocked as sexually tedious. Judith Butler's hip quietism is a comprehensible response to the difficulty of realizing justice in America. But it is a bad response. It collaborates with evil. Feminism demands more and women deserve better.[134]

The *Praxis of Performativity*, despite its obvious disruptive potential, seems fraught with problems when viewed pragmatically, as Out-Siders must view heterosexism. How, then, should Out-Siders proceed?

Focus Problems

The foregoing explication of the *Praxes in re Sexual Identity* suggests some profound disagreements between, among, and within the various praxes about what identity in general, and sexual identity in specific, means for siding with LGBTQ outsiders. The various ways in which identity has been theorized have led to dramatically different perspectives on appropriate strategies for changing the heterosexist environment. This essentialism–social constructionism debate has been the focus of so many books and articles that it seems impossible to offer anything on questions of sexuality at this juncture without at least doffing one's hat to this discussion.

How one should use and interpret sources related to sexuality—indeed, what constitutes the proper subject of inquiry—has increasingly divided traditional philosophers and historians from those studying minority histories, feminists from one another, gay men from lesbians, and gay and lesbian activists from academicians. Many of the "malestream" attitudes that previously induced neglect or distortion of lesbian and gay history and thought still prevail in many quarters. Mainstream philosophers and historians often cite poor scholarship, or they object to groups "studying themselves." Their most prevalent criticism is that minority histories and philosophies are intent on, and lend themselves to, political use, which distorts scholarly integrity. However, as John Boswell pointed out, the exclusion of minorities from history and philosophy before the twentieth century was certainly related to, or caused by, concerns other than those of purely scholarly interest, concerns that would certainly be considered political. Therefore, including minority scholarship now, even for purely political ends, not only corrects a previous political distortion but also provides a more complete source of data and perspectives.[135]

At a more particular level, the struggles among scholars over what role, if any, identity should play for those involved in research about sexual minorities underlies a raging metaphysical controversy. The categories of sexual preference or orientation are interrogated by the realist and nominalist positions described in the foregoing discussion. Because most theorists do not hold these positions absolutely, it might appear that a useful dialogue could denote where their theories agree and, through careful analysis of difference, promote discussion and understanding of these issues.

In reality, the political ramifications of the discussion have hindered such an approach. Realism has been viewed as conservative and reactionary. Nominalism has been regarded as obscure and radical, designed to undercut values, rather than clarify them. The efforts of sociobiology to demonstrate an evolutionary etiology of homosexuality have been denounced by nominalists who regard the task as an effort to convince people that sexual categories are fixed and unchangeable. Activists in the gay movement, however, often see such efforts as the proof that dominant heterosexual groups must come to understand their sexuality as innate and therefore without blame. Adding to the confusion, there is still no agreement in the scientific community about the nature of human sexuality. Whether humans are "homosexual," "heterosexual," or "bisexual" by birth, training, or choice is still an open question.

Both sides of the realist–nominalist debate appear to be paralyzed by words. In fact the "debate" can hardly be characterized as such. As Boswell puts it, "One of the ironies is that no one involved in [the realist–nominalist debate] actually identifies him- or herself as an 'essentialist,' although constructionists (of whom, in contrast, there are many) sometimes so label other writers."[136] In fact, applying the *essentialist* label to a writer seems to foreclose all further serious discussion of his or her work, regardless of the fact that the label ill-fits almost all contemporary scholars.[137] The controversy is, subsequently, rarely a dialogue between essentialism and constructionism, but a largely one-sided critique by constructionists.

Social constructionist critiques of "essentialist" identity politics have often been merciless, disregarding or glossing over the important gains in gay rights made by those same "essentialists" in the thirty years following Stonewall. Butler, Fuss, Sedgwick, and the other extreme social constructionists are not alone in this critique, of course. These were the fundamental complaints of lesbians of color against lesbian feminism, which ushered in the *Praxis of Location*. Even Adrienne Rich, who is often tagged "essentialist" by others, recognizes the violence of making claims about *all women:*

> Some of us, calling ourselves radical feminists, never meant anything less by women's liberation than the creation of a society without domination; we never meant less than the making new of all relationships. The problem was that we did not know whom we meant when we said "we."[138]

The most vitriolic arguments have taken place interpraxes, but there are major intrapraxis issues. Gay males have seen the issues of gays and lesbians as substantially similar, seeking lesbian support of a united political agenda. Lesbians have believed that their concerns, issues, traditions, and sexuality have been subsumed under a political agenda dominated by gay male concerns, seeking women's help just as men have always looked to women to assist in men's projects.

One might assume that such disagreements would have disappeared in the *Praxes of Refusal* and *Performativity,* where all gender boundaries are permeable and where difference is ubiquitous. Yet, Judith Butler concedes the need to explore sexual difference within homosexuality,[139] and Diana Fuss argues that more sophisticated analyses are needed to make important distinctions between male homosexuals and lesbians because the two are frequently conflated in the research on sexual minorities, which is noticeably skewed in the direction of the gay male subject.[140] Conversely, when Michel Foucault was asked in an interview whether such a distinction was needed, his response was, "All I can do is explode with laughter. . . . I find it very amusing. . . . What I will say is that the distinction offered doesn't seem to be convincing."[141] The gay male–lesbian binarism expressed in these constructivist viewpoints seems to echo the previously cited opinions of Marilyn Frye that informed earlier praxes.

Where, then, can Out-Siders presume to stand? The Out-Siders most interested in the practical needs of lesbians and gays tend to work from within the *Praxis of Inclusion* or the *Praxis of Coming Out*, which have numerous theoretical problems. Adherents to the *Praxis of Coming Out* are critical of the conservative stance of the *Praxis of Inclusion* and charge that academicians' efforts in the *Praxes of Refusal* and *Performativity* are far too abstract and morally passive. Almost all the educators in the school systems who have challenged the mis-education of compulsory heterosexuality are working from the *Praxes of Inclusion, Coming Out,* or *Location,* while contemporary academicians, including philosophers of education such as Cris Mayo and Maureen Ford, are operating from the *Praxes of Refusal* and *Performativity.* The struggles between and among the various praxes can, and often have, become a world unto themselves.

Yet, those nagging statistics remain: lesbian and gay teens account for 30 percent of all successful teen suicides; 42 percent of homeless teens are gay or lesbian; a majority of preservice teachers are more homophobic than the general population is. How can Out-Siders work effectively within a theoretically flawed praxis? Conversely, a theoretically sound praxis must be conscious of the consequences involved in the decisions that affect the exigencies of daily life for LGBTQ outsiders. Must not an *Out-Siders' Praxis* be fundamentally pragmatic?

How would insisting on a pragmatic approach change the viability of these *Praxes in re Sexual Identity* for the lesbian and gay community and for academicians researching sexual identity issues? If we heed Aristotle's claim that *phronesis* is not a wisdom sought to *know* the good but one sought to *do* the good, must not any plan of action be concerned with not just intention but effect? How are potential action choices affected when we consider that identities that bring people together are also composed of boundaries that exclude? Further, if one of the core elements for being an Out-Sider is a commitment to responsibility to outsiders that we teach and with whom we live and work, can such responsibility be pursued within an ethical framework that holds the cultivation of the Self to be the most important aim of thinkers? What would happen if the real lives of lesbian and gay people were allowed to challenge the theories? By what method could such an inquiry proceed?

Notes

1. Luce Irigaray, *An Ethics of Sexual Difference*, trans. Carolyn Burke and Gillian C. Gill (Paris: Les Editions de Minuit, 1984; translation, Ithaca, N.Y.: Cornell University Press, 1993), 5.

2. Eve Kosofsky Sedgwick, *Epistemology of the Closet* (Berkeley: University of California Press, 1990), 1.

3. Plato, *Republic*, trans. Allan Bloom (New York: HarperCollins, 1968), 521d–540c.

4. Richard J. Bernstein, *Beyond Objectivism and Relativism: Science, Hermeneutics, and Praxis* (Philadelphia: University of Pennsylvania Press, 1983), 144–48.

5. Bruce A. Kimball, "Liberal Education," in *Philosophy of Education: An Encyclopedia* (New York: Garland Publishing, Inc., 1996), 350–55.

6. Janet M. Atwill, *Rhetoric Reclaimed: Aristotle and the Liberal Arts Tradition* (Ithaca, N.Y.: Cornell University Press, 1998), 16.

7. Atwill, *Rhetoric Reclaimed*, 7.

8. Atwill, *Rhetoric Reclaimed*, 1.

9. Rosemarie Tong, *Feminist Thought: A Comprehensive Introduction* (Boulder, Colo.: Westview Press, 1989), 11–12.

10. See Jane Roland Martin's distinction between the "curriculum proper" and the "hidden curriculum," in "What Should We Do with a Hidden Curriculum When We Find One?" in *Changing the Educational Landscape: Philosophy, Women, and Curriculum* (New York: Routledge, 1994), 154–69.

11. See Linda L. Gaither's discussion of biblical interpretive methods in Susan Birden, Linda L. Gaither, and Susan Laird's "The Struggle over the Text: Compulsory Heterosexuality and Educational Policy" *Educational Policy* 14, no. 5 (November 2000): 638–63.

12. Patricia Donovan, "School-Based Sexuality Education: The Issues and Challenges," in *Family Planning Perspectives* 30, no. 4 (July/August 1998), at www.agi-usa.org/pubs/journals/3018898.html.

13. See People for the American Way, at www.pfaw.org/issues/right/teachingfear 96.shtml.

14. Susan Laird, "Girls and Women, Education of" in *Philosophy of Education, An Encyclopedia* (New York: Garland Publishing, Inc., 1996), 241.

15. Tong, *Feminist Thought*, 71.

16. Emancipatory praxis did profoundly affect the American settlement house movement, however. Settlement houses sprang up in the 1890s and early 1900s to assist the educational and health care needs of immigrant families in major urban areas. Jane Addams' Hull House in Chicago was the best-known and most influential of the settlement houses, but others served important needs as well: the Henry Street House in New York City, established by one of this country's first licensed nurses, Lillian Wald; the House of Seven Gables' Settlement in Salem, Massachusetts, established by Caroline Emmerton; the To-

berman House in Los Angeles; the Kingsley House in New Orleans; the Lutheran Settlement House in Philadelphia; the East Side Settlement House in Manhattan; and the
South End Settlement in Boston. Even though Jane Addams and the other women of the
settlement house movement never addressed questions of sexual identity, they provided a
safe place for single educated women to use their newly acquired college educations and
to live and work together. See Jane Addams, *Twenty Years at Hull-House* (Urbana: University of Illinois Press, 1900); Lutheran Settlement House website, www.libertynet
.org/luthersh/greeting.html; Kingsley House website, www.kingsleyhouse.org/; "Settlement Houses," at www.infoplease.com/ce6/society/A0844555.html; United Neighbor-
hood Houses of New York website, www.unhny.org/; East Side House Settlement website,
www.eastsidehouse.org/commbldg.htm; Toberman Settlement House website, www.tober-
man.org/.

17. Antonio Gramsci, *The Antonio Gramsci Reader*, ed. David Forgacs, trans. Quintin
Hoare et al. (New York: New York University Press, 2000), 317–18.

18. Paulo Freire, *Pedagogy of the Oppressed*, trans. Myra Bergman Ramos (New York:
Continuum Publishing, 1993), 50, 52–67.

19. See Lorraine Code, *What Can She Know? Feminist Theory and the Construction of
Knowledge* (Ithaca, N.Y.: Cornell University Press, 1991).

20. By "epistemological inequality" Martin means inequality in the knowledge itself,
the representation of women in historical narratives and philosophical interpretations.
See Jane Roland Martin, *Reclaiming a Conversation: The Ideal of the Educated Woman* (New
Haven, Conn.: Yale University Press, 1985), 3.

21. Martin, *Reclaiming a Conversation*, 1.

22. Martin, *Reclaiming a Conversation*, 5–6.

23. Martin, *Reclaiming a Conversation*, 195.

24. Martin, *Reclaiming a Conversation*, 198.

25. See Ann Diller, Barbara Houston, Kathryn Pauly Morgan, and Maryann Ayim, *The
Gender Question in Education: Theory, Pedagogy, and Politics* (Boulder, Colo.: Westview
Press, 1996).

26. It would be highly unethical for me to document this point by "outing" anyone
who has chosen to remain and write within the *Praxis of the Closet*, so I will not do so here.
That is not to say, however, that this point is not documentable.

27. Mary Wollstonecraft, *A Vindication of the Rights of Woman* (London: Penguin
Books, 1992; original, 1792).

28. See Alice S. Rossi's "A Feminist Friendship: Elizabeth Cady Stanton and Susan
B. Anthony," in *The Feminist Papers from Adams to de Beauvoir* (Boston: Northeastern
University Press, 1988), as well as Stanton's "Motherhood" and "Introduction to the
Woman's Bible," both reprinted here; see also Eleanor Flexner and Ellen Fitzpatrick,
Century of Struggle: The Woman's Rights Movement in the United States (Cambridge,
Mass.: Balkan Press of Harvard University Press, 1996, original in 1959).

29. Betty Friedan, *The Feminine Mystique* (New York: Dell Publishing, 1963).

30. Tong, *Feminist Thought*, 12.

31. Martha C. Nussbaum, *Sex and Social Justice* (Oxford: Oxford University Press,
1999), 190–206.

32. See Susan Birden, Linda L. Gaither, and Susan Laird, "The Struggle over the Text:
Compulsory Heterosexuality and Educational Policy," *Educational Policy* 14, no. 5
(November 2000): 655–56.

33. This support dramatically increased after Jamie Nabozny was awarded a $900,000 settlement because school officials failed to respond when he was subjected on a routine basis to abuse and violence in school. Anthony R. D'Augelli, "Fear and Loathing in High School," at www.psu.edu/ur/oped/daugelli.html.

34. See Sharon Lerner, "Christian Conservatives Take Their Antigay Campaign to the Schools," at http://traversearea.com/GLSEN/articles/art63.htm.

35. See the Boston Women's Health Book Collective, Our Bodies, Ourselves (Boston: New England Free Press, 1971; New York: Simon and Schuster, 1973); Our Bodies, Ourselves, rev. and exp. ed. (New York: Simon and Schuster, 1984); The New Our Bodies, Ourselves (New York: Simon and Schuster, 1992); Our Bodies, Ourselves for the New Century (New York: Simon and Schuster, 1998); Ruth Bell and other coauthors of Our Bodies, Ourselves and Ourselves and Our Children, with members of the Teen Book Project, Changing Bodies, Changing Lives, rev. and upd. (New York: Vintage Books, 1988); Norma L. Chaska, The Nursing Profession: A Time to Speak (New York: McGraw-Hill, 1983); Paul Starr, The Social Transformation of American Medicine: The Rise of a Sovereign Profession and the Making of a Vast Industry (New York: Basic Books, 1982); Tamsin Wilton, "Healing the Invisible Body: Lesbian Health Studies," in Straight Studies Modified, ed. Gabriele Griffin and Sonya Andermahr (London: Cassell, 1997); and Mariamne H. Whatley, "Images of Gays and Lesbians in Sexuality and Health Textbooks," in Coming Out of the Classroom Closet, ed. Karen M. Harbeck (New York: Harrington Park Press, 1991).

36. See Susan Moller Okin, Justice, Gender, and the Family (New York: BasicBooks, 1989).

37. See Saul M. Olyan and Martha C. Nussbaum, eds., Sexual Orientation and Human Rights in American Religious Discourse (Oxford: Oxford University Press, 1998).

38. See Martha C. Nussbaum, Cultivating Humanity: A Classical Defense of Reform in Liberal Education (Cambridge, Mass.: Harvard University Press, 1997) and Sex and Social Justice (Oxford: Oxford University Press, 1999).

39. Nussbaum, Cultivating Humanity, 9–11.

40. Nussbaum, Cultivating Humanity, 249.

41. Nussbaum, Cultivating Humanity, 249–56.

42. Nussbaum, Cultivating Humanity, 239–45.

43. Saul M. Olyan and Martha C. Nussbaum, eds., Sexual Orientation and Human Rights in American Religious Discourse (Oxford: Oxford University Press, 1998).

44. Nussbaum, Sex and Social Justice, 184–210.

45. Jane Roland Martin, Coming of Age in Academe: Rekindling Women's Hopes and Reforming the Academy (New York: Routledge, 2000), 136–38.

46. Martin, Coming of Age in Academe, 139.

47. Martin, Coming of Age in Academe, 139.

48. Mary Daly, Beyond God the Father (Boston: Beacon Press, 1985).

49. Dennis Altman, Homosexual: Oppression and Liberation (New York: Outerbridge and Dienstfrey, 1971), 229.

50. Amanda Udis-Kessler, "Identity/Politics: Historical Sources of the Bisexual Movement," in Queer Studies: A Lesbian, Gay, Bisexual, and Transgender Anthology, ed. Brett Beemyn and Mickey Eliason (New York: New York University Press, 1996), 53.

51. John Boswell, Christianity, Social Tolerance, and Homosexuality: Gay People in Western Europe from the Beginning of the Christian Era to the Fourteenth Century (Chicago: University of Chicago Press, 1981) and Same-Sex Unions in Premodern Europe (New York: Vintage Books, 1995).

52. See for instance, Paul Gordon Schalow, "Male Love in Early Modern Japan: A Literary Depiction of 'Youth'"; "Russia's Gay Literature and Culture: The Impact of the October Revolution"; and "Migrancy and Male Sexuality on the South African Gold Mines," all in *Hidden from History: Reclaiming the Gay and Lesbian Past,* ed. Martin Duberman, Martha Vicinus, and George Chanuncey Jr. (New York: Penguin Group, 1990).

53. See Edwin J. Haeberle, "Swastika, Pink Triangle, and Yellow Star: The Destruction of Sexology and the Persecution of Homosexuals in Nazi Germany," in Duberman, Vicinus, and Chanuncey, *Hidden from History.*

54. John D'Emilio, *Sexual Politics, Sexual Communities: The Making of a Homosexual Minority in the United States, 1940–1970* (Chicago: University of Chicago Press, 1998).

55. Amanda Udis-Kessler, "Identity/Politics: Historical Sources of the Bisexual Movement," in *Queer Studies: A Lesbian, Gay, Bisexual, and Transgender Anthology,* ed. Brett Beemyn and Mickey Eliason (New York: New York University Press, 1996), 53.

56. Lillian Faderman, ed., *Chloe plus Olivia: An Anthology of Lesbian Literature from the Seventeenth Century to the Present* (New York: Penguin Group, 1994), vii.

57. See Faderman, *Chloe plus Olivia; Surpassing the Love of Men: Romantic Friendship and Love between Women from the Renaissance to the Present* (New York: Morrow, 1981); *To Believe in Women: What Lesbians Have Done for America—a History* (Boston: Houghton Mifflin, 1999).

58. Martha Vicinus, "Distance and Desire: English Boarding School Friendships, 1870–1920"; and San Francisco Gay and Lesbian History Project, "'She Even Chewed Tobacco': A Pictorial Narrative of Passing Women in America," in Duberman, Vicinus, and Chanuncey, *Hidden from History.*

59. See Adrienne Rich, *Of Woman Born: Motherhood as Experience and Institution* (New York: W. W. Norton, 1995); and "Compulsory Heterosexuality and Lesbian Existence," in *Blood, Bread, and Poetry* (New York: W. W. Norton, 1986).

60. See Mary Daly, *Beyond God the Father: Toward a Philosophy of Women's Liberation* (Boston: Beacon Press, 1985); and Josephine Donovan's discussion of Daly's existentialist feminism in *Feminist Theory: The Intellectual Traditions of American Feminism* (New York: Continuum Publishing, 1994), 126–29.

61. See Mary Daly, *Gyn/Ecology: The Metaethics of Radical Feminism* (Boston: Beacon Press, 1990); Donovan, *Feminist Theory,* 153.

62. See Janice Raymond, *A Passion for Friends: Toward a Philosophy of Female Affection* (Boston: Beacon Press, 1986).

63. Sarah Lucia Hoagland, *Lesbian Ethics: Toward New Value* (Palo Alto, Calif.: Institute of Lesbian Studies, 1988).

64. See Irigaray, *An Ethics of Sexual Difference;* and *je, tu, nous: Toward a Culture of Difference,* trans. Alison Martin (New York: Routledge, 1993; original in French, 1990).

65. See Charlotte Bunch, "Not By Degrees: Feminist Theory and Education," in Bunch and Pollack, *Learning Our Way,* 248–60.

66. Marilyn Frye's Oklahoma roots are a great encouragement to many of us living and working for change on issues of lesbian and gay prejudice in the Bible Belt. She and Cornel West are two wonderful examples of radical thinkers from Oklahoma.

67. Marilyn Frye, "Lesbian Feminism and the Gay Rights Movement: Another View of Male Supremacy, Another Separatism," in *The Politics of Reality: Essays in Feminist Theory* (Freedom, Calif.: Crossing Press, 1983), 128–29.

68. Frye, "Lesbian Feminism and the Gay Rights Movement," 130.

69. See Birden, Gaither, and Laird, "The Struggle over the Text," 658.

70. Adrienne Rich, "It Is the Lesbian in Us . . . ," in On Lies, Secrets, and Silence, 199.

71. Lorraine Code, What Can She Know? Feminist Theory and the Construction of Knowledge (Ithaca, N.Y.: Cornell University Press, 1991), 299.

72. Nussbaum, Cultivating Humanity, 110–11.

73. Judith Butler, Bodies That Matter: On the Discursive Limits of "Sex" (New York: Routledge, 1993), 188.

74. See Audre Lorde, "The Master's Tools Will Never Dismantle the Master's House" and "Age, Race, Class and Sex: Women Redefining Difference," in Sister Outsider (Freedom, Calif.: Crossing Press, 1988), 110.

75. Lorde, "The Master's Tools," 11.

76. Lorde, "The Master's Tools," 110–13.

77. Frye, "To Be and Be Seen: The Politics of Reality," in The Politics of Reality.

78. Frye, "On Being White: Thinking toward a Feminist Understanding of Race and Race Supremacy," in The Politics of Reality, 110.

79. Frye, "On Being White," 114–15.

80. Frye, "On Being White," 116–17.

81. Adrienne Rich, "Notes toward a Politics of Location" and "Split at the Root: An Essay on Jewish Identity," in Blood, Bread, and Poetry (New York: W.W. Norton, 1986), 215.

82. Rich, "Notes toward a Politics of Location," 217–31.

83. Patricia Hill Collins, Black Feminist Thought: Knowledge, Consciousness, and the Politics of Empowerment (New York: Routledge, 1991), 225.

84. Collins, Black Feminist Thought, 225–26.

85. For an interesting approach to a gay- and lesbian-themed writing course, see Harriet Malinowitz's book Textual Orientations: Lesbian and Gay Students and the Making of Discourse Communities (Portsmouth, N.H.: Heinemann, 1995).

86. Some feminists have been extremely critical of the need for men's studies courses, claiming that the academy as a whole is a men's studies course. However, advocates have insisted that these courses provide safe places not only to discuss issues that men feel uncomfortable addressing in coeducational settings but to provide safe environments in which men can come out.

87. See James Sears and Walter L. Williams, eds., Overcoming Heterosexism and Homophobia: Strategies That Work (New York: Columbia University Press, 1997).

88. Butler, Bodies That Matter, 241.

89. Butler, Bodies That Matter, 241.

90. See Birden, Gaither, and Laird, "The Struggle over the Text," 656–57.

91. See Michel Foucault, Discipline and Punish: The Birth of the Prison, trans. Alan Sheridan (Paris: Editions Gallimard, 1975; translation, New York: Vintage Books, 1997); The History of Sexuality, vol. 1, An Introduction, trans. Robert Hurley (Paris: Editions Gallimard, 1976; translation, New York: Vintage Books, 1990); The History of Sexuality, vol. 2, The Use of Pleasure, trans. Robert Hurley (Paris: Editions Gallimard, 1984; translation, New York: Vintage Books, 1990); The History of Sexuality, vol. 3, The Care of the Self, trans. Robert Hurley (Paris: Editions Gallimard, 1984; translation, New York: Vintage Books, 1988); Madness and Civilization: A History of Insanity in the Age of Reason, trans. Richard Howard (Paris: Librairie Plon, 1961; translation, New York: Vintage Books, 1988); Michel Foucault: Politics, Philosophy, and Culture, trans. Alan Sheridan and others (New York: Routledge, 1990); The Foucault Reader, ed. Paul Rabinow (New York: Pantheon Books, 1984).

92. C. G. Prado, *Starting with Foucault: An Introduction to Genealogy* (Boulder, Colo.: Westview Press, 1995), 25–31.

93. Michel Foucault, "Nietzsche, Genealogy, History," in *The Foucault Reader*, ed. Paul Rabinow (New York: Pantheon Books, 1984), 76.

94. Foucault, "Nietzsche, Genealogy, History."

95. Foucault, "Nietzsche, Genealogy, History," 78.

96. Michel Foucault, *Discipline and Punish,* 170–94.

97. Michel Foucault, "On the Genealogy of Ethics: An Overview of Work in Progress," in *The Foucault Reader*, ed. Paul Rabinow (New York: Pantheon Books, 1984), 340–62.

98. Michel Foucault, "Friendship As a Way of Life," in *Ethics: Subjectivity and Truth*, ed. Paul Rabinow (New York: New Press, 1997), 135–36.

99. Michel Foucault, "Sexual Choice, Sexual Act," in *Ethics*, 142–43.

100. Michel Foucault, "Sex, Power and the Politics of Identity," in *Ethics*, 164.

101. Jana Sawicki, "Foucault and Feminism: A Critical Reappraisal," in *Disciplining Foucault: Feminism, Power, and the Body* (New York: Routledge, 1991), 99–109.

102. John Covaleskie, "Power Goes to School: Teachers, Students, and Discipline," *Philosophy of Education Society Yearbook 1993,* at www.ed.uiuc.edu/COE/EPS/PES-Yearbook/93_docs/COVALESK.HTM.

103. James D. Marshall, "Education in the Mode of Information: Some Philosophical Considerations," from *Philosophy of Education Yearbook 1996*, at www.ed.uiuc.edu/eps/pes-yearbook/96_docs/marshall.html.

104. Michel Foucault, "On the Genealogy of Ethics: An Overview of Work in Progress," in *The Foucault Reader*, 343.

105. Eve Kosofsky Sedgwick, *Epistemology of the Closet* (Berkeley: University of California Press, 1990), 48–50.

106. Sedgwick, *Epistemology of the Closet*, 1–3.

107. Sedgwick, *Epistemology of the Closet*, 3.

108. Sedgwick, *Epistemology of the Closet*, 3–5.

109. Sedgwick, *Epistemology of the Closet*, 5–8.

110. Sedgwick, *Epistemology of the Closet*, 5–8.

111. Judith Butler, *Bodies That Matter: On the Discursive Limits of "Sex"* (New York: Routledge, 1993), 1.

112. Judith Butler, *Gender Trouble: Feminism and the Subversion of Identity* (New York: Routledge, 1990), 139–41.

113. Butler, *Gender Trouble*, 139–41.

114. Judith Butler, "Imitation and Gender Insubordination," in *Inside/Out: Lesbian Theories, Gay Theories*, ed. Diana Fuss (New York: Routledge, 1991), 13–14.

115. Butler, "Imitation and Gender Insubordination," 18.

116. Butler, "Imitation and Gender Insubordination," 20–21.

117. Butler, "Imitation and Gender Insubordination," 23.

118. Butler, "Imitation and Gender Insubordination," 23–24.

119. Butler, "Imitation and Gender Insubordination," 27–29.

120. Butler, *Bodies That Matter*, 218.

121. Butler, *Bodies That Matter*, 227.

122. Butler, *Bodies That Matter*, 227–28.

123. Butler, *Bodies That Matter*, 229.

124. Cris Mayo, "Foucauldian Cautions on the Subject and the Educative Implications of Contingent Identity," *Philosophy of Education Society Yearbook* (1997): 3.

125. Mayo, "Foucauldian Cautions," 5.

126. Mayo, "Foucauldian Cautions," 6.

127. Malinowitz, *Textual Orientations*, 14.

128. Margrit Shildrik, "Queering the Master Discourse: Lesbians and Philosophy," in *Straight Studies Modified: Lesbian Interventions in the Academy,* ed. Gabrielle Griffin and Sonya Andermahr (London: Cassell, 1997), 187.

129. Carole Vance, "Homosexuality, Which Homosexuality?" quoted in the introduction to *Hidden from History: Reclaiming the Gay and Lesbian Past*, ed. M. Duberman, M. Vicinus, and G. Chauncey Jr. (New York: Penguin Group, 1989), 6.

130. Jeffrey Weeks, *Invented Moralities: Sexual Values in an Age of Uncertainty* (New York: Columbia University Press, 1995), 13.

131. Weeks, *Invented Moralities*, 8.

132. Sedgwick, *Epistemology of the Closet*, 41.

133. Nussbaum, *Cultivating Humanity*, 254.

134. Martha C. Nussbaum, "The Hip Defeatism of Judith Butler," *New Republic,* February 22, 1999, 45.

135. John Boswell, "Revolutions, Universals, and Sexual Categories," in *Hidden from History: Reclaiming the Gay and Lesbian Past*, ed. M. Duberman, M. Vicinus, and G. Chauncey Jr. (New York: Penguin Group, 1989), 18.

136. Boswell, "Revolutions, Universals, and Sexual Categories," 35.

137. See Jane Roland Martin's discussion of this controversy in part I of *Coming of Age in Academe: Rekindling Women's Hopes and Reforming the Academy* (New York: Routledge, 2000), 7–24.

138. Adrienne Rich, "Notes toward a Politics of Location," in *Blood, Bread, and Poetry,* 217.

139. Butler, *Bodies That Matter*, 240.

140. Diana Fuss, *Essentially Speaking: Feminism, Nature, and Difference* (New York: Routledge, 1989), 108–9.

141. Michel Foucault, "Sexual Choice, Sexual Act," in *Ethics*, 145.

CHAPTER THREE

Woolf, with Attitude

Out-Sider Issues

Earlier I suggested that Out-Siders need a praxis from which to work as they develop specific interventions intended to mitigate the effects of compulsory heterosexuality across a wide range of configurations of education. An *Out-Siders' Praxis* must be not only theoretically sound but pragmatic. It must be a life practice that can meet theoretical challenges. Further, its theories must not only shape strategies for change but also remain sufficiently malleable so that practice can ground it in experience.

Virginia Woolf conceptualized an Outsiders' Society that is praxis in all these respects. The Outsiders' Society is theoretically sound and pragmatically focused. Its flexibility is evident since it can be employed in a number of scenarios and it can be shaped to meet the specific demands of circumstance, which in turn informs theory. In addition, Woolf's conceptualization of the Outsiders' Society both demonstrated her acquaintance with the specific circumstances and details of her subjects, the daughters of educated men, and advocated strategies that held the potential for being profoundly disruptive in situations where abuse occurred. The Outsiders' Society allowed its members to exercise great creativity in choosing specific methods and arenas for its employment. Woolf also made clear that this Outsiders' Society would transform the Outsiders themselves even as the Outsiders transformed the world.

Notwithstanding the value of this Outsiders' Society for the daughters of educated men, it does not constitute an effective praxis for Out-Siders, who want to mitigate heterosexism, anti–lesbian and gay prejudice, and compulsory heterosexuality. Praxis, by definition, is time- and location-dependent. As a result, a praxis that developed in pre–World War II England for a group of upper-middle-class white women would require translation to be accessible for any other group sixty years later. Further, the development of praxis demands that its practitioners be conversant with specific practical considerations so that choices about the best intervention for particular situations are timely and creative. Woolf met these requirements for praxis about the daughters of educated men, but she did not consider—indeed, could not have considered—the practical circumstances of a gay teen in a North American high school.

Out-Siders, then, cannot simply adopt the methods and goals of Woolf's Outsiders' Society as their own, nor can those goals be effectively translated into this situation. Nevertheless, Woolf's methods for inquiry and the types of sources that she employed are instructive for my purposes here. Consequently, I adopt Woolf's approach and utilize similar kinds of sources in defining the needs, goals, and form an *Out-Siders' Praxis* will take that can meet the demands that the daily exigencies of lesbian and gay outsiders place on those who side with them. Therefore, in what follows I describe in greater detail the kinds of sources to which Woolf turned and the methods she used for inquiry. Further, I explain how and why those sources and methods are employed in my own inquiry.

When Woolf envisioned the Outsiders' Society, she claimed that a careful view of the world would reveal Outsiders already at work for the betterment of society. I argue that the same could be said of Out-Siders, and I describe six primary ways that theory and practice are integrated in research on sexual identity. As I examined each of these praxes in chapter 2, it became clear that the several ways theorists understood identity produced dramatically different strategies for changing heterosexist environments. It seemed conceivable at the outset of the analysis that one of the six *Praxes in re Sexual Identity* would fulfill the requirements for an *Out-Siders' Praxis*. Nevertheless, as I studied each of the praxes, theorists' critiques revealed conceptual problems, gaps in scholarship, or pragmatic weaknesses. From a theoretical perspective it appears inevitable that an *Out-Siders' Praxis* will have to be conceptualized that can overcome the problems of the existing praxes.

Because praxis integrates theory and action, so must an analysis of the *Praxes in re Sexual Identity* scrutinize practical strategies. Since action shapes theory in praxis, just as theory molds action, testing the practical strategies of the *Praxes in re Sexual Identity* against the circumstances of lesbian and gay outsiders' lives will indicate whether theorists' critiques of the praxes are valid. Further, a pragmatic approach forces a distinctive perspective with regard to theory. That is, from a pragmatic perspective, theoretical disparity is meaningless if no practical difference can be detected when one view is held, rather than the other. In pragmatism, theories are simply instruments, not answers.[1] Therefore, if the theoretical problems identified in one or more of the *Praxes in re Sexual Identity* are not reiterated in practical contexts, that praxis may still be useful to Out-Siders. Failing that, such an analysis will provide insight about how to address those actions in an *Out-Siders' Praxis*.

If an *Out-Siders' Praxis* is to be genuinely useful to those who side with lesbian and gay outsiders in their work to challenge heterosexism, it must consist of more than picking and choosing favorite points from each praxis. I am mindful of John Dewey's challenge to his fellow philosophers of education:

> It is the business of an intelligent theory of education to ascertain the causes for the conflicts that exist and then, instead of taking one side or the other, to indicate a plan of operations proceeding from a level deeper and more inclusive than is represented by the practices and ideas of the contending parties.
>
> This formulation of the business of the philosophy of education does not mean that the latter should attempt to bring about a compromise between opposed schools of thought, to find a *via media,* nor yet make an eclectic combination of points picked out hither and yon from all schools. It means the necessity of the introduction of a new order of conceptions leading to new modes of practice.[2]

For an *Out-Siders' Praxis* to lead educators into new orders of conceptions and new modes of practice, it must be able to resolve the major theoretical problems of the *Praxes in re Sexual Identity* as they affect practice.

With this objective in mind, I focus my practical questions on the weaknesses of the theoretical positions described in chapter 2. For instance, critics of the *Praxis of Inclusion* charge that liberal political theory's commitment to extend rights does not challenge the structure of society. Those who are loath to support the *Praxis of Coming Out* claim that its dependence on identity politics is, by definition, essentialist and exclusionary. Detractors argue that identity politics promotes the idea that people can only sympathize and understand those in their own identity group, dooming society to competitive pluralities. The *Praxis of Location*, with its composite view of identity, seems to satisfy the concerns of adherents to the *Praxis of Inclusion* but suffers from the same essentialist labels from social constructionists. Finally, activists and theorists alike have charged that the *Praxes of Refusal* and *Performativity* are too abstract and morally passive. Are educators actually finding practical ways of "queering the discourse"? These theoretical concerns will focus my practical tests of the *Praxes in re Sexual Identity*.

Out-Sider Sources

In *Three Guineas* Woolf considered what ordinary people might do to prevent war. When she looked at education and the practice of the professions, she saw competition, jealousy, self-advertisement, and profit motives, all of which were actually increasing the predisposition for war. The Outsiders' Society that she conceived served as part of her solution.

What was it that allowed Woolf to grasp the connection among competition and strife on university campuses, greed and pugnacity in the professions, and society's propensity to war when other people, seemingly better educated and with more political clout, failed to comprehend it? Her genius aside, I argue that the sources Woolf consulted and her method of inquiry permitted a different vantage point, allowing a view from the margin, across the grain.

To which sources, then, did Woolf turn? To find a perspective about how to prevent war that was different from those opinions so prevalent in public debate, Woolf turned to people who had never been part of war, who had never been part of the university, who had only been part of the professions in the recent past and then only in its lowest rungs. She turned to the words, experiences, and material facts of women's lives. By using their words, Woolf used details of life in the private house and in the public exclusions that the daughters of educated men experienced, to test accepted definitions, to challenge educational and philosophical ideals. That is, she forced specificity on ideals and definitions held to be abstract, faceless, locationless, genderless, and classless.

Typically, if a philosopher wanted to prevent war, he would call on the words of great experts: historians, politicians, and philosophers. Had Woolf been able to find the daughters of educated men among the great experts, she might have been inclined to use them. But as Woolf convincingly argued, the daughters of educated men would not be called on to give their opinions as experts in the political, philosophical, or historical realm; for they were, in Woolf's words, not part of the "intelligentsia" but part of the "ignorantsia." They were second-class citizens within a privileged class, whose knowledge was trivialized and whose brains were thought "too small to pass the Civil Service Exam." To engage the daughters of educated men, Woolf turned away from the experts, privileging the words and experiences of the daughters of educated men.

Woolf did refer to several recognized historical and political authorities, but much of her source material was drawn from over fifty biographical sources found in various forms: autobiographies, memoirs, collected letters, diaries, biographies. In addition, Woolf used source material, such as memoranda from universities, student handbooks, rulings by court justices, and even *Whitaker's Almanac*. Woolf called these documents and the newspaper, one of her most frequent and convincing sources, "history and biography in the raw."

Of course, as Woolf was keenly aware, most of what might conceivably end up in a history book is found in headlined articles that focus on the movements of nations, governments, and famous people. However, headlines seldom drew Woolf's interest. Instead, the stories that caught her attention were local news items and editorials that spotlighted some ordinary person for a moment of fame. Woolf was interested in quotes by a little-known Mayoress of Woolrich or in the mention of a women's lacrosse league. These statements of fact (mixed with fiction), expressions of opinion, and records of actions, uncensored by historians and biographers, allowed Woolf to draw close to the actual voices of her "subjects," women, the daughters of educated men. Woolf's sources were rich with unusual details and surprising perspectives. By listening to them, consciously looking at situations from the vantage point of the women whose lives she studied, she saw things that allowed her to assess the situation of war differently from how her male counterparts would.

In fact, Woolf's use of women's words, experiences, and the exclusions to which they had been subjected permitted Woolf to understand the epistemological significance of the sex of the knower. This importance, implicit in Woolf's analysis, was demonstrated explicitly some fifty years later in Lorraine Code's epistemological work *What Can She Know? Feminist Theory and the Construction of Knowledge*.[3] When Woolf, and later Code, used real people, women, to fill the roles of the knowers in "malestream" theoretical concepts, the universality of those concepts buckled under the weight.

For instance, epistemology uses a basic premise, "'S' knows that 'p,'" where "S" represents any "normal" knower. Epistemology has traditionally focused on the necessary and sufficient conditions for the possibility and justification of knowledge claims. Philosophers have proposed methods for arriving at truth and criteria for determining the validity of claims to the effect that "'S' knows that 'p.'"[4] The search for truth inquires about the nature of, and conditions of, human knowledge. According to Code, "Questions about the circumstances of knowledge acquisition serve merely to clutter and confuse the issue with contingencies and other impurities. The question 'Who is S?' is undoubtedly such a question."[5] That is, "Who is S?" is regarded in "malestream" philosophy as neither legitimate nor relevant.

Woolf, however, ignored the propriety of such a question. Using as examples Arthur and his sister, she inserted first Arthur, then Arthur's sister, into a hypothetical situation that could have been represented by "'S' knows that 'p.'" By forcing specificity on this abstract premise, Woolf demonstrated that in practice, when the "p" in "'S' knows that 'p'" is anything more complex than a "red book"—say, "liberty," "war," or "the campus at Eton"—the knowledge that comes from empirical observation or from a priori reasoning may well differ according to whether it is Arthur or his sister who fills the role of "S." Woolf's deconstruction of this philosophical universal normal knower amounted to a claim that the sex of the knower is indeed epistemologically significant, a claim explicitly argued by Lorraine Code.

Similarly, Woolf used the specific details of women's lives to challenge the ideological concept of scientific neutrality and objectivity. Objectivity has been touted as that which distinguishes knowledge from belief, opinion, testimony, and fantasy. In objective inquiry, then, there is a complete split between the knower (subject) and the known (object). It is assumed that neither placeholder is affected: the knower is not affected by knowing; the known is not affected by being known. Invoking the help of photographs of dead bodies and ruined houses sent twice weekly from the Spanish government, she reminds the reader: "Those photographs are not an argument; they are simply a crude statement of fact addressed to the eye."[6] Woolf proposed that the "fact" of these photographs creates an emotional response in the so-called objective observer. Her intent is to suggest that neither the Cartesian thinker nor the Kantian disciple can will away the neurological connections of the brain that link value-laden emotions with a culturally dependent intellect. That emotional responses are more basic than the will of the intellect prompts Woolf's claim that "facts" may not be purely objective. Facts, like novels, appear to be part truth, part fiction.[7]

Following Woolf's lead means that I, too, must listen carefully to the voices of my subjects. Like the daughters of educated men, lesbians and gays in this country's educational system have been accorded second-class status. They are rarely the subjects of educational inquiry. Their words or experiences rarely warrant more than a footnote, if that, in traditional educational textbooks and curriculum. Consequently, like Woolf, I rely heavily on biographical sources to find accounts of their words, experiences, and public exclusions.

Like fiction, biography has been used infrequently in traditional philosophical inquiry. This thinking has changed in the last forty years, principally because of the ongoing scholarly research conducted by various unrepresented constituencies. Because these unrepresented constituencies, like the daughters of educated men and lesbians and gays in education, have held "expert" authority only rarely, nondominant cultures have looked for, and found, wisdom in nonconventional people and places. To that end, fiction has become, if not a common tool, at least an accepted one.[8]

Biography and autobiography, from whence came Woolf's primary sources, have been used far less than fiction has, but in some philosophically notable ways. For instance, educational philosopher Jane Roland Martin undertook a convincing gender analysis based on Richard Rodriguez's autobiography, *Hunger of Memory*.[9] Karen Maloney has used the life and work of Charlotte Perkins Gilman in her philosophical research and, with Connie Titone, has compiled the book *Thinking through Our Mothers: Women's Philosophies of Education*, which gives similar treatment to the life and work of seven women who are philosophers of education.[10] Susan Laird has drawn on autobiographical writings by May Sarton and Alice Koller to theorize about curriculum concerning single life for women;[11] Deanne Bogdan has constructed her feminist theorizing about literature education around autobiographical narratives of her own classroom teaching.[12] Madeleine Grumet and Jo Anne Pagano pioneered a feminist genre of curriculum theory grounded in autobiographical reflection,[13] and Susan Douglas Franzosa has conceived educational autobiography itself as a form of theorizing[14] in which she and Laird, with Wendy Kohli and other contemporary feminist educational theorists, have also engaged.[15] Harriet Malinowitz even utilized student autobiographical narratives from the lesbian- and gay-themed writing class that she teaches.[16] Thus, while the practice of using biographical narrative as primary source material for philosophical analysis is not commonly used, it is certainly not without precedent.

I am cognizant of the fact that in turning to these sources I am not finding all that can be said. Thus, I am consciously avoiding the modernist mistake of assuming that I am highlighting a representative sample of gay and lesbian people in North American education. Rather, I am fully aware that these accounts, interviews, sources are mediated by what could be said, given the circumstances. Kevin Jennings, the editor of *One Teacher in Ten*, was also very aware of this limitation as he compiled the stories of lesbian and gay educators:

> Editing this book showed me that times had changed. . . .
>
> Yet, in other ways, I was reminded that some members of the gay and lesbian community are not as free as others, even if times were changing. Three institutionalized barriers—regionalism, sexism, and racism—became painfully evident as I put this collection together. In my native South, few teachers were willing to contribute, even anonymously, so heavy is the hand of homophobia in the Land of Dixie. . . .
>
> Similarly it became quickly apparent that women felt much more at risk than men in sharing their stories. The final collection is over sixty percent male, even though education is a female-dominated field. Furthermore, of the women who contributed, one-third felt the need to use pseudonyms for themselves or their hometowns, while only one man did so. Clearly, male privilege continues to exist.

Finally, my inability to bring greater cultural diversity to the collection was a tremendous disappointment. Over and over, gay and lesbian teachers of color expressed their tremendous anxiety over contributing to the book. In the process, they educated me on how homophobia, racism, and sexism can intersect in an individual's life in truly powerful and destructive ways. At one point, seven of the potential contributors, or approximately twenty percent, were people of color. But, as the deadline drew near, the bulk of those individuals felt compelled to withdraw . . . more often than not, out of fear of the consequences of publishing their stories, even under assumed names. As a community, we have a long way to go before all of our members feel equally safe in leaving the closet behind.[17]

Jennings was writing only about the contributors to one specific book, but his observations could just as well be said of all the biographical and autobiographical sources that I use to tell the stories of gay and lesbian teachers and students. These narratives only represent the people whose circumstances have allowed them to be open enough to share their stories. There is no way of knowing the stories and circumstances of those who feared loss of employment or community by contributing their narratives. And what of those people who are so closeted that an editor, researcher, or news reporter would have never asked them? Clearly, there are many lesbians and gays in our nation's educational system whose experiences will not be represented in this inquiry, whose voices will not test the *Praxes in re Sexual Identity*. Given the silence that still surrounds lesbian and gay lives in many parts of our society, there is no way of knowing if the narrative accounts that serve as my primary resources are representative of the gay and lesbian experience in North American schools and colleges. They are simply the accounts that exist.

Sources Used for Primary Materials

I draw extensively on ten sources that contain autobiographical interview accounts of lesbian and gay experience in education.[18] These sources provide interview accounts or autobiographical narratives of lesbian and gay teachers, students, administrators, and academicians; children of same-sex parents; and heterosexual teachers, priests, and ministers who have worked with lesbian and gay people. They are the best sources available to date dealing with the lesbian and gay educational experiences across a wide range of configurations of education.

Two of these sources—*Out and about Campus: Personal Accounts by Lesbian, Gay, Bisexual, and Transgendered College Students*, edited by Annie Stevens and Kim Howard; and *One Teacher in Ten: Gay and Lesbian Educators Tell Their Stories*, edited by Kevin Jennings—are collections of autobiographical narratives. Toni McNaron's *Poisoned Ivy: Lesbian and Gay Acade-mics Confronting Homophobia* is autobiographical, but she supplemented her own story in academia with information garnered from qualitative research conducted with over three hundred lesbian and gay faculty members.

Four sources contain extensive narratives derived from in-depth interviews: *Gay Parents/Straight Schools: Building Communication and Trust,* by Virginia Casper and Steven B. Schultz; *The Last Closet: The Real Lives of Lesbian and Gay Teachers,* by Rita M. Kissen; *School's Out: The Impact of Gay and Lesbian Issues on America's Schools,* by Dan Woog; and *Lesbian Teachers: An Invisible Presence,* by Madiha Didi Khayatt.

Three of these sources are accounts and analyses of educational interventions designed to combat heterosexism and homophobia: *Coming Out of the Class-room Closet: Gay and Lesbian Students, Teachers, and Curricula,* edited by Karen M. Harbeck; *Queering Elementary Education: Advancing the Dialogue about Sexu-alities and Schooling,* edited by William J. Letts and James T. Sears, editors; and *Overcoming Heterosexism and Homophobia: Strategies That Work,* edited by James T. Sears and Walter L. Williams. The individual contributors to these volumes rely on extensive interviews with lesbian and gay students, teachers, and het-erosexual teachers who have worked with lesbian and gay students.

Outsider "Attitude"

Woolf's sources and methods were inextricably linked. She did not find the voices of the daughters of educated men in scholarly books and journals. She did not find them writing reviews in which one great expert comments on the work of other great experts. Because the voices she chose to privilege were not typical to philosophical thought in 1938, she was forced to invent a method appropriate to her sources.

Simply stated, Woolf challenged standard definitions of several concepts, demonstrating that the idea of a "normal," universal knower was actually syn-onymous with "male" knower, and that "neutral" and "objective" inquiry was perhaps neither neutral, nor objective. She then envisioned how education and the practice of the professions could be transformed in order to promote a disposition to peace instead of encouraging a propensity for war. Woolf's two-pronged approach was made up of deconstruction and re-visioning.

Although Woolf's project in *Three Guineas* predates Michel Foucault's eth-ical inquiries by more than forty years, these two thinkers were, in fact, using methods that were remarkably similar. Foucault dubbed his method for inquiry in volumes two and three of *The History of Sexuality* "thinking with 'atti-tude.'"[19] Foucault said that "thinking with 'attitude'" consisted of two phases.

In the first phase, *problematization*, the goal is primarily deconstructive. The second phase, which is primarily constructive, Foucault called *ethical inquiry*.

In the problematization phase, the philosopher comes to understand where change is possible and desirable by questioning established truths and developing alternative accounts or critical analyses of targeted facts, concepts, principles, canons, natures, institutions, methodological truisms, and established practices. In the last two volumes of *The History of Sexuality*, Foucault's problematization consisted of a genealogical approach, which he described as "gray, meticulous, and patiently documentary. It operates on a field of entangled and confused parchments, on documents that have been scratched over and recopied many times."[20] Foucault's problematizations led him to assert that knowledge is historical, particular, and perspectival, constituting not *truth* but *truths* without epistemological foundations.

Woolf, like Foucault, problematized several concepts: liberty, war, education, fact and fiction, and influence. Her problematization showed gaps in the accepted definitions of these words, definitions that had been culturally constructed in the service of the dominant class of males. Through problematization Woolf challenged the notion that women's subjugation is pre-ordained, natural, and inevitable; she demonstrated that objectivity and neutrality function as accolades, just as Foucault later suggested of reason. "Objective" and "neutral" "facts," she observed, were actually part fact, part fiction, riddled with hidden power motives and subjectivity. She related these faulty paradigms to equally faulty public education and professional practices that increased competition and strife. Having revealed gaps in dominant ideology, Woolf argued that the subjugation of women, the reverence for objectivity and neutrality, and the deficiencies of traditional education were directly correlated. Public education was actually mis-educative, preparing emotionally barren men to practice their professions with greed, pugnacity, and malice, thereby contributing to a mature predisposition for war.

I am not suggesting that Woolf was some sort of early postmodern thinker, for Woolf was firmly committed to the notion of individual agency and still held out hope for successful and lasting state intervention in some situations. Even though she understood the locatedness of the daughters of educated men, postmoderns would still view them as an identity category. Further, Woolf did not engage in a full-scale Foucauldian genealogical study into the nature of the subject. Woolf did, however, engage in problematization.

When Foucault used problematization, he was focused on emancipating obscured knowledges from subjugation to make them capable of opposition against the coercion of a theoretical, unitary, formal, and scientific discourse. When Woolf used problematization, she suggested that the knowledge gained from the unpaid-for education, constituting the lowest rung of the hierarchy of knowledge, could bring much-needed human understanding and communication to public education and the practice of the professions. Woolf's problematization suggested that knowledge is particular and perspectival and that education and the practice of the professions creates a mature predisposition for war. Foucault's problematization suggested that knowledge is historical, particular, and perspectival and that education, with multiple other institutions in society, has created the modern soul.[21]

Problematization is, however, only the first phase of "thinking with 'attitude.'" The second phase consists of ethical inquiry. When Foucault engaged in ethical inquiry, he meant experimenting with the kind of relationship you ought to have with yourself: how an individual constitutes himself as a moral agent. Notably, the potential for the agency of individuals in his ethical works is considerably greater than that in his previous purely genealogical works.[22] Agency, for Foucault, was about creating one's self as a work of art, rather than conforming to some moral code. Thus, his inquiry into Greek and Roman sexuality and ethics was not undertaken to find models for imitation, for they too are historically and culturally specific. Rather, exploring ancient practices of the self suggested to Foucault that contemporary mechanisms of subjectification are culturally specific, creating a conceptual gap into which alternative ideas of self-constitution might enter in the future. Engaging this method of "thinking with 'attitude,'" Foucault claimed that having understood the extent to which individuals have been subjectified and subjugated by institutionalized powers (phase one), individuals can create opportunities to conceive and enter into positive, enabling subjectification (phase two).

Woolf's ethical inquiry, like Foucault's, worked within the conceptual gaps created by her problematization of education and the practice of the professions. Her deconstruction suggested that the unpaid-for education of the private house, low on the hierarchical scale of knowledge, might be linked to preventing war. Like Foucault, she invested an obscured knowledge with potential for working against the coercion of formal, scientific discourse. When Woolf examined the practice of the professions, she saw aggression and competition as something that is not inevitable but culturally specific. Through ethical inquiry, she envisioned the Outsiders' Society as an alternative to the prevailing societal mode of working in the public world. Woolf hoped that the Outsiders' Society, like Foucault's ethical models, would serve as a living experimental alternative to mainstream ideology, not a normalizing strategy to be imposed on the masses, but tenets to which people would voluntarily adhere. The Outsiders' Society provided a means by which the daughters of educated men could constitute themselves as moral agents. However, moral agency, as conceived by Woolf, was not without constraints, for Woolf said that the Outsiders must not allow themselves to be separated from the un-paid-for education that had enabled them to see differently. Assenting to abide by these constraints allowed Outsiders to practice the professions in an ethically responsible way that allowed for maximum growth of the Outsiders and maximum contribution to the development of other Outsiders. The tenets of the Outsiders' Society were designed to produce what Foucault later called "positive, enabling subjectification."

This approach, "thinking with 'attitude,'" serves my purposes well in this research for several reasons. First, like Woolf and Foucault, in turning to the words of lesbian and gay outsiders for my primary sources, I too will privilege hidden knowledge, subjugated experience, and silenced words. Second, "thinking with 'attitude'" is thoroughly practical. As a matter of fact, educational philosopher Clive Beck has charged that the postmodern approach, as epitomized by Foucault, is *too* practical. Beck is troubled by the fact that in postmodern thought, "attitude" is more highly regarded than cognition. He believes that postmodernism has too strong a methodological component, suggesting approaches rather than outlooks. Further, Beck finds the post-modern approach fraught with problems since it involves both "a working understanding of reality and life" and is, in part, autobiographical and heav-ily dependent on pragmatism.[23] Although Beck's comments are intended as criticism, it is just this attention to "approach," "attitude," "practicality," and the heavy dependence on "a pragmatic approach" that makes Foucault's method perfect for my purposes here. Michel Foucault has said:

> I have always been concerned with linking together as tightly as possible the historical and theoretical analysis of power relations, institutions, and knowl-edge, to the movements, critiques, and experience that call them into question in reality. If I have insisted on all this "practice," it has not been in order to "apply" ideas, but in order to put them to the test and modify them. The key to the personal poetic attitude of the philosopher is not to be sought in his ideas, as if it could be deduced from them, but rather in his philosophy-as-life, in his philosophical life, his ethos."[24]

In addition, as Foucault makes quite clear, in the interview entitled "Prac-ticing Criticism,"[25] this approach is intended to be theoretical and practical. Foucault is adamant that "thinking with 'attitude'" is not critique for the sake of critique. Foucauldian critique serves a political function, the "deep transformation" of society.

This critical approach is consistent, then, with my aims in examining the *Praxes in re Sexual Identity*. Any effective praxis for Out-Siders must be thor-oughly pragmatic if it is to address the exigencies of life for lesbian and gay outsiders. Further, just as Beck suggests, a "working understanding of reality and life" is inherent in Out-Siders' sense of responsibility to the outsiders with whom they teach and learn. Finally, if we are to believe Foucault and Woolf, all scholarly inquiry is in part autobiographical. Scholars have value-laden emotions and culturally dependent intellect, negating pure objectivity.[26] In Woolf's words, scholarly inquiry is part fact, part fiction, formed of perspective and history. No scholar, however much she or he tries, can escape autobiography, culture, emotion, perspective, or history.

Therefore, "thinking with 'attitude'" is consistent with a pragmatic approach that allows the particulars of lesbian and gay lives an opportunity to test the positions adopted in the *Praxes in re Sexual Identity*, to pry open for analysis any conceptual gaps that are revealed by looking across the grain. Those conceptual gaps offer the opportunity to engage in ethical inquiry about what ideas and acts should constitute a praxis for those who would call themselves Out-Siders. My critique of the *Praxes in re Sexual Identity* is therefore premised on the need to develop an *Out-Siders' Praxis* that can be used as a theoretical base for curriculum development and educational practice that will mitigate the mis-educative effects of compulsory heterosexuality in North American education.

In the two chapters that follow, I engage in "thinking with 'attitude.'" Chapter 4, the first phase of this method, will problematize the *Praxes in re Sexual Identity*. The voices of lesbian and gay outsiders, privileged in this chapter, test the conclusions of theorists and critics, as summarized in Chapter 2. Chapter 5 is an ethical inquiry into the kind of praxis that Out-Siders need to practice to work effectively toward the goal of mitigating the effects of compulsory heterosexuality in this nation's educational system. The *Out-Siders' Praxis* constitutes an alternative way of understanding our roles as teachers, colleagues, teacher educators, and the host of others involved in education across its many configurations. The *Out-Siders' Praxis* offers opportunities for creatively intervening in the educational system and re-creating ourselves in the process.

Notes

1. William James, *Pragmatism* (New York: Dover Publications, 1995; original, 1907), 21.

2. John Dewey, *Experience and Education* (New York: Touchstone, 1997; original, 1938), 5.

3. See Lorraine Code, *What Can She Know? Feminist Theory and the Construction of Knowledge* (Ithaca, N.Y.: Cornell University Press, 1991), 1–26.

4. Code, *What Can She Know?* 1–2.

5. Code, *What Can She Know?* 1–2.

6. Virginia Woolf, *Three Guineas* (San Diego, Calif.: Harcourt Brace Jovanovich, 1938), 11.

7. See Lorraine Code's deconstruction of scientific neutrality and objectivity in "The Autonomy of Reason," in *What Can She Know?*

8. See Maxine Greene, *Landscapes of Learning* (New York: Teachers College Press, 1978); Garrison, *Dewey and Eros*; Butler, *Bodies That Matter*; Sedgwick, *Epistemology of the Closet*; Susan Laird, "The Concept of Teaching: *Betsey Brown* vs. Philosophy of Education." *Philosophy of Education 1988* (Urbana, Ill.: Philosophy of Education Society); Susan Laird, "The Ideal of the Educated Teacher: 'Reclaiming a Conversation' with Louisa May Alcott," in *Curriculum Inquiry* 21, no. 3 (1991): 271–97; Susan Laird, "Teaching in a Different Sense: Alcott's Marmee," *Philosophy of Education 1993* (Urbana, Ill.: Philosophy of Education Society).

9. Jane Roland Martin, *Reclaiming a Conversation: The Ideal of the Educated Woman* (New Haven, Conn.: Yale University Press, 1985).

10. Connie Titone and Karen E. Maloney, eds., *Thinking through Our Mothers: Women's Philosophies of Education* (Upper Saddle River, N.J.: Merrill, 1999).

11. Susan Laird, "Women, Single Life, and Solitude: A Plea to Rethink Curriculum," in *The Center of the Web: Women and Solitude*, ed. Delese Wear (Albany: State University of New York Press, 1993).

12. Deanne Bogdan, *Re-educating the Imagination: A Poetics, Politics, and Pedagogy of Literary Engagement* (Toronto: Boynton Cook 1992).

13. Madeleine Grumet, *Bitter Milk: Women and Teaching* (Boston: University of Massachusetts Press, 1988); Jo Anne Pagano, *Exiles and Communities: Teaching in the Patriarchal Wilderness* (Albany: State University of New York Press, 1990).

14. Susan Douglas Franzosa, "Authoring the Educated Self," *Educational Theory* 42, no. 4 (Fall 1992): 395–412.

15. Susan Douglas Franzosa, *Ordinary Lessons: Girlhoods of the 1950s* (New York: Peter Lang, 1998).

16. Harriet Malinowitz, *Textual Orientations: Lesbian and Gay Students and the Making of Discourse Communities* (Portsmouth, N.H.: Heinemann, 1995).

17. Kevin Jennings, ed., *One Teacher in Ten: Gay and Lesbian Educators Tell Their Stories* (Los Angeles: Alyson Books, 1994), 11–13.

18. See appendix for annotated bibliography of these sources.

19. Michel Foucault, "On the Genealogy of Ethics: A Work in Progress" and "Polemics, Politics, and Problematizations," from *The Foucault Reader*, ed. Paul Rabinow (New York: Pantheon Books, 1984).

20. Foucault, "Nietzsche, Geneaology, History," in *The Foucault Reader*, 76.

21. Michel Foucault, *Discipline and Punish: The Birth of the Prison*, trans. Alan Sheridan (original, Paris: Editions Gallimard, 1975; translation, New York: Vintage Books, 1997), 27–31.

22. Especially *Discipline and Punish* and *The History of Sexuality*, vol. 1.

23. Clive Beck, "Postmodernism, Pedagogy, and Philosophy of Education," *Philosophy of Education Society Yearbook* (1993): 3–6.

24. Michel Foucault, "Politics and Ethics: An Interview," in *The Foucault Reader*, 374.

25. In *Michel Foucault: Politics, Philosophy and Culture*, ed. Lawrence D. Kritzman, trans. Alan Sheridan et al. (New York: Routledge, 1990).

26. See Code's *What Can She Know?*

CHAPTER FOUR

———

Problematizing the
Praxes in re Sexual Identity

I ended the review of the *Praxes in re Sexual Identity* by highlighting some of the most profound disagreements between, among, and within the various praxes about what identity in general, and sexual identity in specific, means for LGBTQ outsiders and Out-Siders. Identity, theorized in a variety of ways, led to dramatically different strategies for addressing a heterosexist environment.

Out-Siders most interested in the practical needs of the lesbian and gay community tend to work from the *Praxes of Inclusion, Coming Out,* or *Location*. Yet, theorists in these praxes have challenged one another, and all have faced serious charges of essentialism by social constructionists. Many theorists, however, have indicted the *Praxes of Refusal* and *Performativity* as too abstract, thereby encouraging moral passivity.

When I inquired into the ways in which the *Praxes in re Sexual Identity* have affected the configurations of education, several patterns emerged. First, the configurations of education deal with sexual identity in ways that are overwhelmingly consonant with the *Praxis of the Closet*. Second, Out-Siders working within the *Praxes of Inclusion, Coming Out,* and *Location* have enjoyed more practical success in mitigating the effects of compulsory heterosexuality across a broader spectrum of the configurations of education than have Out-Siders within the *Praxes of Refusal* and *Performativity*. Third, the *Praxes of Refusal* and *Performativity* have become quite influential in academia.

After studying these *Praxes in re Sexual Identity*, I suggested that, to be genuinely helpful in addressing the exigencies of daily life for lesbian and gay outsiders, praxis must be fundamentally pragmatic. Further, I questioned whether an insistence on a pragmatic approach would alter the viability of any of the *Praxes in re Sexual Identity* for use in the configurations of education. I went on to ask: What would happen if the real lives of lesbian and gay people were allowed to challenge the theories? By what method could such an inquiry proceed?

In chapter 3, I discuss the method "thinking with 'attitude,'" which I will use to inquire into the stories of lesbian and gay people. In keeping with the methods employed by Woolf and Foucault, I proposed to use problematization, the first phase of "thinking with 'attitude,'" as a way of allowing the real lives of lesbian and gay outsiders to "test" the theories of the *Praxes in re Sexual Identity*. Further, I suggested that, once armed with the "test" results accumulated from the problematization, I would engage in ethical inquiry, as Woolf and Foucault had done, to theorize an *Out-Siders' Praxis* that could serve as a useful theoretical base from which to develop curriculum aimed at abating compulsory heterosexuality's mis-educative potential.

Therefore, in keeping with this scheme, I undertake that problematization in this chapter. Foucault said that as conversations, ideas, and actions of, and toward, those people whose thoughts have not been deemed worthy of the discipline's label are unearthed, one can begin to understand that formal discourse is less unified, less consistent, less reasonable than the ways in which it presents itself. Problematization allows petty details, malice, and the use of reason and logic as an accolade to surface. Foucault used problematization to focus on obscured knowledge by revealing how formal discourse has shrouded thought that contravened the official story, how experiential knowledge has been subjugated on low rungs of the knowledge hierarchy, and how potentially useful ideas were abandoned because of political maneuvering. Woolf, however, used problematization to focus on obscured knowers. She allowed the actions and words of obscured knowers to surface in her analyses, and in the process she demonstrated how silencing and ignoring anomalous knowers had perpetuated unjustifiable gaps in epistemology.

My own problematization in this chapter follows Woolf's method more closely than it does Foucault's by consciously listening to the voices of outsiders and Out-Siders who have not gained entrance to the formal conversations circling around the *Praxes in re Sexual Identity*. Formal discourse has silenced lesbian and gay outsiders in education so frequently that it is easy to assume that they do not exist. If one were to listen to the voices of these outsiders, those people most affected by the formal discourse of the *Praxes in re Sexual Identity* but least represented in it, one may find it possible to reopen discourse around certain facts, concepts, and established practices. The words of outsiders may shed light on how to conceive an *Out-Siders' Praxis*.

In the sections that follow, voices will surface that have been obscured in North American education. In some cases, the stories of lesbian and gay people will animate the theoretical discussions of the *Praxes in re Sexual Identity*, supporting critiques of theorists; in other cases, the outsiders' experience will point to areas where theorists have been remiss. Sometimes these outsiders force abstract thought, sometimes global thought. But, in all the accounts that follow, the real lives of lesbian and gay outsiders challenge us never to forget that theories have consequences.

The Curriculum of the Closet

In chapter 2, I claim that most of Western philosophical thought was conceived in the Closet and that the North American educational paradigms that are built on that philosophical thought have remained in the Closet. The Curriculum of the Closet, then, contains curriculum designed in conformance with the *Praxis of the Closet*. However, as I use the term, the Curriculum of the Closet will include not just that curriculum that springs from the *Praxis of the Closet* but also that which simply conforms to the organizing principle of compulsory heterosexuality.

It is possible, in fact it is common, to design lesson plans, courses, curriculum, and even entire systems of education that have no basis in praxis whatsoever. Praxis combines theory and action concerned with one making wise choices, those requiring in-depth acquaintance with the practical considerations so that one may proceed skillfully, creatively, in a timely manner to intervene in the practical problems of human beings. Further, praxis is always time- and location-dependent, suggesting not only that it is inseparable from the subject who creates and enables it but that it also redefines the subject through its practice.[1] In praxis, theory and action shape each other, building a framework for understanding situations and sorting options. Praxis is a considered yet active, inventive yet interventive, way of life undertaken by individuals within a reflective community.

While little of our continent's educational practice conforms to these considerations, I could point to certain educational practices that embody praxis, such as much of feminist pedagogy, Freire's work with Brazilian peasants, and even several experiences in my own educational history. Yet, the fact that one must think to come up with such examples indicates that most contemporary education does not proceed from praxis but from some combination of traditional and progressive educational paradigm adhering to one brand or another of developmental psychology.

Therefore, just as the *Praxis of the Closet* is highly diverse but united in its failure to address sexual identity in a direct way that supports LGBTQ people in coming out, so is the Curriculum of the Closet highly diverse. As the heir of liberal education, the Curriculum of the Closet is not based on any unified philosophical system; rather, it consists of books, methodologies, and curricula tied to the project of transmitting culture, literacy, and numeracy. Consequently, whether teachers develop educational practice with or without roots in praxis, deliver the message explicitly or implicitly, or promote it through the hidden curriculum or curriculum proper, its failure to mitigate compulsory heterosexuality earns it a place in the Curriculum of the Closet.

Of course, every curriculum has its successes and failures, but supporters of various curricula tend to focus on success stories. The adherents to the Curriculum of the Closet are no exception. They highlight chosen images: those well-adjusted, appropriately masculine and feminine heterosexuals residing in, or destined for, marriage and family. These images loom prevalently, if most often wordlessly, in public discourse about "the means of correct training."[2] This said, it may well appear that the Curriculum of the Closet has nothing to offer Out-Siders. Nothing could be further from the truth.

The chosen images that populate the histories of those successfully educated in the Curriculum of the Closet are closely aligned with the "normal knowers" that Woolf, and later Code, critiqued. Woolf and Code concluded that an epistemology based on the universality of "S" as a normal knower is hopelessly flawed when the identity of the knower figures into the conditions that make knowledge possible. Like those normal knowers, the chosen images of the Curriculum of the Closet—male and female, black and white, average and gifted—are nonetheless reductive, abstracted, and universalized.

Woolf's problematization of "normal knowers" demonstrates what happens to universal and abstract knowledge when philosophers consider "anomalous knowers." Following her lead, problematizing the Curriculum of the Closet first means bringing to the foreground those whom advocates of the Closet normally keep in the background. Second, it seems appropriate to question whether the public mien of the Curriculum of the Closet veils any conversations found too low in the knowledge hierarchy, or deemed otherwise unfit, for inclusion in its formal discourse.

Clearly, as the name of the Curriculum of the Closet implies, educational configurations contain, in addition to chosen images, closeted images. Do these closeted images reflect the failure of the Curriculum of the Closet? Not at all. The closeted images actually lend their support to the Curriculum of the Closet in two important ways. First, because the harm inflicted by the Curriculum of the Closet is a carefully guarded secret among those who remain closeted, the harm does not challenge the Closet's success. Second, by failing to challenge the Curriculum of the Closet, those closeted images become publicly identified as success stories, allowing others to count them among the chosen images, thereby reinforcing the claim of the Closet's near-universal success.

If the Curriculum of the Closet counts closeted images among its successes, where should one look for the failures? Clearly, the failures did not adhere, at least publicly, to the teaching of the Closet. The failures are lesbian, gay, bisexual, and transgender people who have refused the Closet, who have refused silence, who have refused to keep the Closet's secrets. Because LGBTQ people are potentially disruptive, those who advocate for the Curriculum of the Closet must exercise extreme vigilance in managing depictions of them. Those LGBTQ lives must serve as deterrents to those who might be tempted to walk out of the Closet. Consequently, adherents of the Curriculum of the Closet have a vested interest in depicting its failures, LGBTQ people, as completely abjected, thereby reinforcing rigid boundaries between heterosexual and homosexual. In fact, the binary opposition of chosen versus abjected images creates the need for the Closet. The Closet is the effect, the consequence, of a chosen–abjected (heterosexual–homosexual) binary.

Therefore, practitioners of the Closet must portray chosen and abjected images routinely and powerfully. Fortunately for the practitioners of the Closet, the near-universal success of its curriculum requires little creative thought to perpetuate the necessary binary. Mr. Lockett's experience demonstrates how routine denigration of lesbian and gays in educational settings promotes callousness toward students those institutions are charged with educating:

> Teaching at what he called a million-dollar school on the waterfront, [Mr. Lockett] heard three colleagues pass his open door telling "faggot" jokes loudly enough to hear. "It was repulsive. I was surprised, yet at the same time I wasn't. The school had scored low on an educators' report on our recognition of cultural differences and the needs of minority students. One day we spent an hour discussing the report in a faculty meeting, and the very next issue was kids on the playground getting hurt playing 'smear the queer.' The principal brought up the topic, and didn't say a word about the name of the game!" That time, Mr. Lockett had spoken up. However, no one had gotten excited. It was as if they didn't know what he was talking about, or else it made no difference to them. At Shoreline, gay and lesbian concerns were a non-issue.[3]

"Faggot" jokes sustain the Closet. They solidify the camaraderie of a group that supposes its right to dominance, and they warn of impending victim status to any who are thinking of straying from the closet. "Smear the queer" and related games serve equally crucial functions. Children and faculty alike learn through such normative games that it is entirely appropriate to show disdain for "queers."

The following story of a West Virginia schoolteacher demonstrates that rumor and innuendo can serve as allies to the Closet in the absence of real lesbians or gay men to portray abjection.

> [Linda] Conway was forced to resign her job because of the reputation in the community that she was a lesbian. It stemmed mostly from the way she looked. Because she taught in a cafeteria where she had to lean over tables to teach, she preferred not to wear dresses. . . . Her clothes were perceived as offensive, her new haircut inappropriate. Finally, when she allowed a recently separated woman to move in with her, school officials and parents insisted that she had to be released.[4]

Jokes, games, rumors, and innuendo are all important, but they play only a supporting role in the Curriculum of the Closet. The leading role in the Closet's warning system must succinctly typify the horrors of nonconformance. The following account by Lewis Gordon illustrates the power of abjected images:

> Some years ago I visited a cousin whose kidneys no longer functioned after his three-year struggle with AIDS. My cousin sat up, alert, looking ahead as the dying do. I have seen that look too often; it is similar to airline passengers on standby. He wiped a tear that was trickling down his cheek.
> "Black men got it bad in this town," he said.
> Just then, a nurse opened the door. She knelt, her hand carefully protected by latex gloves, and shoved a tray of food along the floor into the room. The door gently closed behind her.
> My cousin didn't make a fuss. His eyes, holding onto his dignity as best he could, said a lot. He looked at the tray. For him, feeling sorry for himself required resentment, which he refused to feel. I decided to change the subject.[5]

This story vividly portrays abjection. Further, these images appear not just in educational settings but in the media and in every major institution in society. By continually defining the boundaries of the acceptable, abjected faces perform an invaluable service within the Curriculum of the Closet.

Lest one assume, however, that the Closet enforces boundaries only through abjected images, consider the strategic discontinuous support that emboldens anti–lesbian and gay rhetoric in the public arena. During the past decade, promoters of "citizen initiatives" have mounted antigay campaigns in dozens of states and municipalities. In four states—Colorado, Oregon, Idaho, and Maine—these referendum questions reached the ballot. Voting yes on these questions generally meant voting to deny gay people the right of protection from discrimination in housing, employment, public accommodation, and credit. With similar initiatives that failed to gather enough signatures or succumbed to legal challenges, these referenda have stirred up considerable public sentiment against lesbians and gay men.[6]

General society-wide endorsement of heterosexism, supported by specific anti–lesbian and gay initiatives and reinforced by abjected images, constitutes a powerful warning system for the Curriculum of the Closet. As a result, the actual teaching practice need not be particularly violent or malevolent. In fact, as the following account by Nathaniel, a senior in high school, suggests, a benign countenance works very effectively:

> In my sociology class we were talking about AIDS. One guy said, "I think gay guys are just sick. How could they do that? It's wrong!" One of my friends who is gay asks, "Why do you think it's wrong?" Well, everyone looks over to Miss L., our teacher, for what she thinks. She says, "I have no comment. I'm not even going to get into this discussion. I'm going to keep my opinion to myself."[7]

Miss L., in this example, did not add fuel to the hate language; she simply failed to participate. It is not clear from this story what Miss L. thinks about gay men. She may agree with the vocal young man in her class; she might be in the closet herself. Regardless of her opinions, however, her refusal to counter the hate speech in her class taught important, if hidden, lessons, all the while maintaining a neutral façade.[8] The students learned that regardless of how hate speech toward other groups might be handled in the classroom, they could count on Miss L. to tolerate anti–gay and lesbian sentiment. Her toleration acted as tacit approval. The students also learned that the concerns, opinions, and feelings of the gay student in this classroom are less important than the heterosexual students' freedom of expression. They learned that heterosexual privilege permits lack of consideration for the feelings of gay students.

Miss L.'s silence in this example effected two fine examples of compulsory heterosexuality as mis-education. Dewey said that the quality of an educative experience should have not only an immediate aspect of agreeableness, which means not repelling the student, but also an effect of promoting opportunities for desirable future experiences.[9] The gay student in this example had an immediately disagreeable experience and will likely dodge any such future class discussions. He learned to keep silent, to draw no attention to himself, and to shun classroom participation.

However, the heterosexual students in Miss L.'s class have also experienced mis-education by compulsory heterosexuality. Dewey indicated:

> Any experience is mis-educative that has the effect of arresting or distorting the growth of further experience. An experience may be such as to engender callousness; it may produce lack of sensitivity and of responsiveness. Then the possibilities of having richer experience in the future are restricted.[10]

The events that transpired in Miss L.'s classroom not only engendered callousness and lack of response toward gay people but also made that callous attitude seem entirely appropriate to a heterosexual majority.

Of course, the presentation of the Curriculum of the Closet does not always come through hidden curriculum and does not always present such a benign face. Franklin, who lives in a predominantly black South Carolina rural town, remembers incidents involving his high school physics teacher, Mr. Jenson.

> Mr. Jenson would usually drift away from the subject. He'd often bring up homosexuality. He mainly talked about the wrongs of it and how it was such a sin and that they should be condemned. I felt really bad.[11]

While Miss L.'s refusal to counter the negative effects of anti–lesbian and gay prejudice in her classroom constituted an implicit and informal instantiation of the Curriculum of the Closet, Mr. Jenson's habit of airing his personal opinions on homosexuality instantiates explicit and informal Curriculum of the Closet. What, then, is an *explicit* and *formal* Curriculum of the Closet?

Owen Garcia's story typifies the experience of an outsider in an environment that makes compulsory heterosexuality part of the curriculum proper. Owen was a young Mormon attending Brigham Young University (BYU). Since his father had earned a doctorate there, Owen seemed destined for BYU from birth, and the school actively recruited him with an early admission and full scholarship. But Owen's most compelling reason to attend BYU had nothing to do with family tradition or scholarship money. Owen feared he might be gay and was looking for spiritual help to overcome it, help he thought must be available at a bastion of religion such as BYU.

> At the counseling center, I was told, "Many men report great success with a program we call reparative therapy." They added that even though homosexuality was no longer considered a diagnosable disorder, it was still a behavior one could overcome. Through counseling with an appropriate male figure, I could repair my weak male self-concept, which was what led me to believe I needed male partners. . . . According to the therapist, I was a promising candidate because I was ego dysdonic, or self-hating, which is the first condition for success in the program. . . . "Saying it makes it real," I was told, so I voiced this miraculous change in my life to my closest friends. When I came out to my friends as a recovered homosexual, I received great praise and immediate superstar status for being diligent and valiant, an example and a witness to the truth of the Gospel of Christ.[12]

Unfortunately, saying it didn't make it real for Owen, nor did the appropriate male figure, nor the superstar status as a recovering homosexual. His continued attraction to other male students wracked him with guilt.

> I kept trying to believe in something, but little came of my will to believe. I did keep pouring my heart out to God in prayers. I kept bearing [sic] my soul to my bishop. And I beseeched the Holy Spirit, hoping my attraction to men would, after years of suffering, be wiped out.[13]

Feeling very alone and questioning his faith, Owen found distraction in school. Then, he received an offer to teach philosophy at a local high school. Leaping at the chance to redirect his energies and make a difference in someone's life, he threw himself into teaching. The school was a small private high school, so teachers and students frequently had dinner together. On one occasion a student's parents invited Owen for dinner. The student picked Owen up at his apartment. One of the boys to whom he had confessed his "recovering homosexual" status saw Owen leave with this young man and suspected Owen of acting as a sexual "predator." He reported his suspicions to the bishop. Through a series of events, Owen was "disfellowshipped," lost his right to participate in church ordinances, and was censored. On the evening of Owen's censoring, the vice president of BYU said, "Heavenly Father has not accepted your sacrifices." Owen said he was prepared to be censored, but he was not prepared for the vice president's claim on God's behalf. Suddenly, Owen recalled that he thought:

> How did he know that? He claimed inspiration, but how did he get it? With such limited knowledge of what had happened in my heart over the last four years, how could he claim to know God was unsatisfied. The most significant part of that evening was the little thought that crept into my mind after he'd said those words: *I don't need you to tell me what God thinks.* In the moment when it seemed God had betrayed me and that I'd lost everything I had strived for at BYU, I began to realize what I *really* needed to learn at BYU: to love myself, even if I'm queer.[14] [emphasis in original]

The stories of young lesbian and gay people from conservative backgrounds echo the guilt, self-loathing, and torment expressed in Owen's words. Owen escaped from the closet. Now he is one of the abjected. For many others the Closet door remains so tightly sealed, with the environment on the other side rendered so treacherous, that they never escape.

Victor Anderson, the pastor of a church with a black congregation, tells the story of another young man's struggle in the closet. Anderson refers to this boy who was part of his congregation simply as "S."

S was a very bright, creative, and popular teenager. He had excellent grades and was active in our church as the director of the youth choir. He was also black and gay. . . . S was a sissy. In the black churches, sissy is a euphemism for "faggot." Only a few of us knew S's secret. His popularity and active participation in the church led him to conceal his sexual identity from his family, friends, and church.

I had known S's terrible secret. I talked with him, and he would talk with me about his feelings and fears. They were expressed more as anxieties or worries than as declarations. . . . I began to hear from S's friends and parents that he was becoming withdrawn and that his grades were declining. He had only to complete the spring quarter of high school to graduate. However, on a spring day in April, only a couple of months before his scheduled graduation, I received a phone call that has haunted me to this day. S was found dead in the basement of his home . . . dead from a self-inflicted bullet to the head. . . . I have always suspected that S's inability to come to terms with being black and gay led him into a silence that ended with a gunshot.[15]

These are two vivid illustrations of what living in the closet—facing abjection on one side, a lie on the other—means for many people. Further, these voices and those cited earlier point to a factor that looms large for those in the closet—throughout the configurations of public education, the academy, and church and community education—a factor that educational philosophers often dismiss: religion.

Those philosophers associated with the *Praxis of the Closet*—Dewey, Marx, Freire, Gramsci—as well as those feminist philosophers in liminal positions within the *Praxis of the Closet,* rarely mention religion. Does the fact that these educational philosophers write from a secular perspective mean that they should overlook the power that conservative religion's condemnation of homosexuality still holds over many people? Does religion matter for educators in the United States since the U.S. Constitution separates church and state? Does not adherence to the Constitution obligate public and community educators to consult only secular sources?

Susan Laird has pointed out that the U.S. Constitution's mandate for separation of church and state could logically justify public educators' invocation of the primacy of a secular perspective in the formation and implementation of policy and curriculum regarding compulsory heterosexuality, since arguments that cite the Bible in legislative and school contexts violate the Constitution. However, she further argues that doing so, especially in the Bible Belt, would be naïve since constitutional freedoms of free speech, press, and assembly still protect the freedom to ground popular opinion in biblical interpretations of issues.[16]

Judith Plaskow's assessment reiterates Laird's position. She argues that religious and public policy dimensions of sexual orientation are so thoroughly intertwined that it is almost impossible to disentangle them.

> Religious injunctions against homosexuality have shaped negative public attitudes toward bisexuals, gays, and lesbians and have been used to justify repressive civil legislation. The contemporary gay rights movement emerged in reaction to the pervasive homophobia of the American culture, a homophobia formed and fueled by religion.[17]

Saul Olyan and Martha Nussbaum also demonstrate the extent to which debates about sexual orientation within several religious traditions have significantly affected public policy. They cite, as an example, the legal debate surrounding Colorado's "Amendment Two," a law prohibiting state and local agencies from passing laws protecting lesbians, gay men, and bisexuals from discrimination. At the trial, the state's witnesses included prominent Roman Catholic and Jewish theological scholars who testified about the relationship of the law to the state's interest in protecting religious freedom and public morality.[18]

Philosophers of education have conceived the theory that informs the *Praxis of the Closet* in secular terms. Yet, hearing the voices of closeted outsiders makes it clear that for many people religion plays a major, if not decisive, role in their decisions to stay in the closet. For many lesbian and gay outsiders who come out, their decision to do so forces them to cope with their religious qualms either by coming to a point of self-acceptance, regardless of the official doctrines of their religions; by changing religions; or by turning their backs on religion altogether. The fact that coming out requires many people to negotiate religious questions suggests that the *Praxes in re Sexual Identity* need to be more subtly theorized with regard to religiosity. The real lives of lesbian and gay outsiders suggest that philosophers' dismissive attitude toward religion, inherent in the theoretical underpinnings of all the *Praxes in re Sexual Identity*, may evidence callousness tantamount to miseducation by supporting a gap in scholarship.

The fact that religion is conspicuous in the Curriculum of the Closet—whether perpetuated implicitly or explicitly through hidden curriculum, or explicitly in the curriculum proper—suggests that the theoretical position of the Curriculum of the Closet is not primarily epistemological but essentializing. Further, a profound inconsistency structures its essential nature. The beliefs of most fundamentalist religions regard homosexual behavior as pathological or depraved. Nonetheless, many of these groups work toward legal repression of homosexual behavior, evidencing a paradoxical belief that such behavior is potentially ubiquitous in the human population.[19]

Other religions that are not associated with fundamentalism but still repress homosexuality engage in equally inconsistent discourse. For instance, James P. Hanigan states that Roman Catholic theologians have come to recognize the importance of sexual orientation:

> With little or no thanks to theology [Roman Catholic theologians now understand] that there is a reality that is appropriately called a sexual orientation, and to understand that one's sexual orientation, whatever it may be and however it comes to be, is fundamentally not a matter of conscious free choice or preference.[20]

Hanigan continues explaining the awakening of Roman Catholic theologians by asserting that they have come to understand that sexuality is not an accidental feature of human nature and human personality but a constitutive element, a mode of being in the world. Yet, Hanigan reports that the Roman Catholic Church, at least in its official teaching, remains convinced of the immorality of homosexual conduct and continues to describe the homosexual orientation as ontically disordered. Hanigan reiterates his belief that nothing he has read or heard has convinced him that the official teaching is false or should be challenged.[21]

These positions on homosexuality may be philosophically incoherent, but they are nonetheless extremely influential on popular culture. In fact, most of the "citizens initiatives" that have mounted anti–lesbian and gay campaigns draw their backing from conservative political organizations and right-wing fundamentalist groups such as the Christian Coalition, Phyllis Schlafly's Eagle Forum, and Colorado's Focus on the Family. They base their actions on the existence of a "gay agenda," in which, these groups claim, homosexuals and their supporters have concocted a plan to take over the country.[22]

One further aspect of this philosophically incoherent position warrants attention. This nation's "don't ask/don't tell" policy regarding homosexuals in the military presents a position just as philosophically incoherent as any of these conservative religious viewpoints. Judith Butler inquires about the significance of such a seemingly illogical position.[23] She has suggested that this policy has allowed the military to retain control over what the term *homosexual* means by allowing it to describe others but not one's self. That is, homosexuals in the military are prohibited from defining themselves. Further, when a homosexual declares, "I am a homosexual," these words are legally and officially construed as homosexual speech and homosexual conduct. That is, the military's policy has defined the words "I am a homosexual" as contagious and offensive. Apparently hearing "I am a homosexual" translates into the hearer's mind as "I want you sexually."[24]

One might assume that since this strange inconsistency takes place in the military that other configurations of education evidence none of its effect. However, this military policy is writ large in the actions of many "liberal-minded" heterosexuals.

> There was [a] lesbian at my school, a bright and well-loved teacher. Everyone knew that she lived out in the country with a woman who taught in another district, and that they had a big garden where they raised most of their food. As far as I can remember, neither the teacher nor her colleagues ever used the word "partner" or "lover." They were just "Cindy" and "Lynn," who lived together.
>
> In 1982, my children and I were among the hundreds of thousands . . . who traveled to New York City to participate in the march for nuclear disarmament. When I learned that Cindy and Lynn were planning to go, I invited them to spend the night with us and avoid the long drive to town where we would board the buses in the morning. It was a festive evening; we were full of exhilaration at the approaching end of the school year and the next day's great event. Cindy and Lynn entertained us with stories of the people in their small farming community, but they never once talked of their life together as a couple, nor did we ask. When the hour grew late, I opened the sofa bed in our living room and said I hoped they'd be comfortable. It was the first time all evening that I'd felt awkward, as if I were breaking the taboo of silence around their lives as lesbians.[25]

Secular scholars may seem to have nothing to gain and everything to lose by even contravening the "don't ask/don't tell" taboo. Academia as a whole evidences a profound disinterest in questions of sexual identity. It even seems logical and understandable when scholars resist being mired in debates built on such obvious inconsistencies, especially when "God's will" can so easily foreclose the dialogues. These two issues taken together, however, have produced an area of educational philosophy that remains undertheorized. Further, the conservative religious positions so frequently voiced in school districts all over the country continue without serious challenge from the academic community.

Given the dire consequences that the Curriculum of the Closet poses for LGBTQ outsiders, those who choose to side with the out do not have the luxury of such neglect. Foucault suggested that one should refuse to privilege the intent of philosophical constructs and purposes, focusing instead on the effects. Considering the *Praxis of the Closet* in this light obviates the fact that many well-intentioned scholars, by their failure to recognize and seriously engage sexual identity and the religious components inherent in the Curriculum of the Closet, perpetuate a mis-educational tradition. When teachers and academicians pretend that lesbian and gay outsiders do not exist; when they pretend not to hear the anti–lesbian and gay jokes, games, rumors, and innuendos; when they fail to counter abjected images; when they ignore the impact of religion on anti–lesbian and gay prejudice evidenced in their classes, they have failed to side with the out in their classes, on their campuses. As a result, the contribution of scholars in the mitigation of heterosexism and anti–lesbian and gay prejudice is roughly comparable to Miss L's contribution in her high school sociology class.

Exclusivity in Inclusion

The liberal foundation of the *Praxis of Inclusion* privileges the "right" over the "good," allowing Out-Siders to work toward maximizing individual freedom even for people with whom they do not agree, so long as the community's welfare is not jeopardized. Within this praxis the dialogue that takes place in public spaces is key to wise decision making. Arendt says that, through such dialogue, is continuous acknowledgment that I must finally come to agreement with these others, constituting the essence of political life.[26] Therefore, Out-Siders working within the *Praxis of Inclusion* seek a place for LGBTQ people in the democratic dialogue. Further, they argue that the basic rights and privileges of all citizens should be extended to LGBTQ citizens on the basis of a shared humanity.

Certainly the Out-Siders in the *Praxis of Inclusion* are espousing worthy goals. Legislation and policy should accord lesbian and gay outsiders the rights to live safely, own property, and obtain equal employment protection. In spite of the criticisms leveled against this praxis by those working within other praxes, all Out-Siders agree on these basic necessities. "Right" over "good," then, seems to be a logical goal. Can the lives of outsiders themselves shed any light on this political strategy? The following are two opinions typical of much of the discourse that holds to the principle of "right" over "good."

David Novack:

> As for secular penalties against those who engage in homoerotic acts, I think there is some consensus even among those who otherwise disapprove of homosexuality that such penalties are socially counterproductive. For better or

for worse, unlike religious communities which really do not have any notion of a "right to privacy" . . . our secular society has more and more assumed that there is such a right. To effectively penalize homoerotic acts between consenting adults would entail such massive invasions of privacy that many other rights would be threatened. And these rights, which unlike the right to engage in any sexual act with whoever agrees to do so with one, are accepted by popular opinion and tradition (for example, the right to privileged communication).[27]

Cheryl J. Sanders:

While the sexual conduct of gays and lesbians has not been endorsed by most of the African American religious community, the quest for human dignity and civil rights has been viewed as all-inclusive. Analogous to this position is the treatment of women in the African American churches; while there remains a strong resistance to accepting the full equality of women in the church, especially in leadership roles requiring ordination, few have argued against the right of women to equal treatment and access in the public sphere. In view of the fact that gays and lesbians have participated in the life of these churches at all levels, perhaps most visibly in music ministries, the general ecclesial stance of black churches can perhaps best be described as acceptance without advocacy.[28]

Without being reductive, I think it is fair to say that the assertion of "right" over "good" evidenced in this discourse hardly leaves the impression that heterosexuals welcome lesbian and gay outsiders into the "dialogue of humanity" with open arms. Novack's concern about potential domino effects that such breaches of privacy would portend for the heterosexual community prompts willingness to end criminal penalties for homosexual behavior and extend the right of safety to lesbians and gay men by supporting anti-gay-bashing legislation. Likewise, Sanders explains that the church, a central force in so much of the African American community, supports protection for lesbians and gay men in public but remains "opposed to licensing, ordination, or approving of persons in leadership actively involved in this lifestyle."[29]

These two speakers are theologians. This praxis's focus on secular concerns tempts one to dismiss the importance of theological discourse for public settings. However, as previously discussed, such religious views are highly influential, not only in the religious traditions that they represent, but in popular culture as a whole. Although both speakers support legislation benefiting LGBTQ persons, they nonetheless endorse continuation of a hierarchical social status that privileges heterosexuality over nonheterosexuality.

In so doing, their assent to basic rights and freedoms for LGBTQ persons does nothing to interrupt the belief in heterosexuals' right to dominance.

How does this subordinate position affect the crucial dialogue of humanity that thinkers such as Dewey, Rorty, Gadamer, and Arendt have considered critical to democracy? Dewey believed that finite creatures grow wiser only if they share perspectives with one another.[30] He insisted that dialogues across differences are essential for those who desire to grow. Rorty said the conversation of humanity takes place not because there is a specific goal but because conversation is an activity that is its own end.[31] Gadamer conceived his conversation of freedom based on mutual respect, recognition, and understanding.[32] Arendt stressed the element of wooing in persuasive speech.[33] Sharing perspectives across difference, dialoguing in and about freedom, wooing others in political conversation that constitutes the essence of political life are conceived in each case as dialogue between equals. What happens to the theoretical ease with which one can conceptualize such critical conversation when domination remains entrenched?

When the liberal premise, which intends to offer greater political freedom to LGBTQ people, is problematized, the *telos* of democratic dialogue is less sure. In fact, as Lorraine Code has pointed out, the liberal ideals of individualism and autonomy, portrayed as the opportunity for individuals to make of themselves what they will, seem even to eschew biological determinism.[34] But this promise, she suggests, cannot be fulfilled when terms of race, sex, socioeconomic circumstances, or expert status become part of the mix. I submit that the discourse cited earlier argues convincingly that even if lesbians and gay men were to receive basic rights, the heterosexual–homosexual binary would remain intact and therefore prohibit dialogue among equals.

The theory of democratic dialogue among equals is, in practice, fraught with multiple hierarchical systems that privilege certain races, ethnic groups, sexes, and sexual orientations over others. Further, if Dan Woog's observations can be trusted, then we can accept that when two people hierarchically equal in class, sex, race, and expert status share perspectives, the one who espouses a politically unpopular cause often slips into a subordinate status.

> It's . . . one thing for a teacher to say, "I'm straight, but I support the rights of my gay colleagues and students to exist in a safe school environment" on the East or West Coast, another to do so in America's heartland or in the wilds of Montana.[35]

Intersections of authority based on expert status, race, sex, ethnicity, religion, age, ability, sexual orientation, and even opinion create a hierarchical dilemma for democratic discourse that liberal notions of "right" over "good" seem ill-prepared to handle. What happens when the ideal of democratic dialogue is replaced with merely working for basic rights and certain legal protections? One lesbian teacher had this to say about an equal protection clause:

> [It] would make me feel more secure, I suppose, in my choices, but in the long run, isn't it the way we are relating to the people around us that is important? A protection clause is actually probably going to polarize people more—I don't know. I'm not at all sure about political action as a means to sensitivity and understanding. But I would suggest that it would be a good thing from the point of view if there—and there is sure to be one rising up from the ashes soon with all the fundamentalist stuff coming up—there is sure to be someone who goes on a witch-hunt soon for the sake of the witch-hunt and his or her own viciousness, and a protection clause would be absolutely necessary in that case because people would lose their jobs left, right, and center. . . . A law never gets to people's hearts, and that's where your greatest liberalizing force comes from, and if their hearts are tight and narrow and restricted, no law is going to change that.[36]

Another lesbian teacher stated the problem more succinctly, saying that with an equal protection clause,

> I would be protected from firing. I would not be protected from ostracism, or harassment, or from students, or from colleagues.[37]

These teachers' words suggest that while changes in legislation and policy are needed, this political maneuver alone is far from enough. The last quoted teacher said it best: law does not address the hearts and minds of people. This is not news. The Civil Rights Act has been in force for thirty-seven years, and there is still rampant race and gender discrimination. Even defenders of liberal ideology recognize these weaknesses.

The words of LGBTQ outsiders resonate with postmodern thinkers' distrust of reason and dialogue. Further, the experiences of those who suffer the consequences of exclusion and those who are marginally included reiterate one of the common criticisms that the *Praxes of Coming Out* and *Location* have directed toward the *Praxis of Inclusion:* The mere inclusion of diverse groups into an institution, state, or form of government does nothing, in and of itself, to transform society. The circle of inclusion may continue to enlarge, admitting more and more people at its margins, but the failure of liberal political thought to ask critical questions about society's structure means that the center has not been impeached. Despite the best efforts of liberal political thought, hegemonic ideology is still thoughtlessly white, male, heterosexual, physically able, educated, and socially and economically privileged.

Out of the Closet, into the Fire

The painful experiences of the closet, coupled with the ineffectiveness of isolated individuals trying to fight the system of heterosexism alone, propelled gay men and lesbians into coming out and organizing for political survival. Theorists have argued convincingly that the *Praxis of Coming Out*, with its inherent commitment to identity politics, is deeply and irrevocably flawed. Are these flaws borne out by the experiences of those ordinary lesbians and gay men in North American education?

Coming out was conceived as the central political act of resistance to lesbian and gay oppression.[38] As a result, it is the unifying tenet of the *Praxis of Coming Out*. Therefore, a logical starting point for this discussion is the story of how one such outsider, Rodney Wilson, chose to come out to his students.

> I have known I was gay since I was seven. Seventeen years later, after much effort to become straight as well as hundreds of prayers pleading for a dispensation of straightness, I came to understand that I was simply meant to be gay and that the God and Parent of us all was not concerned about the issue. . . .
>
> The only place where I was still closeted was at work. However, in the fall of 1991, a classroom exercise prompted me to seriously consider coming out to my students. In class, we debated various civil rights issues, including whether or not a lesbian couple should be allowed to adopt children. I was taken aback by the students' overwhelmingly negative response. Some proclaimed that they would burn down the house of any lesbian couple who moved near them. I felt it was my duty at the time to tell my students that I was gay: they needed a human face behind the word *homosexual*. I thought of the following analogy: if I were an African American in Montgomery in 1956, teaching blind white students who did not know my racial heritage, I would be morally compelled to reveal my blackness to help them overcome their prejudice. Similarly, I felt compelled to tell my "blind" students in 1991 that I was gay, but could not.[39]

Rodney decided to attend the NEA conference in Washington entitled "Affording Equal Opportunity to Lesbian and Gay Students through Teaching and Counseling." Realizing that he was no longer willing to participate in his own oppression, he decided to be honest with his students when he returned.

During my absence, I had asked my substitute to show the film *Escape from Sobibor*. An engrossing account of the only successful mass escape from a Nazi death camp, the film captures and holds the students' interest. I was aware that during my stay in D.C., they were watching a film about one of the most horrific chapters in human history, one that took place because one group of people felt justified in hating another group—a group that included gays who had perished by the thousands in the Nazi-led Holocaust. . . .

We began class by watching the final fifteen minutes of the film. Afterwards, I pulled my chair to the front of the room to begin discussion. I began to talk about crimes against humanity. I noted the different groups the Nazis had persecuted, using [a Holocaust Museum poster] as my visual aid. . . . The room was absolutely silent. Then I pointed to the pink triangle and said, "If I had been in Europe during World War II, I would have been forced to wear this, and I would have been gassed to death." And so I came out to my students.

I went on to tell them that thousands of gays had been killed in the Holocaust by the Nazis. . . . I waited nervously for their reaction. Absolutely none of them responded negatively. M. raised his hand and said, "I respect you a lot for having the courage to say what you just said." . . . Others followed with more personal questions. . . . Three female students began to cry: the tears, I learned, came from the level of emotion in the room, not from anger or prejudice. . . .

As the exhausting hour came to an end, I felt at peace with my decision. The moral universe had opened a window through which I had just traveled, and the students had applauded my journey. . . . Finally, the truth was known, and I felt freer than ever before.[40]

Others who have come out while working as school personnel made the decision as Rodney Wilson did, to come out because of a deeply felt need for authenticity. But some have based their decisions on the need to help their students. Such was the case of Pat McCart's experience of coming out as a lesbian:

I was fifty-three, a secondary school principal. Outside the gay community, I was out to my immediate family, a few close straight friends, and a few trusted people at work. I was out to, and had the support of, my boss. I had worked patiently and quietly to get sexual orientation included in the school's nondiscrimination policy. I had the Names Project poster [the organizational custodian of the AIDS Memorial Quilt] in my office. I thought I was out enough.

It was the fall of 1988. One of my advisees was to give the year's first senior speech to the student body. She had chosen the topic of homophobia and at the end planned to say that her mother was lesbian, and to tell how proud she was of all the risks her mother had taken, and all the work she had done to confront the prejudice and bigotry. This student had been my advisee for three years. I knew her mother was a lesbian but the student and I had never talked about it. She hadn't told a soul in the school. When the time came to practice the speech in the empty auditorium, she realized she wouldn't be able to say, "My mother is a lesbian." She came to my office crying, devastated that she couldn't say it. She was afraid of what others might think, say, do . . . afraid of the homophobia that might be lurking under all those good manners.

Well, there I sat on my own personal road to Damascus. I was the school adult responsible for the bright, young woman who wanted so much to make a public statement. I was the adult responsible for the group she was afraid to tell about her mother. And I was a lesbian.

I was struck by two things. One, I had never related my lack of public openness about my sexual orientation to my authenticity as a teacher and a role model. I had mistakenly thought that part of my success was due to how well I kept the two issues separate. And two, that by not being fully, publicly identified as a lesbian, I was maintaining my comfort at the expense of the youth—the very group I had spent my adult life working for and with. My fear, my privatization helped keep the fear, misinformation, prejudice, and homophobia alive among these adolescents, whether they were straight or gay. I was not out enough.[41]

Pat McCart's decision to come out was well received. Her students rewarded her with affection for her honesty, and she believes that lesbian and gay students in her school can now more easily accept who they are.

Six-year-old Jake reaps rewards every day from his mothers' difficult decision to be out with his elementary school teachers. The teachers, learning about Jake's home situation, purposefully placed Jake in a classroom with two other children with same-sex parents, much as they would do with other culturally diverse children. Jake's assessment? "I would feel worse if there were no other two-mom families. What if I wanted to feel like other kids and nobody was like me?"[42]

These stories point to the positive effects of the decision to privilege authenticity over safety. These stories serve as the chosen images of the *Praxis of Coming Out* in much the same way that smiling heterosexual couples serve as the chosen images for the Curriculum of the Closet. They present what is best about coming out and demonstrate that environments are frequently less hostile than imagined. Rodney Wilson and Pat McCart talk about their trepidations, but the underlying message is this: these people came out, walked through their fears, and so can you!

However, problematization challenges one to unearth exclusions, petty malices, details covered over by the public face of whatever knowledge is being examined. Therefore, while acknowledging the good that can result from coming out, one needs to look at stories that have less positive endings.

Students have not targeted Michael, a closeted gay teacher in a suburban high school, but he is well aware of what happened to his gay predecessor, Curtis.

> They would put things on his door, you know, like "This is Curtis the fag's room." They would call him "fag," they would shout it down the hallway. They would call up his phone several times a day. . . . He'd pick it up and [they'd] say, "Fag." . . . My worst-case scenario is that I would be treated the way Curtis was treated.[43]

The consequences of coming out as a lesbian or gay college student often go beyond the verbal harassment Curtis endured. For instance, one college student came out to a few friends on a campus in upstate New York. She was packing her car for a trip off campus with her girlfriend one weekend when she went back to the car to find windows smashed, tires flat, and lights broken. Scrawled across the hood was the word *DYKE*.[44] Another lesbian college student, who came out to her roommate, describes returning to her dormitory room to find her side of the room trashed. Water had been poured on the bed, the posters on the wall were wet, and the word *DYKE* was written on her poster of Barbara Jordan.[45] A young gay college student, seen going into the LGB office on campus, was beaten nearly to death while the group of his assailants yelled derogatory gay epithets.[46] These accounts are as common as they are alarming.

However, not everyone finds such stories to be especially problematic. Take, for instance, the opinion of a Florida legislator quoted in an article in the *Tampa Tribune*:

> Gay students lobbying for discrimination protection in Florida schools got a jolting civics lesson Monday from a lawmaker who welcomed them into his office only to declare: "God . . . is going to destroy you."
>
> "I don't understand why the gay population is becoming so vocal," state Rep. Allen Trovillion, R-Winter Park, told the Orlando-area high school students. "You are going to cause the downfall of this country that was built on Christian principles." . . .
>
> Thomas Gentile, 19, sought to give the lawmaker a better sense of what gay students contend with in Florida schools each day. He described how he was beaten during his freshman year in a Boca Raton high school classroom by assailants who targeted him because of his sexual orientation. School administrators suspended the attackers for one day. They also suspended Gentile, he said, suggesting he provoked the violence by being "too openly gay."
>
> Trovillion was unswayed. "You have to suffer the consequences of your actions."[47]

The anti–lesbian and gay sentiment fueling this representative's words is replicated, unfortunately, in academic circles. Often applicants are not taken seriously when they are open about their sexual orientation during the hiring process. A lesbian professor of English working at a graduate university in the Midwest writes as follows:

> A couple years ago I was on a search committee and very excited that an out lesbian scholar was among the applicants. She emerged as one of the two top candidates and was interviewed at our yearly conference. However, before it was decided who would be invited to campus, everyone on the committee was asked to read her newest book and comment on whether her approach was important and broad enough to be useful to graduate students. We were not asked to do anything similar for the other candidate. I told chairs of the recruitment team and the department that it was homophobic to treat an out lesbian candidate differently than other candidates. But they were on their liberal "we need the best candidate" horse and wouldn't get it.[48]

A widely published science professor who was the fourth woman to be tenured at a historically all-male private school reports with some resentment:

> I publish under two names—one for my regular science work and one for writing on gay/lesbian subjects. I do that because I'd lose my grant funding for my scientific research if my sexual identity was known.[49]

A professor of communication for fifteen years writes the following:

> Being a lesbian has taken away job opportunities from me—has led to my not receiving tenure at one institution and has curtailed my research in that I have been hesitant to publish anything feminist—let alone lesbian.[50]

One gay man, having published twelve books and over twenty-four articles on gay-related topics, was repeatedly passed over for academic positions where persons with almost no experience were hired. Finally he removed all titles from his vita that were gay-related and applied for a job. With this embarrassingly bald vita, he was granted an interview and the position, in his words, "virtually in the blink of an eye."[51]

None of these lesbian or gay males wanted to live a closeted existence. They believed their silence to be hypocritical and unhealthy. Coming out in an accepting and supportive environment, as did Rodney Wilson and Pat McCart, is certainly the ideal of the *Praxis of Coming Out*. Yet, for many lesbian and gay people at all levels of education, lives, property, and careers are, or would be, severely and irreparably damaged by coming out. What does this say about the *Praxis of Coming Out*'s universal prescription for full disclosure? Does not this mandate, just like its converse, that of being forced to remain closeted, arise from the same image of Virginia Woolf's Dictator? She said, "It suggests that we cannot dissociate ourselves from that figure but are ourselves that figure."[52]

Obviously, all people who come out face risks. Those risks, however, are not the same in every location, in every household, in every community. It is one thing to be out in San Francisco, Los Angeles, New York, or Boston, and quite another to be out in the small towns and rural communities that still make up most of the United States.[53] Nor is the risk the same for those who are self-employed; employed in large, diverse organizations; or employed in rural school districts. The universal prescription for coming out has been voiced overwhelmingly by whites in large, liberal cities on the East and West coasts. What do we make of the fact that the costs and benefits are distributed so unequally?

One of the more extensive areas of inquiry in lesbian and gay studies examines adult attitudes toward homosexuality and homosexuals. These studies often report the relationships between attitudes and personality traits or demographic variables. Though such studies are not without conflicting data, there are consistent patterns. One correlation that emerges repeatedly is that those people harboring negative attitudes about homosexuality are more likely to have grown up in the Midwest or the South, in rural areas or small towns.[54]

This research suggests that a universal prescription for coming out imposes a greater burden on those gays and lesbians in parts of the country least equipped with support systems. The geographic concentration of lesbians and gays in large urban centers is one of the things that makes coming out a more livable choice, personally as well as politically. Yet, the universal prescription to "come out" that is part and parcel of the *Praxis of Coming Out* displays little sensitivity to one particular aspect—namely, the relative risks versus benefits of coming out in geographic locations where there are few other lesbian or gay people to serve as supports. Is the universal prescription for coming out rife with regionalism?

Most studies on homosexuality have been conducted with gay men and with people who know them. Lesbians typically have been far less public. In part these decisions have been based on lesbian mothers' needs to protect their children from public scorn. Further, sex alone makes lesbians more vulnerable to domestic and public violence. Nonetheless, many lesbians object to the entire coming-out strategy on other grounds. For instance, Khayatt's sociological study with lesbian teachers indicates an intense disdain not only for the term *lesbian* but for any label whatsoever. For her, labeling

> seems to put a boundary around it when you use the term *lesbian*. I can't say what I see that boundary as being, but it creates a general image which I don't think fits all women who are attracted to or who live with other women.[55]

Another woman put it like this:

> One word I'm still reluctant to use is *lesbian*. It's another label. It's a label like all other labels. I'm a teacher. I'm a lesbian. I'm X.[56]

Is the universal prescription for coming out rife with sexism?

A number of social scientists indicate that scientifically measuring homosexuality and homophobic attitudes in any population is difficult. However, this problem is particularly difficult among African Americans, who are usually excluded from major statistical research studies on sexuality.[57] Further, Victor Anderson describes an African American preoccupation with a "cult of black masculinity." He suggests that the cult of black masculinity inscribes on black moral consciousness a hierarchy of virtues that favors race loyalty and the good of the race over one's loyalties to gender or sexual goods. It favors an unmitigated commitment to race over the claims that one's sexual desires, preferences, and orientation make on one's communal choices. The virtues of this cult of black masculinity exhibit a universality that transcends the particularities of black women's commitments to one another when such women become threatened by domestic abuse and violence or encounter sexual harassment by black men. Furthermore, this cult of black masculinity trumps the preferences of black gays and lesbians for sexual association and the fulfillment of their desires for same-sex unions.[58] Is the universal prescription for coming out rife with racism?

Jose Manuel, the son of a prerevolutionary Cuban bourgeois family and an activist in the gays-of-color community, indicates that the typical white situation is different from the Latino experience regarding homosexuality:

> Cuban society is *machista*, but if you grew up with money and power the norms of the poor man did not apply. True, we were often forced to marry and have children against our wishes, but we also had our own lives. We could have all kinds of sex on the island. . . . We were very Americanized, so we had a very U.S. view of sexuality, but with more freedom to experiment than your aver-

age American. Coming to the U.S. was a downer because my family lost all its money, and being a refugee you had to be very careful. It took me years to get an education and money to be able to come out. I find that upper-class Latinos have always been able—as most upper-class people all over the world—to do more with their sexuality than the middle class.[59]

The reverse was true of Xochil, a lesbian from a Guadalajara middle-class family, currently studying in a Los Angeles college:

My father is a university professor in Mexico. He works at a private university. If I had come out in Guadalajara he would have probably lost his job because his boss is very Catholic. It would have been me or his job. Here in L.A. I am a lesbian. In Guadalajara I am straight.[60]

Is the universal prescription for coming out rife with nationalism?

Working-class men and male peasants in Mexico and in other parts of Latin America have constructed very particularized concepts about homosexuality. In these settings a "homosexual" refers to the male who is penetrated during same-sex intercourse, whereas the male who penetrates does not compromise his "straight" identity. Thus class, as well as race, determines to a great extent whether one would even feel the need to come out as homosexual. Is the universal prescription for coming out rife with classism?

Religionism, regionalism, sexism, racism, nationalism, classism. The message of the *Praxis of Coming Out* claims that anything less than full disclosure is dishonest and dishonorable. Yet, the experiences of many LGBTQ individuals suggest that the practical aspects of full disclosure may add to the theoretical problems of identity politics. That such a basic tenet of the gay movement is permeated with insensitivity to sex, geography, race, and class indicates why the gay movement, especially after the AIDS onslaught, suffered from lack of cohesion. This praxis's reliance on identity politics simply precluded it from managing the demands of composite identity. Therefore, even though the act of coming out is imbued with profound significance for most lesbians and gay men who choose to do so, the "cost to benefit ratio" varies significantly among those who come out. It is a praxis that holds great potential and great risk.

Multiple Locations, Multiple Problems

The theoretical need to manage composite identities prompted the development of the *Praxis of Location*. Eschewing the identity politics of the *Praxis of Coming Out*, advocates of this praxis argue for forging coalitions around common concerns. Kevin Kumashiro considers the difficulties people with composite identities have in finding a place for themselves:

> While in elementary school, I internalized many stereotypes and messages about who I was supposed to be and, consequently, read (that is, made sense of) my identities and experiences through these normative lenses. For example, I read myself through a racist lens that viewed white Americans as the norm in U.S. society while stereotyping Asian Americans as the smart, hardworking minority. I read myself through a sexist lens that valued a particular form of masculinity while denigrating other expressions of masculinity and all expressions of femininity among boys. And I read myself through a heterosexist lens that defined heterosexuality as "normal" and "normative" while characterizing queer sexuality as something to fear, hate and avoid.[61]

Learning to form coalitions based on common needs among diverse groups has proven to be a task that requires considerably more acumen than that necessary for promoting political causes based on simple identity. For instance, J. Craig Fong writes about coalition building in which the nation's largest Asian Pacific Islander civil rights group, the Japanese American Citizens League (JACL), passed a resolution supporting same-sex marriage, allying it with the gay and lesbian community on one of the most controversial human rights issues faced in the United States. Fong states unequivocally that the gay and lesbian community often ignores people of color until LGBTQ national leaders decide that the support of people of color is necessary for completing a project or for passing some piece of legislation. Because the National Gay and Lesbian Task Force supported the JACL's efforts to secure financial redress for Japanese Americans who were interned by the U.S. government during World War II, the two groups found each other through the efforts of a handful of heterosexual JACL leaders and a few Asian Pacific gay advocates acting as go-betweens.[62]

Other groups have formed similar alliances to good effect. For instance, the Reform and Reconstructionist movements of American Judaism passed resolutions advocating military service for gays and lesbians, opposing anti-gay civil rights referenda, and most recently advocating civil gay marriage. Since 1993, Reconstructionist policy guidelines have affirmed the holiness of committed same-sex partnerships, placing them on equal footing with committed heterosexual relationships.[63]

The commitment to located identity has created a facile relationship between multiculturalism and feminism, as well as between multiculturalism and sexual identity. However, Katha Pollitt believes that such unions can be problematic:

Feminism and multiculturalism may find themselves allied in academic politics, where white women and minority women and men face common enemies (Great Books, dead white men, old boy networks, job discrimination, and so forth). But as political visions in the larger world they are very far apart. In its demand for equality for women, feminism sets itself in opposition to virtually every culture on earth.[64]

Susan Moller Okin argues that multiculturalism, suffused with advocacy of group rights for minorities, overlooks the fact that minority cultural groups, like the societies in which they exist, are gendered and thus create substantial differences between men's and women's respective power and advantage. Further, those same advocates of group rights pay almost no attention to the private sphere, where the group's need to create or maintain a "culture of its own" neglects the different roles that such cultural groups impose on their members, especially since most cultures have as one of their principal aims the control of women by men. Okin questions why women from more patriarchal cultures who come to the United States should have less protection from male violence than do other women.[65]

Will Kymlicka has distinguished two types of group rights. One is based on *internal restrictions*, wherein the ethnocultural group's claims prohibit its own members, especially women, from questioning, revising, or abandoning traditional cultural roles and practices. The second is based on *external protections*, in which the minority group claims its vulnerability to the economic or political power of the larger society. Kymlicka suggests that while a democracy such as ours should endorse the second, it cannot accept internal restrictions violating the autonomy of individuals and creating injustice within the group.[66] Agreeing with the basic positions of Okin and Kymlicka, Joseph Raz adds the following observation: "Repression of homosexuality is probably as widespread as discrimination against women."

How, then, has the facile conflation of multiculturalism with politics of location played out in the educational arena? In schools, most teachers continue to wrestle with how to deal with a child that has two mothers or two fathers. They still struggle with the wishes of parents from ethnic and racial minorities who live in areas populated by the dominant culture. Dealing with both can be fairly overwhelming for schoolteachers who have had little leadership from academicians.

June, a lesbian mother with a first-grade child, complains that schoolteachers are not handling even relatively simple identity issues successfully.

The problem is that a lot of people presume that they're treating the child from a gay family just like everybody else, and they don't realize all the number of times they are referring to "mommy and daddy families." Then they aren't treating that child like everybody else. They're systematically ignoring that child. . . . It would be like teaching colors to a nursery school class and saying, "This is flesh color," holding up one of those pink colored crayons when half your class isn't that color.[67]

Some teachers have found that adopting a multicultural curriculum is in many ways politically and practically easier than dealing with children of same-sex parents. Multiculturalism actually disturbs the traditional classroom far less, for two reasons. First, when dealing with questions of sexual identity or same-sex parents, much of the traditional language, many of the conventional stories and approaches, require radical change. Tense local debates often accompany those changes. Second, teachers often address multicultural issues by simply introducing special lessons into an established curriculum. This additive approach, while admittedly insufficient, requires no fundamental reconceptualization of classroom methods, values, or goals.

The New York City Board of Education's attempt to initiate the *Children of the Rainbow: First Grade* curriculum epitomizes the kinds of competing values and goals that arise between gay parents and their supporters on the one side and conservative district superintendents and their adherents on the other. This curriculum attempted to include gay-headed families in citywide curriculum. The controversy erupted after Community School Board Twenty-Four president Mary Cummins sent a letter to district parents asking for their participation in a protest against the curriculum. She viewed any references to lesbians or gay men as endorsements of homosexuality and sodomy, and she was quoted as saying, "I will not demean our legitimate minorities, such as blacks, Hispanics and Asians, by lumping them together with homosexuals in that curriculum." Cummins then banned the use of the entire guide. As a result, the majority of New York City districts altered, eliminated, or postponed until the upper grades any part of the curriculum that mentioned lesbian and gay parents and people. A revised policy separated "multicultural" curricula from "antibias" curricula and removed lesbian and gay topics from the latter.[68]

That the curriculum was developed by the New York City Board of Education indicates the complex dynamics at work in current struggles over multiculturalism. While the majority of school districts altered this curriculum to exclude the lives of lesbian and gay people, the results of a poll conducted shortly after this rupture found that teaching about lesbian and gay families was supported by 72 percent of adults in New York City.[69] Clearly the decision to exclude lesbian and gay identities from the curriculum was based on successful attempts of the few, rather than on the will of the many.

Common themes emerge when groups oppose inclusion of gay and lesbian issues in the early grades. The most basic presumption equates gayness with sexuality. Opponents cite religious and moral reasons, as well as children's inability to comprehend the "far off" concept of gayness. Both sides argue about what constitutes "developmentally inappropriate" subject matter. Academics testify as "expert" witnesses by interpreting what Jean Piaget, Erik Erikson, or Lawrence Kohlberg might have said about exposing young children to gay issues.[70] These tense situations point to the danger of simply including lesbian and gay concerns under a multicultural label. They also reiterate the fact that opponents of lesbian and gay issues can mount successful coalitions with far less conceptual and political work than that which is required to produce coalitions supporting equality for nonheterosexuals.

Robert Parlin talks about his struggle to discuss lesbian and gay issues in a high school in Newton, Massachusetts. Parlin served on the high school's Committee on Human Differences. Over a three-year period the committee had sponsored sessions on anti-Semitism, racism, sexism, classism, and attitudes toward foreign students.[71] When the issue of homophobia was raised, the other committee members responded less than enthusiastically:

> You know, I don't think this school is ready to deal with homophobia. Newton may be a fairly liberal suburb, but I don't think the parents will approve of this type of work.

> Perhaps we need to discuss this issue more amongst ourselves. The timing just doesn't seem right to me.

> This is so divisive, I'm afraid we'll do more harm than good if we try to talk about gay and lesbian issues here at school.

> Sexual orientation seems like an issue that is more appropriate for discussion at the college level. High school is too soon.

> I've been a guidance counselor at this school for more than twenty years, and I don't ever recall a student coming to me and telling me that he or she was a homosexual. I don't think we have any gay kids here.

> I'm actually not that certain that having a program on homosexuality is that relevant to us here. Maybe communities in other parts of the country—say in California—are struggling with this, but we don't have a problem here.[72]

As the public discourse around the Rainbow Curriculum and this incident in a Boston suburb suggest, Out-Siders cannot assume that multicultural approaches will mitigate gender inequality or discrimination against lesbians and gays. The adoption of a multicultural stance toward educating children or college students does not guarantee women-, lesbian-, and gay-friendly positions. In fact, conservative political agendas can employ multicultural approaches with great success.[73] Thus, although the *Praxis of Location* stands on much firmer theoretical ground than that of the *Praxis of Coming Out*, these scenarios illustrate that employing these praxes in educational contexts can destine these efforts to abysmal failure, especially when they are employed in educational contexts in which mitigating anti–lesbian and gay prejudice is not the teacher's primary political concern.

Multiculturalism premised on internal restrictions, as theorized by Kymlicka, is almost always antithetical to equality for women and sexual minorities. However, multicultural approaches based on the need for external protections, necessary because the cultural group has little economic or political power, promote equality for all the members of nondominant cultures. Women's and gender studies classes have been champions of just this sort of multiculturalism since the inception of the *Praxis of Location*. Audre Lorde believes that difference paves the way for creativity:

> Difference must be not merely tolerated, but seen as a fund of necessary polarities between which our creativity can spark like a dialectic. Only then does the necessity for interdependency become unthreatening. Only within that interdependency of different strengths, acknowledged and equal, can the power to seek new ways of being in the world generate, as well as the courage sustenance to act where they are no charters.
>
> Within the interdependence of mutual (nondominant) differences lies that security which enables us to descend into the chaos of knowledge and return with true visions of our future along with the concomitant power to effect those changes which can bring that future into being.[74]

Of note are the women who founded the Combahee River Collective, a black feminist group that formed coalitions with other progressive organizations and movements to fight racism, sexism, heterosexism, and classism. Seeing these major systems of oppression as interlocking, these women believed that only an integrated analysis and practice could challenge such oppression. However, these women also realized that political work intent on addressing a whole range of oppression presented difficulties that simple identity politics did not face.[75]

Bernice Johnson Reagon, a black lesbian feminist, realized that even women for whom she cared deeply—black women who were part of her primary identity group—were homophobic. She realized that they, too, must be challenged. Reagon makes it clear that coalition politics is not for sissies.

> You don't go into coalition because you just *like* it. The only reason you would consider trying to team up with somebody who could possibly kill you, is because that's the only way you can figure you can stay alive. . . .
>
> Coalition work is not work done in your home. Coalition work has to be done in the streets. And it is some of the most dangerous work you can do. And you shouldn't look for comfort. Some people will come to a coalition and they rate the success of the coalition on whether or not they feel good when they get there. They're not looking for a coalition; they're looking for a home! They're looking for a bottle with some milk in it and a nipple, which does not happen in a coalition. You don't get a lot of food in a coalition. In a coalition you have to give.[76]

As these Out-Siders in the *Praxis of Location* argue, multiculturalism must be supported; but it must be a multiculturalism committed to equality for all its members. The work is not easy.

Consequential Refusals and Performances

I examine the *Praxes of Refusal* and *Performativity* together. Because the theoretical base for these approaches grows from the same postmodern roots, the primary distinctions between the praxes rest on two issues: first, the sorts of literature and events that have been designated for deconstruction; second, the approach toward activism taken by the praxes' adherents.

When considering what is appropriate material for deconstruction, the theorists of the *Praxis of Refusal* concern themselves to a great extent with unearthing hidden discourse so that they can demonstrate how the modern subject has been constructed by societal constraints. Conversely, theorists in the *Praxis of Performativity* focus less on little-known historical facts or literature. They concentrate their efforts on reconfiguring psychoanalytic discourse and on extracting new interpretations from critiques of literature that instantiate heteronormative practice, coded gender bending, and permeable boundaries of sex and gender. Out-Siders in each of these praxes intend to demonstrate that sex and gender do not exist *before* discourse but are formed *through* discourse. Each praxis is informed by a belief in the provisional, precarious, and dependent constitution of sexuality, which is based on unstable relations of unconscious forces, changing social and personal meanings, and historical contingencies.[77]

These two praxes also differ in their approach toward activism. Adherents to the *Praxis of Refusal* demonstrate far more faith and dependence on collective social action than do those in the *Praxis of Performativity*. While both groups of Out-Siders find identity collectives to be theoretically problematic, those Out-Siders in the *Praxis of Refusal* continue to lend their active support to such work despite their concerns. Several of the best-known early Out-Siders in the *Praxis of Refusal*, such as Michel Foucault, Jeffrey Weeks, Jonathan Katz, and Dennis Altman, emphasized sexual experimentation and embraced erotic diversity in every imaginable form. As queer theory has matured, it has actually become less theoretical. Jeffrey Weeks has expressed this change as the "rise of a sort of leather S/M chic where style obliterates content."[78] The importance of style, coupled with queer theory's embrace of erotic dispositions that challenge even progressive attitudes toward sexuality (pedophilia, public sex, S/M, erotic pornography), explains why schools and many university settings have shunned queer theory. Many lesbian feminists and a host of others have sought to distance themselves from these highly stigmatized sexual practices.

Conversely, queer theorists in the *Praxis of Performativity* depend heavily on reconstructing psychoanalytic theory. Where the *Praxis of Refusal* has become somewhat passé in academia, the *Praxis of Performativity* has become increasingly trendy and academic. In fact, feminists and lesbian feminists alike worry openly that the scholarship of the *Praxis of Performativity* is so academic that it is inaccessible to the LGBTQ people who might benefit most from its insights. These feminists are also wary of this praxis's dependence on terminology and hypothesis, its creating an environment where only a tiny circle of colleagues can participate in the discussion.[79] Although the adherents to the *Praxis of Performativity* declare the need for continued collective activism on social issues, it is clearly a tangential issue. This praxis focuses on disabling the master canon and unseating heterosexuality from its hegemonic position.

This said, the teachers, students, and academicians who proceed from a position of extreme social construction may operate from either or both of the *Praxes of Refusal* and *Performativity*. Little in these praxes indicates what specific ends they hope to achieve in education. Butler, Sedgwick, Fuss, Weeks, Foucault, and Cixous have all focused on *disturbing* and *de-centering* heteronormativity. For most educators, at any level, to understand how to undertake such propositions, these Out-Siders need to specify what "queering the discourse" means in terms of goals. The work of the extreme social constructionists implies that such goals are individualized and constantly shifting, making such definitions radically useless.

Regardless, I suggest that because it is so difficult for most of us to even conceptualize what a child reared by advocates of the *Praxis of Refusal* and *Performativity* might look like, "queering the discourse" paralyzes many Out-Siders who are otherwise interested in mitigating the effects of compulsory heterosexuality. Therefore, at the risk of essentializing one such story, let me begin with a rather lengthy but valuable account of a child reared by family and friends who refused heteronormativity.

Steph is an eight-year-old girl in Australia who is being "queerly raised" by her biological parents, who identify as heterosexual. She travels between multicultural worlds and multisexual worlds. "Queerly raising" a child, according to Steph's mom, interrogates the taken-for-grantedness of fixed categories and the way society divides people into normal/abnormal, natural/unnatural. It means constructing a nonheteronormative space and subverting society's heteronormative framework.[80]

What happens when such a child then attends a school where sexual diversity is still considered deviant? Plenty! Steph's mom recalls a discussion before school one morning in which Steph wanted to know about artificial insemination. This subject quickly evolved into how so many gays and lesbians can become parents without having sex with people of the other sex. The discussion was followed by Steph's dismay about what was missing from the "sex education" lessons at school—the clitoris!

> But why didn't they show it in the book at school? I looked for it but the teacher acted like nothing was there. I know it's there. . . . They don't say all the truth at school but I know it anyway.[81]

Steph attends Mardi Gras each year in Sydney. One year she posed as the daughter of Alan and Malcolm, donning a purple fairy suit and waving a gay flag. Her teachers are now used to Steph's writing about these occasions in her journal and her shouting happily on the Friday afternoon before the event: "I'm going to Sydney to the Mardi Gras!" Steph's current teacher worried about the response of other children toward Steph, but after voicing this concern in the staff room, Steph's first teacher in the parish replied, "Oh don't worry. She knows how to handle it. And the kids are used to her. She's teaching them a thing or two."[82]

Her teachers began to call Steph a "political activist." It is Steph, after all, who

> tells the girls that it's a dumb game to dare each other to run up to the school fence and yell out "I'm a lesbian!" She can't understand the dare. She quite happily stands at the fence and yells out, much to the shock of passersby, "I'm a lesbian!"

Often she hears words like *gay* and *lesbian* being used in other "weird" ways, and she tells the kids what they mean. Like the time she's walking down the street with me and one of her school friends. Steph's feeling happy and runs up to a streetlight and hugs and kisses it. Her friend yells, "You're a lesbian!"

Steph looks at her incredulously. "Lesbians don't kiss poles. Lesbians are women who love women."[83]

These sorts of comments usually silence friends who are shocked, stunned, and curious all at once.

This final account about Steph seems shocking to those of us living in a culture fed by compulsory heterosexuality because Steph's mother responds in a way that appears so counterintuitive.

One evening, as we wait for Steph's computing class to begin, three girls around twelve years old come cheerily in to collect some material for their next class. They look confident and speak assertively, arms and hair swinging. I notice Steph has taken my hand and is squeezing it.

I look across and notice a faint shy blush on her face. "What's up, Steph?"

Steph is still staring at the girls. She whispers, "Which one do you like?"

"All of them. They look like really nice, smart young women."

Steph persists. "No! I mean, which one do you like?"

"Which one do you like, sweetie?"

Steph nods her head toward the long-haired girl in jeans and T-shirt who's doing most of the questioning in articulate computer-speak. "Do you like her too?"

"Yes, I do," I reply.

Steph smiles shyly. She shrugs and looks at me with embarrassment. I squeeze her hand. "It's okay, Steph. She's gorgeous, and if you think that, that's fine. Enjoy those feelings, there's nothing wrong with them."

In the meantime, Steph also has crushes on two boys. Getting out of the car one afternoon with a friend who's come to play, she looks at the houses across the street and declares, "I wish Peter lived there and Anthony lived there. Then I could see both of them."

Her friend looks scornfully at her. "You can only love one person."

"Who says?"

"That's the way it is. Unless you're a lesbian."

"If I was a lesbian, I'd want Peter and Anthony to be girls. Anyway, maybe I'll love no one. Maybe I'll love girls or boys, or both. Maybe lots of both!" And she laughs cheekily as her friend remonstrates.[84]

I suggest that Steph's early childhood education demonstrates a *disturbed* and *de-centered* heteronormativity. Steph illustrates what all that *disturbing* and *de-centering* might look like. Further, in her daily "performances" she continually *disturbs* her friends' mis-education by compulsory heterosexuality. (She also serves to justify conservative political groups' greatest fears!) If we take Steph as a temporary goal, or end, to which educators may look, what other kinds of refusals and performances might have this de-centering effect on heteronormativity?

Children don't always bring up issues directly to the teacher, but when they do, a well-prepared and creative teacher "performs" in a variety of ways. For instance, Cathy, an early childhood educator, teaches Elly, a child with two moms. Cathy gives an example of how to use dramatic play as a fertile area for exploring and understanding out-of-school roles. In the following, Cathy supports the two children in dramatic play, while acknowledging Elly's family structure.

> Elly was playing in the dramatic area with a couple of other kids. [Janie] came over to me really upset. She said, "I wanted to be the mommy and Lizzie said that she's the mommy, and I wanted to be the mommy." And then Elly came over to me and said to both of us, "Well, I told Janie that we could have two mommies and that I could be the mommy and she could be the mommy too." And I said, "Janie, that sounds like a great idea. Why don't you both be mommies?" And then they went, "Okay," and they both went back and they were both mommies, I guess.[85]

In the following example Janet de-centers heterosexuality in a simple statement on the first parents' night through this performance:

> We are proud to have diverse families in our center. Children with special needs, racially mixed families, children with two moms, and children with two dads. I want to welcome you all.[86]

Another public school principal, Emory, describes the conscious approach of his school:

> [Our school's] general theme is that everybody that we come in contact with is different in some way. He's Black, you're White. She's yellow, he's red. He has parents who are not his birth parents. She has only one parent. Her mother and father died. His mother died. This child happens to have two male parents. This one has two female parents. Put it in a larger context.[87]

Are there other acts of resistance and refusal evident in stories previously considered in this chapter? Certainly! As Eve Kosofsky Sedgwick has argued, living in the closet constitutes a speech act, albeit one that is not going to subvert the effects of compulsory heterosexuality. Coming out is a speech act. Verbally or physically supporting someone who has come out is a speech act. So is walking in a parade; being part of a protest; claiming friendship with an LGBTQ outsider; voting for lesbian- and gay-friendly legislation, policies, and candidates; or insisting on keeping sexual diversity issues in multicultural curricula. Acts of resistance and performance hold out the potential for profound disruption of compulsory heterosexuality. Acts of parody, as Butler suggests, can also decenter the master canon:

> Before he delivers a lecture on gender identity to his philosophy class this semester, Michael A. Gilbert must decide what to wear. Most likely, he will put on a knee-length skirt, a long-sleeved blouse, and low pumps. Standing before a mirror at home, he'll fix his wig and apply some makeup before heading out the door.

Dr. Gilbert is part of a growing cadre of "trans" people on campuses who are going public.[88]

Social constructionists argue that social sanctions and pressures mandate the performance of appropriately gendered behaviors. The experiences of chosen, abjected, and closeted images confirm this pressure. Identified as male or female by the appearance of genitalia at birth, social expectations shape children into conformance with gender roles.

I find it more difficult to make this case for heterosexual or homosexual orientation. No external mark separates infants, making them receive different social conditioning. How does the young man growing up in a pious Mormon family in the Midwest become gay? What in his parents' treatment of him could have set him apart so painfully from other boys growing up in Mormon homes? After all, many gay and lesbian people become distinguishable from others only because of the socially unacceptable nature of the persons to whom they are sexually attracted. Social construction may explain how the norms and categories got there, but I find it unconvincing about explaining individual cases. Some more individualized explanation, whether biological or psychoanalytic, must be invoked.[89]

Butler argues that the categories of "sex" and "gender" should be reconflated since "sex" is, from the start, normative and hence a regulatory ideal. Without acting in conformance with the regulatory ideas, gender and sex would presumably not exist.[90] If this scenario holds true, why does the performance, albeit imperfect performance, of gender not *always* result in gender-appropriate behavior? Why does it not *always* result in gender-inappropriate behavior? What accounts for the differences? What accounts for so many transgender people believing that cross-dressing is not a political statement but a perceived internal necessity? Why do not *all* people growing up with the norms of compulsory heterosexuality respond similarly?

In addition, if the discourse of gender is not universal, then how do we account for the wide generality, if not universality, of compulsory heterosexuality in social constructionist arguments? Granted, the intensity of the compulsion may have interesting regional variations, but do Butler, Fuss, Foucault, and Sedgwick doubt the near universality of the heterosexual regime? Hardly.

Finally, Butler's prescription for action needs to be problematized more than any other. Her goals, subverting and de-centering compulsory heterosexuality, are my goals. However, she endorses actions that I find problematic. For instance, her focus on cross-dressing may subvert heteronormativity in the Castro district of San Francisco. Butler does not argue that cross-dressing should occur only in specific environments but that lesbian and gay people should universally appropriate such actions. However, if this notion is applied universally, then cross-dressing would likely be experienced as a suicide wish in other, less tolerant environments—say, those in the South or Midwest, or in small towns or rural areas.

So it is with Butler's grudging acceptance of identity group politics. Butler makes it appear that lesbian and gay outsiders have won the war of rights and privileges. I submit that this attitude can only be endorsed on a liberal campus in a liberal urban center in a liberal state. How easy to make such claims as a tenured, well-published professor at University of California, Berkeley! Although, as so many of the stories of lesbian and gay outsiders attest, acting solo in conservative environments not only results in few substantive changes but often results in physical harm. As lesbian activist and professor Margaret Cerullo has said, "Don't confuse the access and influence of a few with the safety and security of all. The center of the gay and lesbian agenda must be saving the youth of our country!"[91]

I do not want to undermine Butler's efforts to expose and delegitimize the regime of gender hierarchy and compulsory heterosexuality. Yet, Out-Siders must be careful here, as in the mandate for coming out, of universalizing recommendations, even as theories are further particularized. Universalizing solutions bear the mark of Woolf's Dictator.

Reflections on Problematization

The words of lesbian and gay outsiders have in many respects supported the theoretical conclusions of critics of the various *Praxes in re Sexual Identity*. The Closet seems even more powerful after listening to the words of lesbian and gay outsiders. In addition, it appears that philosophers of education have failed to take sufficient care in theorizing religiosity. Liberal principles, proffered in the *Praxis of Inclusion*, do not challenge societal structures. Theorists told us they would not, and lesbian and gay outsiders confirmed this perception. Heterosexism apparently remains intact even when legislation accords basic rights to lesbian and gay outsiders. The *Praxis of Coming Out* mandates complete disclosure for lesbians and gay men, with little sensitivity to the fact that the circumstances of each person are significantly different and may require a more nuanced approach. The universality of its prescriptions points to racism, sexism, regionalism, nationalism, and classism. These charges about the *Praxes of Inclusion* and *Coming Out* are consistent with theoretical critiques leveled against them.

Lesbian and gay outsiders indicate that the goals of the *Praxis of Location* are even more difficult to implement than theorists suggested. Bernice Johnson Reagon's words about working in coalitions ring with the truth of someone who has practiced, and not merely preached, coalitions. Nor does the facile adoption of multiculturalism present itself as a way of obliterating anti–lesbian and gay prejudice. Out-Siders who work for a multicultural perspective must ensure that it is based in equality for women and sexual minorities.

The criticism that lesbian feminists and gay activists level at the *Praxes of Refusal* and *Performativity* seem justified. They are abstract and largely devoid of pragmatic goals. Yet, when Out-Siders have established temporary and contingent ideals, queering the discourse presents a way to challenge heterosexist thinking at a deep level.

This testing of the *Praxes in re Sexual Identity* demonstrates that none of these praxes is without weakness or fault for Out-Siders committed to mitigating the effects of compulsory heterosexuality over a range of the configurations of education. Problematization has revealed that they all suffer from serious deficiencies for Out-Siders who need a pragmatic, as well as theoretically sound, approach.

The next step then is to engage, as did Woolf and Foucault, in ethical inquiry. Armed with the knowledge produced through these analyses of the theoretical dispositions of the *Praxes in re Sexual Identity*, what remains is to construct an *Out-Siders' Praxis* that proceeds, in Dewey's words, "from a level deeper and more inclusive than is represented by the practices and ideas of the contending parties."[92] With the voices, the concerns, of lesbian and gay outsiders out of the Closet, it is time to forge a praxis that utilizes the practical and theoretical knowledge gained from this intensive work in the *Praxes in re Sexual Identity*. This *Out-Siders' Praxis* must be thoroughly pragmatic, concerned not with what is necessary but with what is best. Mindful of the need to proceed skillfully, creatively, and in a timely manner, this *Out-Siders' Praxis* must be capable of intervening in the practical problems of lesbian and gay outsiders. The choices

Out-Siders make about praxis are critical because the interventive aspect reinscribes its time- and location-dependence. However, these choices are also critical because the very definition of praxis suggests that as Out-Siders change the world, they themselves will be changed by their work.

Notes

1. See Aristotle, *The Nicomachean Ethics*, book 6; and Atwill, *Rhetoric Reclaimed*, 54, 170–71.

2. See Michel Foucault, "The Means of Correct Training," in *Discipline and Punish: The Birth of the Prison*, trans. Alan Sheridan (Paris: Editions Gallimard, 1975; translation, New York: Vintage Books, 1997), 170–94.

3. Dan Woog, "The State of Washington State," in *School's Out: The Impact of Gay and Lesbian Issues on America's Schools* (Los Angeles: Alyson Publication, 1995), 162.

4. Madiha Didi Khayatt, *Lesbian Teachers: An Invisible Presence* (New York: State University of New York Press, 1992), 213.

5. Lewis R. Gordon, "Introduction: Three Perspectives on Gays in African-American Ecclesiology and Religious Thought," in *Sexual Orientation and Human Rights in American Religious Discourse*, ed. Saul M. Olyan and Martha C. Nussbaum (Oxford: Oxford University Press, 1998), 175–76.

6. Rita M. Kissen, *The Last Closet: The Real Lives of Lesbian and Gay Teachers* (Portsmouth, N.H.: Heinemann, 1996), 110.

7. In James T. Sears, "Educators, Homosexuality, and Homosexual Students: Are Personal Feelings Related to Professional Beliefs?" in *Coming Out of the Classroom Closet: Gay and Lesbian Students, Teachers, and Curricula*, ed. Karen M. Harbeck (New York: Harrington Park Press, 1991), 33.

8. See Jane Roland Martin's "What Should We Do with a Hidden Curriculum When We Find One?" in *Changing the Educational Landscape: Philosophy, Women, and Curriculum* (New York: Routledge, 1994), 154–69.

9. John Dewey, *Experience and Education* (New York: Touchstone, 1997; original, 1938), 27.

10. Dewey, *Experience and Education*, 25–26.

11. In James T. Sears, "Educators, Homosexuality, and Homosexual Students: Are Personal Feelings Related to Professional Beliefs?" in Harbeck, *Coming Out of the Classroom Closet: Gay and Lesbian Students, Teachers, and Curricula*, 32.

12. Owen Garcia, "An Unfailing Sufficiency," in *Out and about Campus: Personal Accounts by Lesbian, Gay, Bisexual, and Transgendered College Students*, ed. Kim Howard and Annie Stevens (Los Angeles: Alyson Books, 2000), 107.

13. Garcia, "An Unfailing Sufficiency," 109.

14. Garcia, "An Unfailing Sufficiency," 111.

15. Victor Anderson, "Deadly Silence: Reflections on Homosexuality and Human Rights," in Olyan and Nussbaum, *Sexual Orientation and Human Rights in American Religious Discourse*, 185–86.

16. See Susan Birden, Linda L. Gaither, and Susan Laird, "The Struggle over the Text: Compulsory Heterosexuality and Educational Policy," *Educational Policy* 14, no. 5 (November 2000): 641.

17. Judith Plaskow, "Sexual Orientation and Human Rights: A Progressive Jewish Perspective," in Olyan and Nussbaum, *Sexual Orientation and Human Rights in American Religious Discourse*, 29.

18. Introduction to Olyan and Nussbaum, *Sexual Orientation and Human Rights in American Religious Discourse*, xiii.

19. Birden, Gaither, and Laird, "The Struggle over the Text," 658–59.

20. James P. Hanigan, "Sexual Orientation and Human Rights: A Roman Catholic View," in Olyan and Nussbaum, *Sexual Orientation and Human Rights in American Religious Discourse*, 68.

21. Hanigan, "Sexual Orientation and Human Rights," 68–69.

22. Kissen, *The Last Closet*, 110.

23. Many thanks to Catherine Hobbs for directing me to Judith Butler's incisive analysis of the "don't ask/don't tell" policy in *Excitable Speech: A Politics of the Performative* (New York: Routledge, 1997), 103–26.

24. Butler, *Excitable Speech*, 103–26.

25. Kissen, *The Last Closet*, 1–2.

26. Hannah Arendt, "The Crisis in Culture," in *Between Past and Future: Eight Exercises in Political Thought* (New York: Penguin Books, 1993), 220–24.

27. David Novak, "Religious Communities, Secular Society, and Sexuality: One Jewish Opinion," in Olyan and Nussbaum, *Sexual Orientation and Human Rights in American Religious Discourse*, 24.

28. Cheryl J. Sanders, "Sexual Orientation and Human Rights Discourse in the African-American Churches," in Olyan and Nussbaum, *Sexual Orientation and Human Rights in American Religious Discourse*, 178.

29. Sanders, "Sexual Orientation and Human Rights Discourse," 181.

30. Jim Garrison, *Dewey and Eros: Wisdom and Desire in the Art of Teaching* (New York: Teachers College Press, 1997), 13–15.

31. Richard Rorty, "Pragmatism, Relativism, and Irrationalism" in *Consequences of Pragmatism* (Minneapolis: University of Minnesota Press, 1982), 172.

32. Hans-Georg Gadamer, "Hegel's Philosophy and Its Aftereffects," in *Reason in the Age of Science*, trans. Frederick G. Lawrence (Cambridge, Mass.: MIT Press, 1996), 37.

33. Hannah Arendt, "The Crisis in Culture," in *Between Past and Future: Eight Exercises in Political Thought* (New York: Penguin Books, 1993), 220–24.

34. Lorraine Code, *What Can She Know? Feminist Theory and the Construction of Knowledge* (Ithaca, N.Y.: Cornell University Press, 1991), 179.

35. Dan Woog, *School's Out*, 133.

36. Interview with lesbian teacher quoted in Madiha Didi Khayatt, *Lesbian Teachers*, 207.

37. Quoted in Khayatt, *Lesbian Teachers*, 207.

38. Amanda Udis-Kessler, "Identity/Politics: Historical Sources of the Bisexual Movement," in *Queer Studies: A Lesbian, Gay, Bisexual, and Transgender Anthology*, ed. Brett Beemyn and Mickey Eliason (New York: New York University Press, 1996), 53.

39. Rodney Wilson, "Telling Our Stories, Winning Our Freedom," in *One Teacher in Ten: Gay and Lesbian Educators Tell Their Stories*, ed. Kevin Jennings (Los Angeles: Alyson Books, 1994), 200–201.

40. Wilson, "Telling Our Stories," 201–3.

41. Pat McCart, "'It's the Teachers! The Teachers Are Coming Out!'" in Jennings, *One Teacher in Ten*, 54–55.

42. Quote in Barbara Danish, "Placing Children First: The Importance of Mutual Presence in the Elementary Classroom," in *Queering Elementary Education: Advancing the Dialogue about Sexualities and Schooling* (Lanham, Md.: Rowman and Littlefield, 1999), 195.

43. Quoted in Kissen, *The Last Closet*, 81.

44. Brandi Lyons, "Out in the Boondocks," in Howard and Stevens, *Out and about Campus*, 119.

45. Sapphrodykie, "The Iconoclast," in Howard and Stevens, *Out and about Campus*, 136.

46. Carlos Manuel, "A Deep, Sad Sorrow," in Howard and Stevens, *Out and about Campus*, 48–49.

47. Ann-Marie Manchise, "Senator's Antigay Lecture Shocks Students," *Tampa Tribune*, April 11, 2001.

48. Quoted in Toni A. McNaron, *Poisoned Ivy: Lesbian and Gay Academics Confronting Homophobia* (Philadelphia: Temple University Press, 1997), 76–77.

49. Quoted in McNaron, *Poisoned Ivy*, 104.

50. Quoted in McNaron, *Poisoned Ivy*, 104.

51. Quoted in McNaron, *Poisoned Ivy*, 114–15.

52. Virginia Woolf, *Three Guineas* (San Diego, Calif.: Harcourt Brace Javanovich, 1939), 142.

53. Dan Woog, *School's Out*, 133.

54. James T. Sears, "Educators, Homosexuality, and Homosexual Students: Are Personal Feelings Related to Professional Beliefs?" in Harbeck, *Coming Out of the Classroom Closet: Gay and Lesbian Students, Teachers, and Curricula*, 38.

55. Quoted in Khayatt, *Lesbian Teachers*, 128.

56. Quoted in Khayatt, *Lesbian Teachers*, 127.

57. Rupert A. Francis and others, "Race and Sexuality in the U.S.: Sexuality and Sexual Preference in the African American Population," in *The Psychology of Sexual Orientation, Behavior, and Identity: A Handbook*, ed. Diamont and McAnulty (Westport, Conn.: Greenwood, 1995), 384.

58. Victor Anderson, "Deadly Silence," in Olyan and Nussbaum, *Sexual Orientation and Human Rights in American Religious Discourse*, 187.

59. Quoted in Lourdes Arguelles and Manuel Fernandez, "Working with *Heterosexismo* in Latino/a Immigrant Los Angeles: Reflections on Community Background, Processes, and Practices," in *Overcoming Heterosexism and Homophobia: Strategies That Work*, ed. James T. Sears and Walter L. Williams (New York: Columbia University Press, 1997), 105.

60. Quoted in Arguelles and Fernandez, "Working with *Heterosexismo*," 105.

61. Kevin K. Kumashiro, "Reading Queer Asian American Masculinities and Sexualities in Elementary School," in Sears and Letts, *Queering Elementary Education*, 61.

62. J. Craig Fong, "Building Alliances: The Case of the Japanese American Citizens League Endorsement of Same-Sex Marriage," in Sears and Williams, *Overcoming Heterosexism and Homophobia*, 371.

63. Saul M. Olyan, "Introduction: Contemporary Jewish Perspectives on Homosexuality," in Olyan and Nussbaum, *Sexual Orientation and Human Rights in American Religious Discourse*, 6, 8.

64. Katha Pollitt, "Whose Culture?" in Susan Moller Okin's *Is Multiculturalism Bad for Women?* ed. Joshua Cohen, Matthew Howard, and Martha C. Nussbaum (Princeton, N.J.: Princeton University Press, 1999), 27.

65. Okin, *Is Multiculturalism Bad for Women?* 12–20.

66. Will Kymlicka, "Liberal Complacencies," in Okin, *Is Multiculturalism Bad for Women?* 31.

67. Quoted in Virginia Casper and Steven B. Schultz, *Gay Parents/Straight Schools: Building Communication and Trust* (New York: Teachers College Press, 1999), 155.

68. Quoted in Casper and Schultz, *Gay Parents/Straight Schools*, 20–21.

69. Quoted in Casper and Schultz, *Gay Parents/Straight Schools*, 20–21.

70. Quoted in Casper and Schultz, *Gay Parents/Straight Schools*, 21–22.

71. Robert Parlin, "We Don't Have a Problem Here," in *One Teacher in Ten: Gay and Lesbian Educators Tell Their Stories*, ed. Kevin Jennings (Los Angeles: Alyson Books, 1994), 219.

72. Parlin, "We Don't Have a Problem Here," 219.

73. One has only to look at President Bush's cabinet to see evidence of this claim.

74. Audre Lorde, "The Master's Tools Will Never Dismantle the Master's House," in *Sister Outsider* (Freedom, Calif.: Crossing Press, 1988), 111–12.

75. Combahee River Collective, "The Combahee River Collective Statement," in *Home Girls: A Black Feminist Anthology*, ed. Barbara Smith (New Brunswick, N.J.: Rutgers University Press, 2000), 264, 269.

76. Bernice Johnson Reagon, "Coalition Politics: Turning the Century," in Smith, *Home Girls*, 343–44, 346.

77. Jeffrey Weeks, *Sexuality and Its Discontents: Meanings, Myths, and Modern Sexualities* (New York: Routledge, 1999), 186.

78. Weeks, *Sexuality and Its Discontents*, 216.

79. McNaron, *Poisoned Ivy*, 132.

80. Maria Pallotta-Chiarolli, "'My Moving Days': A Child's Negotiation of Multiple Lifeworlds in Relation to Gender, Ethnicity, and Sexuality," in Letts and Sears, *Queering Elementary Education*, 71–72.

81. Pallotta-Chiarolli, "'My Moving Days,'" 73.

82. Pallotta-Chiarolli, "'My Moving Days,'" 76.

83. Pallotta-Chiarolli, "'My Moving Days,'" 76–77.

84. Pallotta-Chiarolli, "'My Moving Days,'" 78–79.

85. Quoted in Casper and Schultz, *Gay Parents/Straight Schools*, 150.

86. Quoted in Casper and Schultz, *Gay Parents/Straight Schools*, 140.

87. Quoted in Casper and Schultz, *Gay Parents/Straight Schools*, 143.

88. Robin Wilson, "Transgendered Scholars Defy Convention, Seeking to Be Heard and Seen in Academe," in *The Chronicle of Higher Education*, at http://chronicle.com/colloquy/98/transgender/background.htm.

89. Martha C. Nussbaum, *Cultivating Humanity: A Classical Defense of Reform in Liberal Education* (Cambridge, Mass.: Harvard University Press, 1997), 232.

90. Judith Butler, *Gender Trouble: Feminism and the Subversion of Identity* (New York: Routledge, 1990), 139–41.

91. Woog, *School's Out*, 306–7.

92. Dewey, *Experience and Education*, 5.

CHAPTER FIVE

———

Envisioning an *Out-Siders' Praxis*

Theoretical Considerations

I defined Out-Siders as those people who side with the "out." They are teachers, administrators, counselors, therapists, coaches, teacher educators, researchers, students, friends, and family members who may be, but need not be, LGBTQ themselves and who are working to mitigate the effects of the mis-education by compulsory heterosexuality and disrupt the heterosexism that plagues our nation's configurations of education. Out-Siders are a pragmatic lot, concerning themselves with dialogue across difference and ethical responses to situations of abuse, harassment, and inequality in the lives of the LGBTQ outsiders with whom they are in contact: teachers, students, colleagues, and children of same-sex parents. Through their actions Out-Siders honor the difficult and continuous decision of LGBTQ outsiders to be out in a world that stigmatizes their existence.

Charlotte Bunch warns, however, that action is difficult to sustain without a theoretical base. Theory keeps vision alive and helps activists understand how their activities contribute to significant victories in the future. Solid theory helps people develop visions and plans for change that nourish activists who might otherwise become bogged down, overwhelmed, and burned out in day-to-day political activity.[1] However, theory without action accomplishes nothing. Dewey asserted that the dualism that distinguished theory and philosophy as apart from, or higher than, experience and practice tended to serve the purposes of kings, oppressive social practices, and bureaucratic and technocratic experts who set themselves apart by assuming a higher realm of reality and knowledge, beyond reflection on ordinary practice.[2]

Out-Siders need an effective praxis that integrates theory and action. The wisdom of *phronesis*—derived from the theoretical and philosophical wisdom of *theoria* and from the skillful artistic, inventive, and interventive wisdom of *techne*—informs an effective praxis. It means choosing what is best, and it means not just believing in, but doing, the right thing. Praxis assumes acquaintance with the practical considerations needed to proceed skillfully, creatively, in a timely manner to intervene in the practical problems of human beings. The pragmatic approach of praxis means bringing reason, passion, and imagination to bear on a situation to solve problems.

Using the method of "thinking with 'attitude,'" the words and experiences of lesbian and gay outsiders in the world of education problematize the *Praxes in re Sexual Identity*. Problematization reveals several important conceptual gaps and confirms certain problems to which theorists had already pointed. Each of the praxes are found to exhibit crucial weaknesses, prohibiting wholesale adoption by Out-Siders in education. The problem still remains: Out-Siders need a praxis.

It is then in the second phase of "thinking with 'attitude,'" ethical inquiry, that I conceptualize a praxis for Out-Siders. This phase represents the opportunity for vision. Ethical inquiry allows Out-Siders to re-create themselves as works of art, as moral agents entering into positive, enabling subjectification. Further, Woolf and Foucault recognized that this second phase of "thinking with 'attitude'" offers the chance to step assertively into the fissures created by problematization, to address just those problems that other theoretical positions have failed to overcome.

Therefore, in this crucial step of inquiry, my conceptualization of an *Out-Siders' Praxis* is informed by the practice of educators. As this conceptualization proceeds, I theorize several new concepts that coalesce and elaborate on theoretical perspectives that I have not yet discussed. These key ideas for an *Out-Siders' Praxis* underscore the active nature of Out-Siders' work in education. I suggest that when Out-Siders with a commitment to the eradication of heterosexism employ the concepts of *out-citing*, *out-sighting*, *out-siding*, and *out-siting*, concepts that I name and explain in the following sections, they can present a powerful challenge to the mis-education of compulsory heterosexuality that is so prevalent in North American educational systems.

Bridging the Abyss: Out-citing at Its Best

The fissures exposed in the foregoing theoretical analysis and problematization of the *Praxes in re Sexual Identity* provide the starting point for an ethical inquiry that leads toward an *Out-Siders' Praxis*. No greater fissure exists than the abyss that lies between the realist and social-constructionist poles of the *Praxes in re Sexual Identity:* the notion of sexual identity as an innate, natural, biological fact on one side; and sexual identity as an historically situated, contingent, and mutable social construction on the other.

Numerous theorists have undertaken the task of resolving this impasse. Most of them try to take advantage of the recent insights produced about socially constructed gendered identities, while salvaging a liberal commitment to equality under the law and the powerful group dynamics inherent in identity politics. Martha Nussbaum's reformed liberal thought, for instance, acknowledges the many ways in which our genders, identities, emotions, values, relationships, and ways of understanding and making meaning are all socially constructed. While her approach is firmly entrenched in liberal politics' concern with rights, she contends that our consciousness of such socially constructed realities aids, rather than hinders, our commitment to securing equal rights and privileges for all people. A high-profile advocate, she believes that the place to begin is with basic rights for lesbian and gay people.[3] However, Jane Roland Martin believes that Nussbaum's reformed liberal paradigm, although intended to overcome the weaknesses of liberal politics, actually takes for granted many of its principles. Martin believes that her well-intentioned reform addresses many symptoms without ever getting to the root of the problem.[4]

Several social constructionists have suggested theoretical strategies as well. Ann Ferguson argues for "at least ten gender positions" in an attempt to bridge the abyss created by the identity politics–social constructionist debate.[5] These multiple gender positions, however, fail to address the problem of identity any more successfully than simple identity politics and not as well as the *Praxis of Location*.

Jeffrey Weeks has said that social constructionism's greatest weakness is its lack of political belonging.[6] Weeks has suggested that, regardless of the theoretical problems posed by identity politics, a politics of collective identity seems necessary to combat issues of rights in the public sphere. He counsels that theoretical work should continue from a social constructionist view, but practice should evidence an enlarged role for identity politics.[7] To do as Weeks suggests, however, obliterates the integration of theory and action. In this scenario, theory cannot inform practice; and the practice of identity politics, already demonized, is prohibited from informing theory.

Diana Fuss's concerns, like Weeks's, are also considerable, but she is less willing to offer an easy return to identity politics as the solution. Rather, she advocates a "sense of identity, even though it would be fictitious."[8] Fictions of identity, she argues, are no less powerful for the fact that they are fictitious.

It is not so much that we possess contingent identities but that identity itself is contingent. Such a view of identity as unstable and potentially disruptive, as alien and incoherent, Fuss suggests, has the potential for producing a more mature identity politics by militating against the tendency to erase differences and inconsistencies in the production of stable political subjects.[9] While Fuss's notion of a more mature identity politics may sound enticing, as does so much of social constructionist theory, it is completely abstract. The Out-Sider remains in a quandary about what it means to adopt or employ a fictitious identity, how that fictitious identity could disrupt anything, or how it will inform a more mature identity politics. These theoretical positions do not bring Out-Siders any closer to a solution than do the praxes already discussed.

If theorizing collectives is so problematic, why do it? The point is to maintain a viewpoint outside of liberal individualism, which denies the reality of groups and thus obscures oppression. Without seeing LGBTQ people as a group in some sense, it is easy to dismiss the systematic, structured, and institutional aspects of oppression. Unconnected to the fact that almost all similarly identified individuals face similar oppression, the problems of individuals appear to be simply that: individual problems.

This liberal principle is even at work, though unacknowledged, in Foucault's notion of power relations, which has been so influential in social constructionism. Foucault did not conceive of the inequities inherent within power relations to be conspiratorial. On the contrary, he regarded power relations as impersonal; an intense web of relationships; a network of practices, institutions, and technologies in which actions bear on actions, rather than dominant groups wielding power over subordinate groups.

There is an approach that I believe bridges this essentialist–social constructionist abyss far better than the others have done. Iris Marion Young argues that instead of theorizing—that is, conceptualizing systematic accounts that mean to be comprehensive—one should take a more pragmatic orientation to intellectual discourse. By this, she means explaining and developing accounts and arguments that are tied to specific practical and political problems where the purpose of the theoretical activity is clearly related to those problems.[10]

Young suggests that Sartre's seriality concept presents a way out of the identity politics–social constructionist dilemma. Sartre said that it is important to distinguish between two levels of social collectivity: groups and series. He defined a *group* as a self-conscious, mutually acknowledging collective with a self-conscious purpose. Groups arise from, and often fall back into, a less organized and un-self-conscious collective unity, which he called a *series*. Unlike a group, which forms around shared objectives, a series is a social collective whose members are unified passively by the objects around which their actions are oriented.[11]

Sartre used an example of people waiting for a bus. They are a series because they are related to a common material object, the bus, and the social practices of public transportation. They are united only by a common desire to ride the bus. However the latent potential of this series to organize itself into a group will become manifest if the bus fails to come. They will complain about the lousy service, share horror stories of lateness and breakdowns, perhaps assign one of their members to call the bus company, or discuss sharing a taxi. The collective dimension of a series is often experienced as constraint.[12]

Young applies Sartre's notion of seriality to consider the ways in which the collective of "women" may be constituted to form a political presence while avoiding the pitfalls of identity politics, which requires that all women have common attributes or a common situation. Expanding on her concept, consider the practico-inert realities that construct a series of lesbians. Female bodies clearly have something to do with this series, since they are inscribed with meanings and possibilities in all cultures. The structure defining the prescribed bodily practices is compulsory heterosexuality. Choosing other women for sexual partners is also part of what differentiates this series from another series, thereby placing it in an outsider position. Dining, traveling, living with, and loving other women constitutes particular constraints and freedoms. Individual lesbians, then, move and act in relation to these practico-inert considerations, generating a milieu of gendered series that enables and constrains action but does not determine or define it.

Belonging to this series does not name attributes of individual lesbians or primary aspects of their identity, but the practico-inert necessities do force them to deal with these varied structures, even though each person may deal with them differently. Thus, an individual's position in the series "lesbian" can mean that one individual has differing experiences and perceptions from those differently situated. Individuals can relate to those social positionings in different ways; the same person may relate to them in different ways in different contexts or at different times in their lives.[13] Consequently, some lesbians will claim that being lesbian is not an important part of their sense of self. Some may see their race or ethnic relations as more defining their sense of being in the world. Others may regard lesbianism as the critical aspect of their identity as an individual.[14]

Sartre said that groups, as self-conscious collectives, often, if not always, arise on the basis of, and in response to, a serialized condition. That is, groups come into being in response to felt difficulties or constraints arising from their serialized positioning to one another. Once groups form and take action, either they institutionalize themselves by establishing more formal structures, or they disperse back into seriality. Social life consists of constant ebbs and flows of groups from series, and back again. Some groups remain and form institutions that produce new serialities; others disperse soon after they are born.[15]

Consider again the series of lesbians. When the Colorado antigay initiative Amendment Two was being considered, its language explicitly declared homosexuality "unnatural" and made it illegal to present homosexuality as "normal" in public schools.[16] A series of lesbian teachers, with few other connections to one another, experienced Amendment Two as a felt difficulty in lesser or greater amounts, depending on their geographic location, how out they were to colleagues, and how deeply they were committed to the freedom to present homosexuality in a positive light to their students. Nevertheless, the constraints experienced from such legislation prompted many series of lesbian teachers who were targeted by these initiatives to start discussing their reactions to this legislation. They began meeting to determine how they would react and what steps they believed they could take as a group. They decided to undertake some actions on their own and join with other groups of lesbians and gay men in other school districts on other larger issues.[17]

The series–group concept describes this scenario well. However, for this concept to apply to Out-Siders' movement into groups, it must be altered. That is, in Young's concept, it is the felt difficulty of some practico-inert constraint, as is the case with these lesbian teachers, that prompts the movement from series to group. However, Out-Siders often move into groups not because they personally feel constrained by a practico-inert difficulty but because they see lesbian and gay outsiders who are their students, colleagues, or friends coping with these constraints. Thus, the series–group concept for Out-Siders depends on responsiveness to the needs of others—namely, lesbian and gay outsiders—responsiveness not needed in the series–group concept as Young uses it.

It was this kind of responsiveness that prompted teachers who were Out-Siders to take action when they saw evidence that anti–lesbian and gay prejudice was active in Fairfax High School in California. The incident that prompted teachers at this school to take action involved an openly gay male student who had been transferred to Fairfax from another school.

From the day he entered, "Chris" was physically abused by peers, and verbally abused by teachers and peers alike. Finally, "Chris" dropped out of school entirely and turned to the streets, becoming one more casualty of a system that neither understood, nor cared about him. His rejection was a systematic repeat of his experiences at four previous schools.[18]

These incidents were so offensive to several Out-Siders on the faculty and administration that they formed into a group that mobilized to develop a model program, PROJECT 10, to address the needs of self-identified gay, lesbian, and bisexual youth in the school setting. PROJECT 10 has subsequently become a nationwide forum for the articulation of the needs of lesbian, gay, and bisexual teenagers.[19]

The Out-Siders that formed into a group to develop PROJECT 10 exemplify both the functioning of Young's series–group concept and the responsiveness to the practico-inert constraints with which lesbian and gay outsiders are coping. Taken together, these concepts become what I call *out-citing,* which comprises three distinct phases as I have conceptualized the term. First, a series of Out-Siders recognizes injustice, harm, abuse, or violence toward LGBTQ outsiders that has occurred, or may occur, as a result of a particular practico-inert constraint. They cite the constraints endured by outsiders, the difficulties associated with the practico-inert constraint. Out-citing thus resembles inciting: the sense of stirring others to action. Second, the out-citing stirs Out-Siders to take action, effectively moving them from series to group. In the group, Out-Siders cite, or share, their unique perspectives and knowledge about what options are available for addressing the objectionable practico-inert constraint. Finally, in the third phase, having decided on a course of action, Out-Siders cite their assessments to groups and institutions that will be affected and take the actions on which they have agreed.

One does not have to look far to find examples of Out-Siders' out-citing. For instance, Out-Siders at the Hetrick-Martin Institute in New York City— a social service agency for lesbian, gay, and bisexual youth—began to cite recurring problems that they were seeing in their institute. Many of the youngsters they counseled and treated were dropping out of school. When a few staff members began out-citing what they were seeing, other counselors realized they too were seeing high dropout rates. The staff was engaged in the first phase of out-citing.

Through out-citing, the counselors realized that the situation was quite prevalent and that they must take action. At this point, the staff moved from series to group. Meeting together, they understood the full extent of the youths' problems. They realized that the reasons for these youths' lack of attendance in school varied—verbal harassment, physical violence, homelessness—but that the root cause in all the cases was the sexual identity of the youth. The counselors knew that they had to take some action to get these youth back in school if they were to have any hope of becoming productive, well-adjusted adults. They seized on a New York City Board of Education policy that provides for a teacher to be assigned to any social service agency that has at least twenty-two clients who are not attending school. This process of citing problems and potential solutions in the Out-Sider group makes up the second phase of out-citing.

Finally, the Hetrick-Martin staff addressed the Board of Education with its concerns and its solution, thus constituting the third phase of out-citing. The Board of Education eventually granted their request. Teachers were provided for the youth, and the Harvey Milk School was formed—the first high school in the country established solely to serve lesbian, gay, and bisexual youth.[20]

Out-citing solves several theoretical problems for Out-Sider collectives. Based on the series–group concept, out-citing overcomes the liberal problematics of focusing on individual rights and privileges while the reality of systematic, structured oppression remains obscured. The Out-Sider concept itself overcomes group-identity concerns since Out-Siders are LGBTQ and straight, students and teachers, administrators and scholars, parents and continuing education professionals, coaches and counselors, journalists and priests. Their diverse occupations and identities, spread across many configurations of education, preclude group formation based on identity from the outset. Further, when Out-Siders are conceptualized as a group that forms around practico-inert constraints, Out-Siders can forego the more difficult-to-organize coalitions in which Group A agrees to support the cause of Group B to receive Group B's support of Group A's cause. Since Out-Siders' series form into groups around specific practico-inert constraints, there is no necessary trade-off like that of complex coalitions.

Finally, out-citing answers social constructionists' concerns about the tendency of identity collectives and coalitions to grow increasingly inflexible, splintering over time. Out-citing allows Out-Siders to come together around specific issues, resolve them, then dissipate into a series again. Out-citing addresses the contingent nature of circumstance and self-concept, while providing a mechanism for political belonging, a much-needed change in social constructionism. Out-citing allows Out-Sider groups to be contingent and politically effective, since these groups form around specific practico-inert constraints, creating an agenda specific to the particular exigencies of outsider oppression in that context.

Out-citing also recognizes the contingent, temporary nature of goals in a second way. Because the particular practico-inert constraints that energize and motivate the formation of an Out-Sider group will necessarily be different from location to location, the solutions sought and methods chosen will be different as well. Each Out-Sider group's solutions must be particularly sensitive to the constituencies of LGBTQ outsiders, including age, gender, ethnicity, race, religion, and geography. Further, the choices made in each context will be bounded necessarily by the understanding, skills, abilities, and networking of the Out-Siders themselves. There are no universal solutions, because no two situations are the same and no two groups of Out-Siders are the same.

Therefore, I endorse out-citing as an appropriate conceptual model for the collective aspect of an *Out-Siders' Praxis*, with three caveats—that is, an effective praxis must overcome three weaknesses inherent in out-citing. First, out-citing is limited by Out-Siders' ability or willingness to see and react to practico-inert constraints. Second, out-citing alone portrays the inner workings of groups as rather bloodless realities, devoid of the passion necessary to accomplish important work. Third, out-citing does not take power relations into consideration. Consequently, out-citing as a base for an *Out-Siders' Praxis* must be accompanied by *out-sighting*, *out-siding*, and *out-siting*.

Caveat 1: Out-sighting

Because Out-Sider groups form in response to practico-inert constraints, Out-Siders need not be crusaders constantly in search of a mission. Yet, if the effects of compulsory heterosexuality are to be mitigated, Out-Siders must demonstrate the ability and willingness to see abuse, harassment, and violence when it occurs around them. That is, they must engage in *out-sighting*.

Out-sighting, as I have conceived it for use in an *Out-Siders' Praxis*, involves two critical ways of seeing. First, Out-Siders must evidence something akin to what Maxine Greene has described as wide-awakeness. We are all, she counsels, aware of the number of individuals who live their lives immersed in daily life, in the mechanical round of habitual activities, not asking what they have done with their own lives, whether they have used their freedom or simply acceded to the imposition of patterned behavior and an assignment of roles. Unless individuals awaken to the inequities, injustices, oppression, and brutality around them, they are likely to drift on impulses of expediency, rather than identify moral situations and assess the demands that those situations are imposing on one's attention. Greene suggests that the modern feeling of being dominated, and its attendant perception of powerlessness, is almost inescapable unless there is a conscious endeavor to keep oneself awake, to think about the condition of the world, to inquire into forces of domination, to interpret experiences one is having day after day.[21]

Out-sighting, then, calls on this commitment to wide-awakeness. Out-Siders must evidence a willingness to see situations around them that demand a moral response, refusing to live in denial to the mis-educative effects of compulsory heterosexuality.

Those teachers at Newton High School in Massachusetts, discussed earlier, serve as a fine example of a group *failing* to be wide awake. Remember the counselor in that discussion? He said: "I've been a guidance counselor at this school for more than twenty years, and I don't ever recall a student coming to me and telling me that he or she was a homosexual. I don't think we have any gay kids here." This group of school personnel was "awakened" by an Out-Sider who helped them see that there were in fact gay and lesbian students in the school and that they were being harassed. Eventually, the school personnel understood that it had not only a commitment but an obligation to provide a safe school for diverse youth, and they began to develop ways to address the anti–lesbian and gay prejudice in the school.

The second component of out-sighting is related to hidden curriculum in education. In the last chapter I mention two examples of hidden curriculum. Mr. Jenson took time out of his physics lessons to make derogatory remarks about the sinfulness of homosexuality, exemplifying explicit hidden curriculum. Miss L.'s action, or rather lack of action, to address her students' anti-gay rhetoric is an example of implicit hidden curriculum. However, as Jane Roland Martin has counseled, one does not simply find hidden curriculum: one must go looking for it. Since the hidden curriculum surrounding compulsory heterosexuality, like all hidden curriculum, is a set of learning states, it is the result of practices, procedures, rules, relationships, structures, and physical characteristics that constitute a given setting. Martin also counsels those who would challenge the hidden curriculum to be aware that it changes over time.[22] Therefore, Out-Siders must be watchful for instances of compulsory heterosexuality making their way into the hidden curriculum. They must watch for its mis-educative effects so that they can locate its source and recognize its paradoxes.

William Norris's research revealed one such paradox. At Oberlin, an institution with a long proud tradition of commitment to equal rights, Norris's research revealed strong positive attitudes toward lesbian, gay, and bisexual (LGB) students by all race and ethnic groups. Respondents to surveys expressed strong support for working, studying, socializing, and living with LGB peers. Yet, LGB students were confronted with on-going instances of direct discrimination, verbal abuse, physical attacks, and hate language. In 1973,

Oberlin became one of the first institutions of higher learning in the United States to include sexual orientation in its antidiscrimination statement. However, Norris found that beneath its progressive façade, Oberlin had never really taken steps to ensure equal rights for LGB students or faculty. Further, there existed an institutional distaste for bringing sexuality into discussions, partly as the result of Oberlin's religious heritage. Norris found that these issues had contributed to creating what he called "two Oberlins." In effect, what Norris had discovered was anti–lesbian and gay sentiment in the hidden curriculum while the curriculum proper professed strong LGB support.[23]

These two components then play a role in out-sighting: wide-awakeness toward instances of abuse, harassment, violence, inequality, and injustice; and a watchful attitude toward compulsory heterosexuality in the hidden curriculum. When Out-Siders out-sight, they instantiate the penetrating mental vision of insight focused on the practico-inert constraints facing LGBTQ outsiders.

Caveat 2: Out-siding
The best hope that Out-Siders have for the process of out-citing comes when out-citing is combined with *out-siding:* friendship and community that supports passionate and creative thought and action. Young's series–group approach portrays the inner workings of groups as rather bloodless realities. I have already argued that Out-Siders' groups are far from bloodless, established as they are to mitigate the instance of abuse, inequity, and injustice that they see directed toward lesbian and gay outsiders. Certainly, when gay–straight student alliances supported by PFLAG and GLSEN form, their intent to provide support and friendship is far from dispassionate. The people who labor to form these alliances and those who work against their establishment are well aware of the power of friendship. In fact, it is hard to imagine a group's forming over any difficulty more intense than Sartre's example of a bus's failure to arrive, dispassionately working for change, then simply dissipating spiritlessly back into seriality. There must be room in the series–group process for passion and creativity to animate and energize such critical work.

Jeffrey Weeks has made the following observations about the importance of identity collectives for sexual minorities:

> Sexual values are important not because they are either rooted in the "natural" or some revealed truth or foundational given, but because they provide the basis of social and cultural identification which makes possible a meaningful individual and social life, and, where appropriate, moral-political struggles.[24]

Such social and cultural identification, according to Weeks's thinking, forms the basis for community, a much-maligned concept in social constructionism. Poststructuralists have pointed to the desire for community, harmony, and unity within collectives as particular problematics that identity groups and coalitions cannot overcome. The poststructuralists claim that because identity collectives and coalitions need consensus, they will silence not only the voices that they exclude through defining themselves but also the voices at the margins that have notions contrary to the stated aims of the group. Poststructuralists argue that, as a result, identity groups and coalitions are bound to disintegrate, to splinter into ever-smaller groups because the needs of individuals are subsumed under the identity rubric, thereby subverting the sense of community.

Yet, Richard Rorty has suggested that the primary function of community is not to reach consensus but to engage in dialogue. Further, he suggests that it is an antipragmatist conviction that demands that conversation must aim at agreement and rational consensus. Dialogue, he claims, is not conversation whose only aim is to make further conversation unnecessary; rather, the moral virtues lie in our willingness to talk, to listen to other people, and to weigh the consequences of our actions on other people.[25]

Harriet Malinowitz, an avowed social constructionist, reaches conclusions similar to Rorty's. She contends that using the ability to reach consensus about the "correct" choice or path misstates one of the fundamental conditions required for community, since matters of accident, necessity, and convenience hold groups together as well. Internal dissonance, she says, is endemic to community, and identifications that forge community are multiple and overlapping, thereby continually rendering functional cohesion tenuous. "The 'organic unity' of a community is a myth, and consensus without conflict a utopian ideal."[26]

What is the pragmatic effect of considering Out-Sider groups as communities? Brought together partly by chance, partly by design, Out-Sider groups will always be changing, losing and gaining members, contingent and tenuous, conflicted and imperfect. Nonetheless, Out-Sider groups hold out the potential for community and friendship. While it is possible to conceive of groups impersonally forming and disbanding to arrange for a taxi when the bus does not arrive on time, it is more difficult to conceptualize groups working toward substantive, long-term goals without any sense of community or caring. Thus, while it seems entirely probable that Out-Sider groups will form from series based on practico-inert constraints, I suggest that difficult and long-term goals may be insufficient motivators to sustain the group over time, through discord within and challenges without. Out-siding, that sense of community and friendship in Out-Sider groups, is critical to an *Out-Siders' Praxis*. It provides a sense of cultural identification and support that sustains Out-Siders working toward social change.

Such was the case with Doyle Forrister, a world-history teacher in the wilds of Montana, a place he says is known for shooting first and asking questions later. When Forrister decided to attend a National Education Association training program to help teachers counsel LGBTQ students, he could find no other gay or lesbian teachers who were willing to come out enough to attend with him. Finally, he was introduced to Mac Swan, a straight Out-Sider who lived four hundred miles away. They attended the training program together and now work in their very different school environments to mitigate anti–lesbian and gay prejudice. Without continued communication with each other, they both readily admit that their projects would have been scuttled long ago. They have formed a friendship based on their work as Out-Siders that supports LGBTQ students in the process.[27]

Out-siding creates opportunities for individual and group caring, for friendship. Further, friendship as a constitutive element in an *Out-Siders' Praxis* is in no way antithetical to Aristotle's conceptualization of praxis. Aristotle, after all, argued that men who have every good known to man except a friend would choose not to live. He believed that "with friends men are more able both to think and to act."[28] In Aristotle's mind, friendship was necessary for the practical wisdom that leads to praxis.

Likewise, Marilyn Friedman has argued that friendship makes moral growth possible by teaching us to grasp our experiences in a new light or in radically new terms. People test abstract moral guidelines by concrete human lives. Therefore, friendship promotes better decision making by widening the experiential base against which people make these assessments. In friendship exists the possibility of accessing a whole range of experience beyond our own. Friendship allows us to orient ourselves in time when we doubt our own moral rules, values, or principles. At its best, friendship can provide us with invaluable and underestimated foundational resources so that we can construct and reconstruct our moral lives.[29]

Friendship, according to Friedman, not only grounds our moral choices but paves the way for change. By its very nature friendship is approximately egalitarian, relying on voluntariness and trusting in goodwill and good intentions. The social value of the voluntary practice of friendship has the potential to support unconventional values and deviant lives. Many traditional values merit distrust when individuals and groups are being harmed by their practice. Therefore, it is of great importance to cultivate moral reflection that can generate criticism and transformation of oppressive social practices.

Friendship makes a distinctive contribution to this effort by supporting unconventional values, deviant lifestyles, and other forms of nonconforming behavior. The voluntary nature of friendship permits friends to evolve idiosyncratic values or find others who support and affirm those values that have already evolved. The evolution of distinctive values may lead friends to shared perspectives that generate disloyalties to existing social institutions, giving friendship disruptive possibilities within society at large.[30]

Remember Steph, the "queerly raised" child of heterosexual parents? Steph's parents were able to provide life experiences for her that de-centered heteronormativity only because their lives were filled with many LGBT friends. Steph's mother says she "travels within and between multicultural and multisexual worlds . . . supported by a network of multicultural and multisexual friends."[31] Steph's parents had many LGBT friends who helped raise Steph with love and caring; and Steph, in turn, provided friendship and caring to several of their friends during the end stages of AIDS-related deaths.[32] Out-Siders all, they sustained one another.

When Out-Sider groups evolve into friendship groups, they hold the potential for making us, in Aristotle's words, "both more able to think and to act."[33] Out-Siders can make better choices when they share viewpoints among themselves. The best possible choices are needed when Out-Siders are in the position of confronting heterosexist values and morals. Further, because even heterosexual Out-Siders such as Steph's parents and Mac Swan are considered somewhat deviant because of their willingness to undertake unpopular causes, finding friendship within a group of Out-Siders with similar values can support those unconventional moral values and encourage disruptive social transformation. Friendship alone will not vanquish compulsory heterosexuality, but it can equip Out-Siders for the activity of sound thinking and for the thoughtfulness of activity. Friendship can prepare us to choose wisely while inspiring hope, creating energy, and stirring us to full potential.

Friendship is then a constitutive element for out-siding, but Out-Siders would be naïve indeed to believe that even friendship will create Out-Sider groups that function with complete unity of purpose. Dissonances, cross-purposes, and conflict are part and parcel of groups and communities. Out-Siders will understand, however, that those tensions need not spell dissolution but that they are part of its contingent form. John Dewey, in fact, claimed that contingency is the hallmark of an artistic form:

> Form is arrived at whenever a stable, even though moving, equilibrium is reached. Changes interlock and sustain one another. Wherever there is this coherence there is endurance. Order is not imposed from without but is made out of the relations of harmonious interactions that energies bear to one another.[34]

This notion of reaching equilibrium, while being constantly moved and constantly moving, supports the inventive, as well as the interventive, purposes of Out-Siders' groups. Out-citing and out-sighting presuppose activity, variety, constant change, and elements of disorder. The constant threat of dissolution and the perpetual reach for equilibrium provide the potential for growth, but they also threaten imminent demise.

Dewey reminds us that coping with such danger is part of the artistic experience. Since artists care in a peculiar way for the phase of experience in which union is achieved, they do not shun moments of resistance and tension. Artists do not avoid disequilibrium, because the artistic experience can occur only when stability has been de-centered. Therefore, the artist cultivates resistance and tension, not for their own sake, but because of the potentialities they hold for bringing to living consciousness an experience that is unified and total. The artistic experience culminates in that moment of passage from disturbance into harmony. That is the moment of intensest life.[35]

Out-siding must permit artistry in the Deweyan sense. Out-siding does not require artists who create sculptures for museums but artists that innovate curricular approaches to challenge compulsory heterosexuality and anti–lesbian and gay prejudice in ways that make it significant to the life of its intended educational community. Out-Siders who are out-siding have the opportunity to bring their passions to bear on the curricula and projects they create. Audre Lorde suggests that it is only when we bring passion to our work, to our problem solving, that we grow as persons and reach for excellence:

> For the erotic is not a question only of what we do; it is a question of how acutely and fully we can feel in the doing. Once we know the extent to which we are capable of feeling that sense of satisfaction and completion, we can then observe which of our various endeavors bring us closest to that fullness.
>
> The aim of each thing which we do is to make our lives and the lives of our children richer and more possible. Within the celebration of the erotic in all our endeavors, my work becomes a conscious decision—a longed-for bed which I enter gratefully and from which I rise up empowered.[36]

It was this kind of passion and creativity that drove Mara Sapon-Shevin to re-envision the primary music education program at her school. Sapon-Shevin's sensitivity to children's music and her commitment to out-sighting made her realize that since music is outside the "real curriculum," few people have looked seriously at what students are learning from the words they sing in songs. After a thorough critical review of the entire primary music curriculum, and after a great deal of research into music that could serve as replacements, she developed a music program that celebrates diversity in all its aspects, including same-sex relationships.[37]

Although this work was intensive and required a great deal of out-citing to engender support from other faculty and school administration, she believes her work has paid off by creating a more humane and caring environment at her school. To the point, Dewey said that passion must not be eschewed, even in practical reasoning, because it is emotion that animates a person to engage in arduous tasks.[38] He believed that emotions and imagination were integral to intelligent thought since it opened the door for new possibilities through creativity.

Thus, thinking as Dewey might, Out-Siders who are out-siding hold out the potential for creative inquiry about the amelioration of injustice, inequity, abuse, and violence toward lesbian and gay outsiders. Such passionate, creative thought shared among friends bestows value on lesbian and gay outsiders, who have so frequently been regarded as valueless. Dewey wrote:

> The reasonable act and the generous act lie close together. A person entirely lacking in sympathetic response might have a keen calculating intellect, but he would have no spontaneous sense of the claims of others for satisfaction of their desires. A person of narrow sympathy is of necessity a person of confined outlook upon the scene of human good. The only truly general thought is the generous thought.[39]

It was reasonable and generous for teachers to realize that six-year-old Jake might feel more comfortable in a classroom with other children of same-sex parents. It was also an instance of out-citing when those teachers met to talk about how to best approach Jake's education. Those teachers displayed outsight by being wide awake to how Jake might feel in a class where all the other children came from traditional families. However, it was out-siding, the creative and passionate concern for children entrusted to their care, that prompted the teachers to take action, to think generously.

In Deweyan thought, interpersonal understanding is always a possibility; but without sympathy—or in his words, generosity—there is always a danger of misunderstanding. With generosity, the recognition of others' needs, desires, and hopes can propel us beyond the bounds of ourselves. Out-Siders, by definition, must be propelled by hope and must go beyond the constraints experienced in their own lives. Out-siding offers the opportunity for friendship that promotes moral growth and for generosity that works toward interpersonal understanding. Out-Siders who choose out-siding—that active, passionate, creative, and generous approach of life—can engage the perspectives of others to reason with passion and imagination, to envision new possibilities, to hope for things never before even dreamed.

Caveat 3: Out-siting

Young's series–group concept states that practico-inert objects become important; groups form from series; situations are resolved; groups dissolve again into series; and everything goes back to the way it was before the group formed, except that the particular issue was resolved. Yet, if contemporary thinkers have learned anything from Foucault, it is that all people and groups are constituted within a web of power relations. Therefore, when an Out-Sider group forms, works, or dissolves, power relations have been stressed. New areas of resistance will surface; old ones will exert more or less pressure; and other Out-Sider series or groups will be motivated to action. The groups and institutions most affected must either endure the stress that the Out-Sider group's actions place on it; move toward the Out-Siders' aims and thus lessen the stress; or move even further away from the Out-Siders in an attempt to force the Out-Siders to scuttle their agenda. Therefore, understanding power relations is critical for Out-Siders since resistance and backlash are inherent to the functioning of any group because of its relations to other institutions and groups within a field of power relations.

Lorraine Code endorses the concept of "positionality," which was first conceived by Linda Alcoff. Positionality acknowledges postmodernism's potential for offering a free play of differences unhampered by any predetermined gender identity. However, Alcoff fears that in place of the old essentialism, postmodernism risks positing a new form of determinism in which human agents are swept along by a tide of discourse that they are powerless to resist. Alcoff explores a way of reconceptualizing subjectivity in terms of positionality wherein a subject's identity is understood as relative to a constantly shifting context, to a situation that includes a network of elements involving others, the objective economic conditions, cultural and political institutions and ideologies, and so on. Subjectivity, thus conceived, is a relational construct, but it is neither immobilized nor stabilized, as it is in the impersonal structures of androcentric discourse. Rather, positionality resists taking any one position as referent. The point of positionality is not to advocate quiescent liberal tolerance; it is to analyze, assess, and assume accountability for the positions one occupies, while engaging in critical dialogue with, or resistance against, occupants of other positions, in cognizance of their political implications. In this way, identity forms and re-forms in contexts of concrete habits, practices, and discourses, which are at once fluid, unstable, yet amenable to quite precise, determinate articulation at specific historical sites and moments. Specific articulations are open to social and political critique, remapping and renegotiation; at the same time, however, they are also sufficiently stable to permit active political involvement.[40]

Therefore, for Out-Sider groups to function effectively, they must understand their site in the field of power relations. That is, they must understand *out-siting*, which is that process by which Out-Sider groups come to establish and understand their location, their site, as real, tangible, and concrete, even while acknowledging its contingent, negotiable, and temporary character. Out-siting comprises two main elements. First, out-siting means understanding how power relations produce resistance to the changes and recommendations that Out-Siders make to reduce the effects of compulsory heterosexuality. Out-Siders cannot afford naïveté about how power relations function, for groups and institutions typically will change only enough to alleviate extreme stress at one point without creating more stress at an alternate point. For groups or institutions to make a wholesale move toward Out-Sider groups would create enormous tension and resistance from other opposing groups and institutions in the web of power relations. Second, out-siting means locating oneself in alliance with lesbian and gay outsiders. In this second sense of out-siting, Out-Siders consciously establish their site in the web of power relations as friends of outsiders. Out-siting, then, becomes a kind of speech act, a considered challenge to anti–lesbian and gay prejudice.

A powerful example of Out-Siders' need for out-siting occurred in Oklahoma. After contacting the GLSEN chapter in Oklahoma City for help in establishing a gay–straight alliance in Jenks, Oklahoma, Kevin Barker began the laborious process of trying to gain administrative approval for the club.[41] The school principal was opposed to the club but, after talking to the school attorney, understood that the Equal Access Act was clearly on the side of the students. After postponing approval for months, the principal finally relented, and the gay–straight alliance was approved. However, in short order the principal found new ways to circumvent the club's activities. He withheld routine approval for posters and flyers. Words such as *homophobic*, *lesbian*, *bisexual*, and *transgender* were deemed inappropriate subject matter for school hallways.[42]

Kevin and the members of GLSEN were completely taken aback by the underhanded means by which the principal was sabotaging the work of the gay–straight alliance. Had this group understood out-siting—that is, how establishing a stable but temporary position in a field of power relations affected other groups—they could have been more prepared for such backlashes. Knowledge of out-siting could have helped the GLSEN members set expectations and future agendas.

Understanding out-siting means understanding the contingent nature of the group's position and gains. This is not to say that gains will not be made. If Out-Siders believed change was not possible, there would be no point in pouring energy into needed change. Yet, comprehending the way that webs of power relations form around knowledge helps Out-Siders appreciate not only the social constructionists' extreme caution about believing that any cause is ever finally won but also Foucault's endorsement of a "hyper- and pessimistic activism." Out-Siders must understand that social positions are malleable but that change will not be lasting without continuing vigilance. Consciousness of power relations promotes a fuller understanding that contingent situations—whether intractable or resolved—are indeed temporary and mutable.

Thus, out-citing with no basis in out-siting is naïve and ultimately self-defeating. Out-citing must be embedded within this more complex conceptual model of out-siting so that Out-Siders can be provided with a conceptual model for understanding their actions relative to a constantly shifting context of other Out-Sider groups; people working against outsider equality; practical considerations; economic conditions; cultural, religious, and political institutions; and so forth. In this context, out-siting takes no one position or goal as referent, but it allows Out-Siders to be prepared to address practico-inert exigencies when they arise. This relational concept means that the Out-Sider understands and assumes responsibility for the site she or he occupies, while engaging in critical dialogue with, or resistance against, occupants of other sites, in cognizance of their political implications. In this way, Out-Sider sites may be fluid and precise at specific moments in specific locations.

Out-Siders who out-site consciously locate themselves as allies. In so doing they serve the cause of LGBTQ outsiders powerfully. The dean of the chapel at Howard University exemplified out-siting when, after learning of an excellent student's troubles with peers over her lesbianism, he asked her to speak at the Presidential Prayer Breakfast.[43] In another instance, several straight teachers at a Catholic school out-sited when they had a conversation in front of other faculty members about how outrageous it was that Catholic teachers were not supposed to be gay. Jeff, a teacher at the school who had only recently come out to himself, found this conversation assuring and it made him feel less alone.[44] Barbara Barbour, a straight junior high math teacher in Vermont, out-sites through her active membership in the NEA's Gay and Lesbian Caucus.[45] There are as many ways to out-site as there are Out-Siders.

Summary of Theoretical Considerations for *Out-Siders' Praxis*

In summary, this *Out-Siders' Praxis* provides a theoretical framework for overcoming the principal theoretical weaknesses of the *Praxes in re Sexual Identity* as well as the abyss that has been created as a result of the essentialist–social constructionist rift. The *Out-Siders' Praxis* utilizes four major conceptual tools to allow Out-Siders to act effectively and sustain themselves and one another over time: out-citing, out-sighting, out-siding, and out-siting.

In the process of out-citing, Out-Siders form into groups from series, citing the practico-inert constraints in the lives of LGBTQ outsiders that are unacceptable. Once in the group, Out-Siders cite potential ideas and solutions to the problems. When an approach for action has been decided on, Out-Siders then cite their decisions to those in educational configurations that will be affected.

Out-sighting keeps Out-Siders not only wide awake to what is happening to lesbian and gay outsiders around them but also watchful of the ways that heterosexism, anti–lesbian and gay prejudice, and compulsory heterosexuality are manifested as hidden curriculum. Out-siding with other Out-Siders and with lesbian and gay outsiders permits the formation of friendships, which allows for moral development as well as passionate, imaginative, generous interventions. It is the potential for community and friendship that offers the greatest possibilities for sustaining Out-Siders as they work toward disruptive social change.

Out-Siders must also understand out-siting. That is, Out-Siders must have a theoretical grasp of how groups function within a field of power relations. It is within power relations that Out-Sider groups are constrained and afforded the opportunity to effect change.

As Out-Siders stir one another to passion and excellence, their work has the opportunity to restore the continuity between refined and intensified forms of experience that makes works of art from the everyday events and circumstances that form our experience. Our engagement with other Out-Siders toward the end of mitigating the effects of compulsory heterosexuality is an endeavor that is intellectual and creative. By practicing passionate, generous thought, we have the opportunity for free, creative engagement wherein we not only change the world for the better but are ourselves changed in the process of working for a better world.

Practical Considerations

Maxine Greene has written that most modern readers "overlook the fact that domination in the intellectual and social realm, unlike mortality, is alterable. They forget that norms and prohibitions and denials are functions of particular sets of interests at particular moments of time."[46] Out-siting permits Out-Siders to understand that such exclusions and denials are changeable even when they are supported by the terrible oppression in which people acquiesce to, and participate in, their own silencing. Because circumstance and ideology are not only always changing but always changeable, it is crucial for people who work in education to out-sight across its many configurations, in settings formal and informal, with children and adults. That is, Out-Siders must understand and become capable of undertaking the kinds of praxis that bear the potential for transforming that which they find to be deficient, for surpassing what they have found to be abusive or inhumane. Such praxis means, in Dewey's words, "bringing the world closer to the heart's desire."

Not only does education hold the potential for overcoming ignorance and warding off manipulations, but when Out-Siders engage in out-citing, they can also resist the cynicism and powerlessness that can so easily silence our voices and paralyze our energies. Education, if it is to qualify as *Out-Siders' Praxis*, must involve every aspect of out-citing: critical reflection—and action—on a situation to some degree shared by persons with common interests or common needs. Education as praxis involves transformation of situations to the end of overcoming oppressiveness and domination.[47]

An *Out-Siders' Praxis* must involve out-citing as collective self-reflection; there must be discourse wherein present and emergent needs are cited, defined, and interpreted. However, these opportunities for reflection and understanding must give way to realization and fulfillment. The problem for Out-Siders is not simply interpretation of the heterosexism we find in the world; the problem is not simply theorizing yet another explanation of how the world came to be in the heterosexist state it is in today; the problem is not simply deconstructing the "naturalness" of compulsory heterosexuality. The problem for an *Out-Siders' Praxis* is to out-cite. In so doing, they confront heterosexism, challenge compulsory heterosexuality, implement solutions, and change the world that harasses, denigrates, abuses, trivializes, and demonizes LGBTQ outsiders. Anything less, any system of thought, any philosophical insight that does not also involve collective execution of plans toward overcoming oppressiveness and domination is not out-citing and is not praxis.

In addition, just as the theoretical understanding of out-citing, out-sighting, out-siding, and out-siting will influence action, so will Out-Siders' actions influence theory. Focus for a moment on several such actions of Out-Siders:

- In 1989 Massachusetts passed a gay and lesbian civil rights law. The Coalition for Lesbian and Gay Civil Rights soon filed legislation to create an advisory board focusing on youth services, an act of out-citing. Although that legislation died, it influenced the thinking of Governor William Weld who formed the innovative Commission on Gay and Lesbian Youth. Soon, based on out-sight that the research and recommendations of the commission provided, the Department of Education established its out-site and intent to out-side by asking the state's three hundred school districts to establish policies to protect gay and lesbian students.[48]

- During a multicultural education class for prospective teachers, the professor told the students that they would be addressing gay issues in the course. The professor indicated her intent at the outset because she did not want any surprises later on, since "some people do not feel comfortable with homosexuality." Jonas, a student in the class, raised his hand and said: "Excuse me! I just want to say something here right now. *Heterosexuals* really make me nervous. . . . I can deal with it—some of my family—I admit it, most of my family—are heterosexuals. Some of my best friends are heterosexuals. But I just don't know why you people have to talk about it all the time. I have to look at you in the news, I have to look at you in the movies, I have to look at you in the newspapers. It's sickening, okay? Sex, sex, sex, sex, sex. Hetero sex. . . . So I'm just gong to put that out there right now. I'm not going to be happy when we're talking about that stuff."

    Most of the students in the class laughed at the fake tirade. Jonas characterized it as a "preemptive strike," a strategic way to out himself to call attention to the heteronormative lens through which a well-meaning professor was looking.[49]

    Translated into Out-Sider terminology, Jonas acted on the professor's attempt at out-siding to out-cite, to announce his sexual identity in a creative way. The intent of his preemptive strike was to establish the out-site from which he would be acting in class and to prompt out-sight in his colleagues.

- Out-Sider educators have used a training model called a neutral-gender description exercise, intended to increase beginning counselors' empathy for nonheterosexual clients who spend a great deal of time and expend enormous amounts of energy concealing their sexual identity from homophobic acquaintances. In the exercise the trainees are asked to describe a recent "date" without revealing the gender of the person they "dated." The listener is given permission to ask probing questions that tempt the speaker to reveal the gender of the date. After the exercise is over, most of the trainees express frustration at the difficulty they had in using completely gender-neutral terminology and find it difficult to believe how exhausting even a five-minute exercise could be.[50]

    The educators who were out-siding in this example asked the trainees to take up a temporary conceptual position within out-siting to increase the trainees' out-sight and to encourage them to out-side with their lesbian and gay clients.

The actions and exercises in the preceding three examples are strategies associated with three different *Praxes in re Sexual Identity*. The initiation of a safe-schools agenda is a liberal solution situated within the *Praxis of Inclusion*. Jonas's fake tirade was intended, first, to disrupt presumed heterosexuality and heteronormative curriculum, an intent associated with the *Praxis of Performativity*; and, second, to find a way to come out, the principle strategy of the *Praxis of Coming Out*. The neutral-gender description exercise, however, is a sensitivity strategy stemming from the *Praxis of Performativity*. The question then becomes, Which of these actions would Out-Siders want to prevent? If we say that all seemed appropriate for their specific situation, a theoretical dilemma arises. Can an *Out-Siders' Praxis* support action initiatives derived from very diverse theoretical perspectives?

To resolve this theoretical dilemma, action must influence theory. If Out-Siders believe that all these approaches are valid in certain situations, "right" or "wrong" choices do not exist. Taking a pragmatic view of the actions, the approach is judged not by its method but by its effect. Did the instances of out-citing succeed in mitigating some of the effects of compulsory heterosexuality? Did it increase out-sight? Did it challenge heteronormativity through out-siding or out-citing? Did it establish a temporary out-site for resistance to anti–lesbian and gay prejudice? If the answer to these questions is yes, it is inconsequential whether the method was one that might be endorsed by social constructionists, liberals, or identity groups. The only question is, Did it work?

Endorsing this pragmatic viewpoint also means that Out-Siders understand that two groups of Out-Siders out-sited in two locations might choose, indeed probably will choose, to out-cite the situation in substantially different ways. The same group of Out-Siders may choose to out-cite a situation differently at different times or with different groups of learners. In fact, if Out-Siders are to avoid succumbing to mime, they must evidence a peculiar out-sight, a demonstrated sensitivity to exactly what word must be spoken at a particular time.

Understanding the pragmatic construction of an *Out-Siders' Praxis* brings up a crucial point: Out-Siders must be proficient at distinguishing their friends from their enemies. Despite the radically different approaches, insights, and political bases of Martha Nussbaum, Victor Anderson, Marilyn Frye, James Sears, Judith Butler, and Jeffrey Weeks, they are all friends of lesbian and gay outsiders. Engaging in discourse about which one is right and which one is wrong presents a tantalizing theoretical problem, but pragmatically, such polemics must remain a secondary issue to making life more liveable, more equitable, for lesbian and gay outsiders. While Out-Siders discuss, research, and experiment with theories, strategies, and curricula designed to mitigate the effects of compulsory heterosexuality, while they ponder and write about the implications that various views may hold for the present and future, while they consider the consequences of choosing this rather than that, such discussions need not be filled with rancor. Inherent in this pragmatist approach is a healthy respect for different strategies. So, Out-Siders will ask thoroughly pragmatic questions as they choose their strategies and the theories that ground their strategies: "What would it be like to believe this rather than that? What would happen if I believed this rather than that? To what actions would I commit myself if I believed this rather than that?"

A commitment to pragmatism means that an *Out-Siders' Praxis* may utilize approaches drawn from the entire range of the *Praxes in re Sexual Identity*. Out-Siders still need to out-cite for policy safeguards and legislated rights for LGBTQ outsiders, those prime considerations in liberal thought. Like Woolf's daughters of educated men, LGBTQ outsiders do not have a free voice when their livelihoods are constantly threatened because they have no employment protections. Justice requires that Out-Siders work for securing basic freedoms and privileges. Out-Siders must therefore espouse many of the goals of liberal politics.

As I have already argued, liberal politics does not change the heart. However, out-siding does. Out-Siders recognize that securing rights and protections for outsiders does not solve the social situation. Out-Siders must learn and teach understanding and communication across difference. As far as is possible, Out-Siders must commit themselves to multicultural approaches that respect rich, multifaceted cultural diversity. However, Out-Siders cannot espouse multicultural approaches that systematically deny political and moral equality to heterosexual women, lesbians, and gay men, those groups traditionally consigned to second-class status. Such an approach would evidence lack of out-sight. As Nussbaum has succinctly stated the issue: "Cultures are not museum pieces, to be preserved intact at all costs."[51]

Out-Siders, by their very name, must support LGBTQ outsiders' efforts to come out. That is, they must work toward helping LGBTQ outsiders out-cite for themselves by creating environments in which outsiders can come out in safety and security with appropriate support systems. Although, aware of the potential for regionalism, sexism, racism, classism, and nationalism in a universal mandate to come out, and aware of the tendency in all of us to become the Dictator in Woolf's educational treatise, Out-Siders must out-side. They must not arrogantly presume to know best about the level of disclosure that is appropriate for every gay man or lesbian. Coming out is a process that is never really complete, an issue that the out-sight of Out-Siders understands.

Each semester, each new staff member or administrator presents the hurdle of coming out anew. Out-Siders must offer their support and alliance; that is, they must out-side so that LGBTQ outsiders' decisions for authenticity can be easier, but they must not pressure outsiders in their influence to disclose themselves when they are unprepared to do so.

Out-Siders must evidence out-sight by understanding the value of the postmodern resolve to decenter heteronormativity. Realizing that compulsory heterosexuality is mis-educative for all students means that it is crucial to intercept the presumption of one, and only one, correct mode for sexual expression. When "queering the discourse" becomes the goal, it is surprising how many little things can change the educational climate.

The sense that Out-Siders can, indeed must, advocate positions from all of the five *Praxes in re Sexual Identity* that support lesbian and gay outsiders may suggest that I am failing to heed Dewey's advice to "proceed from a level deeper and more inclusive than is represented by the practices and ideas of the contending parties" and rather am making "an eclectic combination of points picked hither and yon from all schools."[52] However, I contend that all these praxes have stayed alive in the discourse surrounding identity because they fulfill needs that other praxes have failed to fill. If Out-Siders are to work for the greatest amount of freedom to live as full citizens, then we must include all of these key issues. In addition, I offer here Eve Kosofsky Sedgwick's support of a similar notion:

> In consonance with my emphasis on the performative relations of double and conflicted definition, the theorized prescription for a *practical* politics implicit in these readings is for a multi-pronged movement whose idealist and materialist impulses, whose minority-model and universalist-model strategies, and for that matter whose gender-separatist and gender-integrative analyses would likewise proceed in parallel without any high premium placed on ideological rationalization between them. In effect this is how the gay movements of this century have actually been structured, if not how they have often been perceived or evaluated. The breadth and fullness of the political gestalt of gay-affirmative struggle give a powerful resonance to the voice of each of its constituencies. The cost in ideological rigor, though high indeed, is simply inevitable: this is not a conceptual landscape in which ideological rigor across levels, across constituencies is at all possible, be it ever so desirable.[53]

Pragmatically, the problem is not to present an ideological approach that is universally embraced but to ask which type of solution is needed for the particular circumstances around which Out-Siders have organized. Out-Siders' practice has informed the theory for the *Out-Siders' Praxis*, helping us to see differently.

Out-Sider practice must inform the theory of an *Out-Siders' Praxis* in one other significant way. It would be highly unlikely that a well-meaning but un-informed group of Out-Siders could out-side effectively to mitigate the effects of compulsory heterosexuality. For Out-Siders to make the best decisions about the practical solutions regarding the exigencies of lesbian and gay outsiders' lives, they require substantial out-sight about LGBTQ issues. Holding general good will toward lesbian and gay outsiders does not mean that one can react effec-tively when a situation arises in a classroom, faculty lounge, or departmental meeting. Out-Siders must reach a level of comfort with the subject matter to be able to work toward subverting compulsory heterosexuality in an educational environment. Of course, no teacher can completely control what happens in a classroom environment when lesbian and gay issues are discussed, let alone a faculty meeting involving peers; but a teacher can promote and encourage an affirmative environment that has the potential of disrupting heterosexism. That is, they can establish themselves in a position of out-siting against heterosexism.

I offer my own suggestions for what teachers and students can do to reach a basic level of preparedness, with the stipulation that none of these ideas is a simple directive for classroom implementation. On the contrary, the sug-gestions have to do with the desire for gaining out-sight, that self-education on critical issues facing lesbian and gay students, colleagues, and students of same-sex parents. My suggestions are then a way of building a base of knowl-edge from which specific practices can grow.

The whole point of praxis is that those who practice it are themselves the developers of it. Out-siding is a creative process requiring one to have dia-logue with others and to have interaction with the specifics of a situation. It is *not* an effort to mime what has been done elsewhere. Developing specific curricula is not only outside the scope of this inquiry but would once again place Out-Siders in a "banking education" environment, where they are ex-pected to spew forth answers developed by someone else under different cir-cumstances at a different time.

Here are some ways that Out-Siders may go about educating themselves:

- Go to a feminist or lesbian-and-gay bookstore in your area, or peruse the lesbian- and gay-themed books found at most of the larger book-stores. Think about which essays and books you might be able to in-clude in your course syllabi.
- Contact your campus Lesbian, Gay, Bisexual, Transgender, and Friends Alliance and ask them for a suggested list of readings. Many women's studies programs can also be useful in this respect. Remember that out-citing includes sharing, not just talking.

- Obtain newsletters from local lesbian and gay organizations and become conversant about the issues contained in those articles.
- Research lesbian and gay studies on the Internet.[54] The links to programs at large universities can provide a wealth of information as can the Center for Lesbian and Gay Studies in New York.
- Go to lesbian and gay cultural events on campus: lectures, forums, literary readings, plays, and films. Out-Siders' presence at these events evidences not only a desire for out-sight but a show of out-siting and out-siding with the out.
- Attend lesbian- and gay-themed sessions at your professional conferences. Again, Out-Siders' presence evidences the desire to out-side, out-cite, out-sight, and out-site.
- Particularly for those educating in the Bible Belt, find out about resistant readings of lesbian and gay experience in religious discourse. This education can provide invaluable out-sight and show a great desire to out-side with LGBTQ outsiders.
- Experiment with adding lesbian and gay discussion topics in classes, and encourage your colleagues to do the same—that is, out-side.
- Bring up lesbian and gay existence in department and committee meetings as a matter of curricular importance.

For those who deplore the absence of more "practical" suggestions, let me point out that such suggestions would not work since recipes do not take the particular circumstances of diverse groups of outsiders into account. Further, as Out-Siders, we must be mindful of a truism that developed during the vintage days of identity politics that is highly relevant in these circumstances, stated succinctly by Audre Lorde:

> Whenever the need for some pretense of communication arises, those who profit from our oppression call upon us to share our knowledge with them. In other words, it is the responsibility of the oppressed to teach the oppressors their mistakes. I am responsible for educating teachers who dismiss my children's culture in school. Black and Third World people are expected to educate white people as to our humanity. Women are expected to educate men. Lesbians and gay men are expected to educate the heterosexual world. The oppressors maintain their position and evade responsibility for their own actions.[55]

Those occupying socially dominant positions place an undue burden on those outsiders in subordinate positions when they expect them to do all the work of deconstructing and rectifying systems of oppression. We tend to be

most aware of oppression when we are the recipients of it, but we are all em-
broiled in the symbolic order that regulates prejudice. Anyone who is interested can become aware of, and work to avert, prejudice. Out-sighting is always possible.

Knowledgeable about LGBTQ issues, Out-Siders can out-side by functioning as allies in educational settings in a number of ways. Numerous studies have substantiated that heterosexual students and colleagues listen to the
suggestions of other heterosexuals about lesbian and gay issues far more in-
tently and respectfully than when those same issues are presented by lesbians
and gays themselves. In an environment that is not particularly lesbian- and
gay-friendly, it is usually far less risky, professionally and personally, for a heterosexual person to out-site as an Out-Sider than it is for a lesbian or gay person to do likewise. Professors, administrators, and teachers can explicitly
present themselves as allies by talking with students and teachers about resources and ideas for dealing with lesbian and gay issues in school situations.

Small gestures mean a great deal to outsiders who are accustomed to being ignored, dismissed, or denigrated. For instance, when Out-Siders show
out-sight about the fact that not everyone they meet is heterosexual, they
can often reduce stress for lesbian and gay outsiders. Heterosexual Out-Siders
need to be cognizant of the ways in which they advertise their own dominant
sexuality through wedding rings, explicit references to "my wife" or "my husband." Merely using these words or wearing a wedding band does not mean
that such representations are detrimental, but Out-Siders should be aware of
the ways in which they announce their dominance and use it for help rather
than harm. One professor who was a lesbian-and-gay ally introduced the subject of homosexuality in class by telling a story in which she mentioned her
husband. She then asked her education students about how they felt about
the fact that she just "came out" to them as heterosexual.[56] She thereby generated a discussion about why, and to what effects, such stories serve to unify
and divide a diverse educational setting, prompting a critique of heteronormativity. This professor was out-siding by introducing this topic in an innovative way. She showed substantial out-sight into her students' thinking and
acted to out-site herself as an ally while out-citing her curricular decisions to
her students.

When Out-Siders become informed about LGBTQ issues, they want to
out-side by representing lesbian and gay issues in teacher education courses.
Representation is a good thing, but Out-Siders must remember: being inclusive is not synonymous with out-sighting. Out-sighting means being aware of
the ways in which difference is framed. For instance, if a professor shows the
film It's Elementary, with the implicit message that it's "Gay Day," the fact

that heterosexuality structures the rest of the classes goes unstated. Including lesbian and gay articles, speakers, and films is important out-citing work, but so is the critical work of analyzing unspoken assumptions. "Gay Day" may bring the issues to the fore, but educating for cultural change is a process, not an event.

We can highlight heteronormativity by asking preservice teachers to observe in classrooms how "compulsory heterosexuality" is being produced. As with those counselor trainees, sensitivity builds out-sight. For instance, do straight teachers mention their spouses in the classroom? Do school memoranda publicly announce a wedding or baby? What family configurations are depicted in school songs, books, and posters? Do teachers assume that girls have "little boyfriends" instead of "little girlfriends"? What would it mean to adopt out-siding by teaching every class, attending every faculty meeting with the assumption that at least one person in that room is either lesbian or gay, will become lesbian or gay, or has a lesbian or gay family member? Many teachers and researchers have shared how *little* it takes for lesbian and gay students, colleagues, or their family members to feel as if they have been seen and heard. Even little changes have the capacity to make a big difference to lesbian and gay outsiders when those changes convey honest attempts to out-side and reveal the extent to which Out-Siders have engaged in creative inquiry on LGBTQ-specific issues.

An *Out-Siders' Praxis* holds out the potential for dramatically improving the lives of the lesbian and gay students and colleagues with whom we all interact daily. By thinking critically, reflectively—that is, by out-citing, out-siding, out-sighting, and out-siting about issues that are important to LGBTQ outsiders—we bestow value on them. By thinking and speaking "generously," in Dewey's words, Out-Siders are not only thinking reasonably but out-siding. By choosing to prepare ourselves through out-sighting to take in hand the situations of abuse and violence that still plague our students and colleagues in educational settings, Out-Siders out-siting are influencing their institutions of learning toward a higher level of morality. In so doing, Out-Siders transform themselves as they transform the configurations of education.

We are presented opportunities every day to refuse small parts of our subjectification and to choose that to which we will subject ourselves. The potential is still available to re-create ourselves as works of art, as moral persons. We can choose to listen to the "voices of poets, answering each other, assuring us of a unity that rubs out divisions as if they were chalk marks only; to discuss with you the capacity of the human spirit to overflow boundaries and make unity out of multiplicity."[57] The *Out-Siders' Praxis* is filled with potential for invention and intervention if we heed the moral imperative therein.

Recapitulation

Outsider to Out-Sider

I began this investigation of the requirements for an *Out-Siders' Praxis* by suggesting that Virginia Woolf's call to action for her Outsiders' Society was useful for contemplating certain ethical values that might apply to lesbian and gay outsiders, but I also argued that the unique circumstances of lesbian and gay people in the current educational environment beg a solution that is fully cognizant of the multiple issues specifically related to sexual identity. I endorsed Woolf's strategy for her Outsiders and set as my goal the creation of an *Out-Siders' Praxis* that could be as philosophically sound and strategically crafted as that which was fashioned by Woolf for the daughters of educated men. Now that this *Out-Siders' Praxis* has been conceived, let us consider if it has included those ethical values that Woolf believed were crucial for transforming society.

Woolf's first vision in *Three Guineas* was of a new education at a new kind of college that would overcome the competitiveness and strife she saw in the great universities of England.

> Let us then discuss as quickly as we can the sort of education that is needed. Now since history and biography—the only evidence available to an outsider—seem to prove that the old education of the old colleges breeds neither a particular respect of liberty nor a particular hatred of war it is clear that you must rebuild your college differently. It is young and poor; let it therefore take advantage of those qualities and be founded on poverty and youth. Obviously, then, it must be an experimental college, an adventurous college. Let it be built on lines of its own. It must be built not of carved stone and stained glass, but of some cheap, easily combustible material which does not hoard dust and perpetrate traditions. . . . Let the pictures and the books be new and always changing. Let it be decorated afresh by each generation with their own hands cheaply. The work of the living is cheap; often they will give it for the sake of being allowed to do it. Next, what should be taught in the new college, the poor college? Not the arts of dominating other people, not the arts of ruling, of killing, of acquiring land and capital. They require too many overhead expenses; salaries and uniforms and ceremonies. The poor college must teach only the arts that can be taught cheaply and practiced by poor people; such as medicine, mathematics, music, painting, and literature. It should teach the arts of human intercourse; the art of understanding other people's lives and minds, and the little arts of talk, of dress, of cookery that are allied with them. The aim of the new college, the cheap college, should be not to segregate and specialize, but to combine. It should explore the ways in which mind and body can be made to cooperate; discover what new combinations make good wholes in

human life. The teachers should be drawn from the good livers as well as from the good thinkers. . . . They would come to the poor college and practise their arts there because it would be a place where society was free; not parceled out into the miserable distinctions of rich and poor, clever and stupid; but where all the different degrees and kinds of mind, body and soul merit co-operated. Let us then found this new college; this poor college; in which learning is sought for itself.[58]

In what ways do the ethical norms of the *Out-Siders' Praxis* conform to the values and conduct that Woolf established for education in her new college? First, both drew their specific data from history and biography since the subjects of their research, outsiders, have not been represented in the standard texts or in the works of great educational experts. Like Woolf's education in the new college, the *Out-Siders' Praxis* is founded on a respect for liberty. It is this passion for liberty that forms the basis for the Out-Siders' responsibility to lesbian and gay outsiders' equality and to their participation in the discourse of humanity. Further, a key aspect of the *Out-Siders' Praxis* is continued work toward extending basic rights and privileges to lesbian and gay outsiders.

Woolf's new college is young and poor. It is founded on an experimental and adventurous attitude, not on tired traditions. Those Out-Siders who have chosen to work toward mitigating compulsory heterosexuality have little choice but to work experimentally, for there are few ready-made resources. Even if tried-and-true recipes were available, however, the solutions that Out-Siders create must reflect the needs of specific groups. Each situation needs creative and specific interventions. Like the education of the new college, then, Out-Siders will not write their solutions in carved stone or stained glass. They know that imitating someone else's solutions could not have served them, so they dare not try to carve their solutions into the foundations of new buildings either. They are bound by one norm only: to mitigate the effects of compulsory heterosexuality wherever they find it. Mindful of the tendency within all of us to perform the role of the Dictator, Out-Siders will build, as Woolf suggested, with easily combustible material. Since contingency surrounds each situation, bricks and mortar are too apt to become traditions that must be followed, methods that must be utilized.

That the teachers and learners of the new college and those working within an *Out-Siders' Praxis* continually look for new books and new pictures is a testament to their constant search for better, challenging ideas. Without constantly challenging our thoughts, the solutions of today become the barriers of tomorrow. Even easily combustible material can become a prison.

Therefore, like those in Woolf's new college, Out-Siders are charged with keeping abreast of new concepts produced by those involved in research about sexual identity as well as education as a whole.

The education of the new college and the *Out-Siders' Praxis* recognize the necessity for creating situations in which discourse, conversation, can take place to forge new understandings among diverse people. It was with this in mind that Woolf argued that the new education must not segregate and specialize, but combine. Out-Siders are likewise committed to combining: combining, instead of separating, peers with miserable distinctions of heterosexual/homosexual; combining by teaching whole students, not disembodied minds; combining by bridging the abyss that has been created between identity collectives and social constructionists; combining by giving all Out-Siders their due respect in working toward social change. The Out-Siders' commitment to out-sighting, to living a life fully awake to injustice, harm, and inequity, helps Out-Siders understand the importance of finding ways to "combine" instead of separate.

Woolf also conceived of an Outsiders' Society, a society of professional women that had as its aim to work toward peace, specifically by finding, exposing, and changing instances of abuse in the professions. Woolf's Outsiders agree to bear certain constraints to work for the betterment of women in society and to thereby transform society in the process. Like the women of the Outsiders' Society, Out-Siders agree to educate themselves not only about professional practices but about the needs and issues of their lesbian and gay students and colleagues. They understand that practicing expertly is key to successfully introducing potentially disruptive topics and ideas. Therefore, like the Outsiders' Society, preparation and experimentation in the classroom are critical.

In addition, the *Out-Siders' Praxis*'s call to out-sighting and out-citing means that Out-Siders, like Woolf's Outsiders, make it their business to make certain that all who are capable are allowed to earn a living wage. In both cases there is resolve to work against discrimination and harassment that keep worthy candidates from gaining or maintaining positions in education. Because these issues are of central importance to Woolf's Outsiders and Out-Siders, both groups refrain from being party to discriminatory practices in their educational institutions, professions, or the societies to which they belong. They both work to be knowledgeable about situations in which institutions only pay lip service to equity, exposing those abuses and urging the groups, societies, and institutions with which they are affiliated to make good on their promises.

Those in the Outsiders' Society and those working within an *Out-Siders' Praxis* assume these constraints voluntarily. In the process, they create a more moral society and a moral way of life for themselves. Finally, Woolf's Outsiders and this discussion's Out-Siders understand the place of the aesthetic, the voices of poets. In the final analysis, Outsiders and Out-Siders alike must create, invent, restore, and intervene with the attitude of artists. Both must come to see the dream of peace, the dream of freedom, and represent it to the world.

Does It Make a Difference?

Now that I have conceptualized an *Out-Siders' Praxis*, the pragmatic question must be raised: Can conceptualizing Out-Sider groups based on out-citing, out-sighting, out-siding, and out-siting make any difference to the outsiders for whom it was designed? Is the multipronged practical approach of the *Out-Siders' Praxis* anything more than an eclectic conglomeration of ideas from various *Praxes in re Sexual Identity*? Further, if we are conversant with the major issues in lesbian and gay lives, does it really matter if that knowledge is grounded in a sound theoretical disposition? Is there any particular value in having the specific curricular designs of teachers and teacher educators grounded in this *Out-Siders' Praxis*, instead of in one of the existing *Praxes in re Sexual Identity* or even in no *praxis* at all?

Rita Kissen, author of *The Last Closet: The Real Lives of Lesbian and Gay Teachers*, is of the opinion that the theoretical foundations of sexual identity do not matter in the practical situations in which lesbian and gay teachers find themselves. She writes:

> In the day-to-day lives of gay teachers, it doesn't matter much whether homosexuality is an identity, a set of behaviors, an essential inborn characteristic, or a chosen "lifestyle." What matters is that vast numbers of dedicated teachers do not feel safe in school, for reasons that have nothing to do with their merit as educators.[59]

While I generally agree with many of Kissen's observations, analyses, and conclusions in *The Last Closet*, I strongly disagree with her assessment on this point.

If it were possible to divorce theory and action completely, Kissen's supposition might be defensible. Feminist philosophers have already demonstrated that such a complete divorce is impossible, even when that is the aim. Just because theory and action are not consciously brought to bear on each other does not mean that the relationship between them simply dissolves. Such is not the case.

Dewey, for instance, maintained that all true reasoning has practical elements. He believed that the philosophical decision to create an intellectual

hierarchy that honored theory over practice was not only ineffective in separating the two but served the purposes of kings of various kinds, including
technocratic and philosophical "experts."[60] Dewey's educational philosophy
maintains that theories are always informed by practice, even when theorists
do not acknowledge it. In fact, much feminist research has charged not only
that this separation has been unsuccessful but that failing to recognize the
connections between theory and practice has produced bad theory and bad
acts. Virginia Woolf demonstrated how failure to recognize the theoretical
foundations of our belief systems has led to faulty sight and thereby faulty
theory. When she inserted "Arthur's sister" into the phrase "S knows that
'p,'" for example, she found that philosophers had unwittingly conceived
"normal" knowers as male, white, educated, Western European, and heterosexual.

Therefore, just as Dewey's and Woolf's observations contribute to our understanding that our theories are always informed by actions, so are actions
always informed by theory. Over twenty years ago Charlotte Bunch recognized the importance of this interplay because of her work as a lesbian feminist academician and as a women's rights activist. She believed that the
women's movement was ineffective in dealing with backlash because of a
failure to understand the specific constructions of the forces that opposed
feminist undertakings and the consequent lack of analysis. Bunch argued
that when feminists despair, burn out, and give up, they often do so because
the theoretical framework did not adequately include the ways in which
individual activities contribute to significant victories.[61]

Does it make any practical difference then to any Out-Sider whether an
Out-Siders' Praxis is based on out-citing and out-siting? I believe it makes a
significant difference. I offer a couple of brief and simple examples. Say that
a group of lesbian and gay teachers meet over lunch (out-siding) and that the
conversation comes around to several incidents that some of the group had
witnessed where gay students were verbally harassed by other students in the
hallways (out-citing). The group of teachers decides to plan some educational sessions to address these concerns (out-citing). They conduct the sessions with the students, and the situation improves (out-citing). Busy with
other school activiⱢies, they go on to other priorities (forgetting out-siting).
Soon they begin witnessing verbal harassment again, this time accompanied
by some physicality (out-sighting). If the teachers did not understand how
their work was out-sited—that is, how it was located on a field of power
relations—they might be inclined to believe that the anti–lesbian and gay
prejudice in the school was completely intractable, and thus fall into a dis-
couraged apathy. Or the teachers might believe that the problem was the ed-

ucational method they used in the sessions. When the teachers understand out-siting, they need not feel either despondent or impotent. Instead, they understand that the backlash is inevitable if they do not maintain that "hyper- and pessimistic activism" that Foucault talks about. They understand where to focus their energies.

Consider one other simple example. Suppose that a university is considering instituting health care insurance coverage for domestic partners. Several lesbian faculty members who support this proposed policy begin meeting and lobbying the administration and other faculty members for support until the policy is approved (out-citing). A few of the women believe their presence has made such a difference (out-sight) that they should continue to meet and work toward other lesbian- and gay-friendly policy initiatives (out-siding); but most of the women in the group vote to disband the group and give their full attention to hectic teaching and research schedules. Without understanding the series–group concept underlying out-citing, the women who wanted to continue meeting are likely to perceive the others as having somehow "betrayed the sisterhood," or they may view the splintering of the group as the inevitable end of identity collectives. When the women understand the series–group dynamic inherent in out-citing, hurt feelings can be minimized by comprehending that the dissolution of the group back into a series is a normal, common, and predictable occurrence. Just because the group dissolves into a series does not mean that the series cannot be motivated into action again when another practico-inert issue arises. Nor does it mean that the group members would be opposed to continued out-siding by sustaining the friendships begun in the group. If the teachers' theoretical understanding of the group was based in the *Praxis of Resistance* or *Performativity*, they might well view the dissolution of the group as a consequence of the ineffectiveness of identity collectives. If their theoretical bases were in the *Praxis of Coming Out* or *Location*, they might despair about women's inability to form lasting friendships in a patriarchal social system or about the difficulty of sustaining coalitions.

Given the foregoing explanation, I believe that Kissen's view—that it makes no difference to lesbian and gay teachers whether homosexuality is an identity, a set of behaviors, an essential inborn characteristic, or a chosen "lifestyle"—ignores a critical fact: we do not simply find our world; we interpret it. Consequently, our theoretical underpinnings do matter, in the ways that we human beings interpret what we see every day and in the strategies we choose to address what we find. The value of the *Out-Siders' Praxis* is not in the practical solutions that it offers but in the theoretical structure it provides, within which such practical solutions may be crafted. As soon as we can no longer think as we formerly thought, transformation becomes urgent, difficult, and possible.[62]

Out-Sider Futures

The *Out-Siders' Praxis* is a challenge to institutionalized, dualistic logic embedded in educational institutions. Such thinking has long served as the ideal framework for our social organization despite the work of numerous feminists and educational pioneers such as Dewey to unseat such dangerous dualisms. Students who equate difference with opposites necessarily equate opposites with good and bad, or better and worse. We need to follow the opening created by the *Out-Siders' Praxis* that chooses to draw action alternatives from many lines of thought. We must carefully examine the ways that we teach our students how to learn, building out-sight.

Therefore, Out-Siders' futures must out-cite about the extent to which our educational experiences have cemented our ideas of student development around behaviors that have been presumed to be "normal." Presumed heterosexuality, when espoused as the norm for social and sexual behavior and identity, is an artifact of oppression that invites Out-Siders to intervene in its continuing mis-educative agenda. Claiming a position as an Out-Sider who is out-siting takes advantage of the ethical benefits of being positioned as an "other," helping us suspend ourselves from full immersion in the assumed consensus of social reality. Therefore, the *Out-Siders' Praxis* motivates us to constant out-sighting by examining the supposed "truths" that we set before children, youth, and adults in our classrooms. It asks us to challenge the arrogant presumption that all people are heterosexual until proven otherwise. Out-Siders sharing their experiences with one another can open dynamic ways of understanding and extracting ourselves from entrenched beliefs.

The narratives of lesbian and gay outsiders indicate that insufficient attention has been paid to the influence of conservative religious thought within the five *Praxes in re Sexual Identity*. If Out-Siders are to out-cite effectively, they must have knowledge about the ways in which, and the extent to which, religion affects outsiders. Further, Out-Siders need to engage in critical research about the effects of sex education programs, particularly when they have been commandeered by organized efforts of religious and political conservatives. Out-Siders lacking this out-sight will be ill-prepared to face well-organized and well-funded opposition to fact-based sex education.

Much of the research on lesbian, gay, bisexual, and transgender youth has been centered on the risks associated with silence about LGBTQ issues. Not enough has been done to consider the risks and costs of extinguishing unique and diverse individuals. We have not yet explored in any detail how dominant groups use and abuse resources to destroy those "others" who serve as the constitutive outside to the inside groups. Studying how heterosexual norms are privileged in educational discourse offers special out-sight into the distribution, use, and abuse of power and privilege.

While I believe that this *Out-Siders' Praxis* has much to offer people in North American education who want to transform situations negatively affecting lesbian and gay students and colleagues, I remain deeply troubled about several issues that are commanding center stage in ongoing work about sexual identity. The abyss between essentialist and social constructionist thought looms large. Several theorists have sought to bridge the gap created by essentialist–social constructionist debates, and I add my efforts with the *Out-Siders' Praxis* to this important work. However, if scholars are to lift themselves from the linguistic paralysis that currently plagues feminism and lesbian and gay studies, this work must be undertaken with vigilance and perseverance.

Out-Siders must be especially careful about stopping conversations that hold the potential for bridge building. While I know of no one writing about gender or sexuality that identifies as essentialist any longer, most of those who are trying to think just short of radical social constructionism fear having an "essentialist" label hung around their necks. Once the "essentialist" label surfaces, discussion is foreclosed even more quickly than when "God's will" is brought to bear on the conversation. Such labels undermine a spirit of inquiry and scholarly discourse. Labels serve the interests of those who do not wish to deal with ideas they find challenging or for which they have no ready answers. It also allows those doing the labeling to forego the work often needed to understand complex ideas by reducing them to a single word and dismissing them out of hand.

Therefore, because social constructionists are now the hegemonic group in secular sexual identity inquiry, they bear a special burden for keeping the conversation open. To do otherwise is to support heterosexist ideology's hierarchical structure, just as surely as whites, heterosexuals, and men have maintained dominance by dismissing "other" thinking without ever making an effort to understand what is being said. The *Out-Siders' Praxis* that I have envisioned holds out the hope that the bridge across the abyss that has formed between identity collectives and social constructionists may not be only a theoretical construct but a path for much-needed conversation.

This task presents practical and intellectual difficulties for social constructionists, for despite the fact that social constructionism has enlarged our thought, the fact remains that as practical matters go, social constructionism is fraught with practical problems. The fact that political conservatives have co-opted this theoretical stance for use in justifying conversion therapies and for combating opposite-sex characteristics in toddlers does not, in and of itself, mean that social constructionism must be eschewed in political strategies.[63] Certainly political conservatives have found ways to co-opt practically every insight about sexual identity. However, conservatives' especial success with social constructionists' formulations indicates that those who work in this arena must thoroughly understand out-siting and tread carefully, if the work is to effect more good than harm for lesbian and gay outsiders.

We live in a culture deeply divided about identity. Cognizant of that fact, we must remember that just because we choose not to *identify* ourselves based on one of any number of identity categories does not mean that we will not be so *identified* by others. Henry Louis Gates Jr. says that it is simply utopian to think that we can now disavow our social identities and dismantle our schemes of difference.[64] It is naïve to think that because one chooses to see race, gender, or sexual orientation as merely a social construct, society will simply follow suit.

Like Gates, I do not deny the importance of social constructionism at the level of theory. Yet, Gates goes on to say

> it's important to remember that "race" is *only* a sociopolitical category, nothing more. At the same time—in terms of its practical performative force—that doesn't help me when I'm trying to get a taxi on the corner of 125th and Lenox Avenue. ("Please sir, it's only a metaphor.")[65]

William Hart also believes that identity categories need to be continually deconstructed. However, his own out-sight has suggested that, politically, more can be done in the name of "nature" than in the name of "construction."[66] That these political issues abound does not mean that the important work in social constructionism should be abandoned. It does mean that Out-Siders must be fully cognizant of the dangers, as well as the potential, inherent in social constructionism.

Further, I share Janice Raymond's concern that we are witnessing a problematic trend that has occurred in other areas of scholarship, namely, that scholars are turning away from the responsibility to generate ideals.[67] Most of the scholarly work that is now being generated on issues concerning identity is invested entirely in deconstruction, reducing questions to analysis of language, while the material facts that concern the daily lives of LGBTQ persons are eschewed as banal and simplistic. Raymond claims that too little "materialism" fosters an abstract consciousness that distracts from the "real" conditions of people's lives.[68] This abstract scholarship, which may be intellectually titillating, is often as far removed from practicality as the modernist analytics to which much of postmodernism has reacted. Abstract philosophy and criticism that make no attempt to out-site, to touch the real concerns of people in jeopardy, is a luxury of the well-fed, fully employed, safely housed, and legally protected. Out-Siders cannot afford to luxuriate at the expense of those who remain emotionally and physically underfed; underemployed; unsafe at work, home, and school, with few legal protections. That means Out-Siders must out-side by connecting with those that stand behind the chosen images of liberal college campuses. I value the enormous potential that "queering the discourse" may have for education. However, if we forget those for whom we are decentering heterosexist ideology, then it becomes simply another academic exercise in which we are showing a complete lack of out-sight.

Jim Garrison has cited similar concerns about appropriating social constructionism in education:

> When postmodernists fail to recognize the practical moral value of the "relatively stable," they fall into nihilism. Instead of enjoying the daimonic dance, they deconstruct frantically. Ironically, if they were more morally responsible, they could be less serious. They lack phronesis. Such practical wisdom allows us to recognize the best possibility, the highest value, or end-in-view, in the precarious that may be actualized in the present.[69]

Garrison goes on to assert a truly pragmatic viewpoint: if deconstruction can contribute to greater joy and meaning in life, then we should delight in it; if it is destructive, then we should shun it. There is always a requirement for critique and possible deconstruction, Garrison says, but we should immediately follow the act of deconstruction with reconstruction.[70] Both are needed for growth. Critique leads to out-sight. But if we are to believe Garrison, Woolf, and Foucault, out-sighting is useless unless accompanied by the action of out-citing, the innovation of out-siding, the way we can effectively set agendas through out-siting.

Social constructionists have typically eschewed the work of generating ideals, since they contend that all knowledge, identity, and realities are temporary and contingent. Garrison, however, suggests that we can work with that which is relatively, if only temporarily, stable. That, too, is the point of understanding out-siting as a framework for the *Out-Siders' Praxis*. It allows one to assume responsibility for the site she or he occupies while engaging in critical dialogue with, or resistance against, occupants of other positions, cognizant of their political implications. Such a construction takes into consideration the ways that ideals may be formed, by out-siding passionately and generously with others, cognizant that those ideals are fluid and precise at specific moments in specific sites.

When the important work of creating ideals is left undone, strategic political problems follow in its wake. Charlotte Bunch advocated a theory-building model for the feminist classroom built on four parts: description, analysis, vision, and strategy.[71] When vision is leapt over, actions tend to be only tangentially related to the analysis and description of the problem because the actor is not completely clear about what it is he or she is trying to accomplish. Thus, if social constructionist insight is to have any impact on the educational field, it must be allowed to benefit from accounts of what discourse looks and sounds like when it has been "queered." Without knowing the goal, one finds it is difficult to design curricular solutions. Educators and scholars must simplify, explain, and show by example what "queer" ideals could mean for education.

Out-Siders recognize the need for making all our theoretical bases in re sexual identity accessible to those they have been designed to help. Popular research in identity politics has not effectively challenged the heterosexual–homosexual binary that places the subordinate term (homosexual) in a deviant position. Queer theory offers a way to out-sight by analyzing lesbian, gay, and other sexual minority issues as by-products of oppression by deeper social, linguistic construction. The out-sights provided by queer theory are simply not available in other praxes of sexual identity. Yet, the difficulty of the texts within which these out-sights are found makes them prohibitive to most of the teachers, and even to many academicians, who might be able to translate them into workable educational goals and strategies. It would be unfortunate for educators to shun the important critiques proffered by queer theory simply because identity discourse is more readily accessible for classrooms.

Michel Foucault talked about the fact that intellectuals must remember that they are paid by society, by taxpayers. To that end, he said, we should make our intellectual work accessible to everyone as much as is possible. He continued:

> Naturally, a part of our work cannot be accessible to anybody because it is too difficult. The institution I belong to in France . . . obliges its members to make public lectures, open to anyone who wants to attend, in which we have to explain our work. We are at once researchers and people who have to explain publicly our research. I think there is in this very old institution—it dates from the sixteenth century—something very interesting. The deep meaning is, I believe, very important.[72]

If education is to benefit from the insights provided by the work of social constructionism, we must take seriously Foucault's cogent advice and make it as accessible as possible to teachers and teacher educators, who have the opportunity to directly and radically affect the practice of education. Out-Siders must provide assistance in translating this difficult theoretical work into potential educational experiments and practical suggestions. Out-Siders must use their commitment to out-siding, the knowledge gained from out-sighting, to out-cite "translations" for educators who have the opportunity to directly impact compulsory heterosexuality.

Finally, Out-Siders must not forget those nagging statistics: lesbian and gay teens account for 30 percent of all successful teen suicides; 42 percent of homeless teens are gay or lesbian; a majority of preservice teachers are more homophobic than the general population. These statistics reveal much about schools and educational practice. They reveal existing and impending tragedies. Those statistics can prompt us, however, to reconsider the acts through which children are taught and the organizational structures that surround teachers and students. They can stimulate Out-Siders' critical assessment of embedded meanings that construct even our simplest classroom methods and approaches.

Through out-sighting, Out-Siders remain wide awake and watchful about the effects and sources of compulsory heterosexuality and the abuses of such ideology in the hidden curriculum of education. Such out-sight offers Out-Siders not only the opportunity for disclosing grand episodes of social injustice but also great opportunities for improved practice.

There is, then, optimism in educational practice that proceeds from the *Out-Siders' Praxis*. It is not optimism that results from believing that things just could not be better; rather, this optimism consists in recognizing that many things are contingent, changeable, temporary, and fragile. When Out-Siders understand that the present is neither unified nor made up of timeless truths, its arbitrary nature seems more assailable, more malleable. Finally, the optimism inherent in an *Out-Siders' Praxis* consists in a profound trust in the efficacy of artists who work to create something new from what is given and who transform themselves through its creation.

Notes

1. Charlotte Bunch, "Not by Degrees: Feminist Theory and Education," in *Learning Our Way: Essays in Feminist Education*, ed. Charlotte Bunch and Sandra Pollack (Trumansburg, N.Y.: Crossing Press, 1984), 248.

2. Jim Garrison, *Dewey and Eros: Wisdom and Desire in the Art of Teaching* (New York: Teachers College Press, 1997), 13.

3. Martha C. Nussbaum, *Sex and Social Justice* (Oxford: Oxford University Press, 1999), 190–206.

4. Jane Roland Martin, *Coming of Age in Academe: Rekindling Women's Hopes and Reforming the Academy* (New York: Routledge, 2000), 136–39.

5. Ann Ferguson, "Racial Formation, Gender, and Class in U.S. Welfare State Capitalism," in *Sexual Democracy* (Boulder, Colo.: Westview Press, 1991), 114–15; quoted in Iris Marion Young, "Gender as Seriality: Thinking about Women as a Social Collective," in *Intersecting Voices: Dilemmas of Gender, Political Philosophy, and Policy* (Princeton, N.J.: Princeton University Press, 1997), 19.

6. To the point, religious conservatives have reduced social constructionist theories of sexual identity as contingent and mutable to "changeable" and have used those ideas in service of reparative and conversion therapies intended to change youth and adults into heterosexuals. Similarly, this focus on changeability has prompted a whole new rash of programs by groups allied with the Focus on the Family to target male toddlers who seem too sensitive or express interest in clothes or music and female toddlers who want to wear boots. Signs of "pre-homosexuality" are being taught to parents and teachers of infants, toddlers, and children in early primary grades. See Sharon Lerner, "Christian Conservatives Take Their Antigay Campaign to the Schools," at GLSEN Online, at http://traversearea.com/GLSEN/articles/art63.htm.

7. Jeffrey Weeks, *Invented Moralities: Sexual Values in an Age of Uncertainty* (New York: Columbia University Press, 1995), 8–13.

8. Diana Fuss, *Essentially Speaking: Feminism, Nature, and Difference* (New York: Routledge, 1989), 104.

9. Fuss, *Essentially Speaking,* 104.

10. Iris Marion Young, "Gender as Seriality," in *Intersecting Voices,* 16–17.

11. Young, "Gender as Seriality," 22–23.

12. Young, "Gender as Seriality," 24–25.

13. Young, "Gender as Seriality," 28–31.

14. Young, "Gender as Seriality," 33.

15. Young, "Gender as Seriality," 34.

16. Rita M. Kissen, *The Last Closet: The Real Lives of Lesbian and Gay Teachers* (Portsmouth, N.H.: Heinemann, 1996), 110.

17. Kissen, *The Last Closet,* 110–12.

18. Virginia Uribe and Karen M. Harbeck, "Addressing the Needs of Lesbian, Gay, and Bisexual Youth: The Origins of PROJECT 10 and School-Based Intervention," in *Coming Out of the Classroom Closet: Gay and Lesbian Students, Teachers, and Curricula* (New York: Harrington Park Press, 1991), 10.

19. Uribe and Harbeck, "Addressing the Needs of Lesbian, Gay, and Bisexual Youth," 10–11.

20. Dan Woog, *School's Out: The Impact of Gay and Lesbian Issues on America's Schools* (Los Angeles: Alyson Publication, 1995), 236–37.

21. Maxine Greene, *Landscapes of Learning* (New York: Teachers College Press, 1978), 42–44.

22. Jane Roland Martin, "What Should We Do with a Hidden Curriculum When We Find One?" in *Changing the Educational Landscape: Philosophy, Women, and Curriculum* (New York: Routledge, 1994), 158–59.

23. William P. Norris, "Liberal Attitudes and Homophobic Acts: The Paradoxes of Homosexual Experience in a Liberal Institution," in Harbeck, *Coming Out of the Classroom Closet*, 81–84.

24. Weeks, *Invented Moralities*, 9.

25. Richard Rorty, "Pragmatism, Relativism, and Irrationalism," in *Consequences of Pragmatism* (Minneapolis: University of Minnesota Press, 1982), 170.

26. Harriet Malinowitz, *Textual Orientation: Lesbian and Gay Students and the Making of Discourse Communities* (Portsmouth, N.H.: Heinemann, 1995), 81.

27. Dan Woog, *School's Out: The Impact of Gay and Lesbian Issues on America's Schools* (Los Angeles: Alyson Publication, 1995), 187–95.

28. Aristotle, *The Nicomachean Ethics*, trans. Sir David Ross (Oxford: Oxford University Press, 1980), 1155.

29. Marilyn Friedman, *What Are Friends For? Feminist Perspectives on Personal Relationships and Moral Theory* (Ithaca, N.Y.: Cornell University Press, 1993), 196–206.

30. Friedman, *What Are Friends For?* 210–19.

31. Maria Pallotta-Chiarolli, "'My Moving Days': A Child's Negotiation of Multiple Lifeworlds in Relation to Gender, Ethnicity, and Sexuality," in *Queering Elementary Education: Advancing the Dialogue about Sexualities and Schooling*, ed. William J. Letts IV and James T. Sears (Lanham, Md.: Rowman and Littlefield Publishers, 1999), 71.

32. Pallotta-Chiarolli, "'My Moving Days,'" 71–80.

33. Aristotle, *The Nicomachean Ethics*, 1155.

34. John Dewey, *Art as Experience* (New York: G. P. Putnam's Sons, 1980; original, 1934), 14.

35. Dewey, *Art as Experience*, 15–17.

36. Audre Lorde, "Uses of the Erotic: The Erotic as Power," in *Sister Outsider* (Freedom, Calif.: Crossing Press, 1988), 54–55.

37. Mara Sapon-Shevin, "Using Music to Teach against Homophobia," in *Queering Elementary Education*, ed. W. Letts and J. Sears, 111–23.

38. Jim Garrison, *Dewey and Eros: Wisdom and Desire in the Art of Teaching* (New York: Teachers College Press, 1997), 80.

39. John Dewey, *Ethics*, LW 6 (original 1932), 270; quoted in Garrison, *Dewey and Eros*, 36.

40. Lorraine Code, *What Can She Know? Feminist Theory and the Construction of Knowledge* (Ithaca, N.Y.: Cornell University Press, 1991), 180.

41. GLSEN Oklahoma press release, March 19, 2001.

42. GLSEN Oklahoma press release, March 19, 2001.

43. Sapphrodykie, "The Iconoclast," in *Out and about Campus: Personal Accounts by Lesbian, Gay, Bisexual, and Transgendered College Students*, ed. Kim Howard and Annie Stevens (Los Angeles: Alyson Books, 2000), 140.

44. Kissen, *The Last Closet*, 147.

45. Woog, *School's Out*, 288.

46. Greene, *Landscapes of Learning*, 25.

47. Greene, *Landscapes of Learning*, 99–100.

48. Woog, *School's Out*, 361–63.

49. Kate Evans, "When Queer and Teacher Meet," in *Queering Elementary Education: Advancing the Dialogue about Sexualities and Schooling*, ed. William J. Letts and James T. Sears (Lanham, Md.: Rowman and Littlefield Publishers, 1999), 238–39.

50. Toby Emert and Lynne Milburn, "Sensitive Supervisors, Prepared Practicum, and 'Queer' Clients: A Training Model for Beginning Counselors," in *Overcoming Heterosexism and Homophobia: Strategies that Work*, ed. James T. Sears and Walter L. Williams (New York: Columbia University Press, 1997), 273–74.

51. Nussbaum, *Sex and Social Justice*, 37.

52. John Dewey, preface to *Experience and Education* (New York: Touchstone, 1997; original, 1938), 5.

53. Eve Kosofsky Sedgwick, *Epistemology of the Closet* (Berkeley: University of California Press, 1990), 13.

54. Center for Lesbian and Gay Studies website, http://web.gsuc.cuny.edu/clags/; LAMBDA Institute of Lesbian and Gay Studies website, www.ualberta.ca/~cbidwell/cmb/lambda.htm; Institute for Gay and Lesbian Strategic Studies, www.iglss .org/index_enhanced.asp; University of Wisconsin, Milwaukee, LGBT Studies website, www.uwm.edu/Dept/GLBCert/; San Francisco State University GLB Studies website, www.sfsu.edu/~bulletin/current/programs/gaylesbi.htm; University of Illinois GLQ Studies website, www.uic.edu/depts/quic/oglbc/resources/gay_studies.html; GLSEN website, www.glsen.org/templates/index.html; PFLAG website, www.pflag.org/.

55. Audre Lorde, "Age, Race, Class, and Sex: Women Redefining Difference," in *Sister Outsider*, 114–15.

56. Kate Evans, "When Queer and Teacher Meet," in *Queering Elementary Education*, ed. W. Letts and J. Sears, 245.

57. Woolf, *Three Guineas* (San Diego: Harcourt Brace Jovanovich, 1938), 143.

58. Woolf, *Three Guineas*, 33–35.

59. Kissen, *The Last Closet*, 4.

60. Garrison, *Dewey and Eros*, 13.

61. Bunch, "Not by Degrees," 248.

62. Michel Foucault, "Practicing Criticism," in *Michel Foucault: Politics, Philosophy, and Culture*, ed. Lawrence D. Kritzman, trans. Alan Sheridan et al. (New York: Routledge, 1990), 155.

63. See Sharon Lerner, "Christian Conservatives Take Their Antigay Campaign to the Schools," at GLSEN Online, http://traversearea.com/GLSEN/articles/art63.htm.

64. Henry Louis Gates Jr., *Loose Canons: Notes on the Culture Wars* (Oxford: Oxford University Press, 1992), 37.

65. Gates, *Loose Canons*, 37–38.

66. William D. Hart, "Sexual Orientation and the Language of Higher Law," in *Sexual Orientation and Human Rights in American Religious Discourse*, ed. Saul M. Olyan and Martha C. Nussbaum (New York: Oxford University Press, 1998), 210.

67. Janice Raymond, *A Passion for Friends: Toward a Philosophy of Female Affection* (Boston: Beacon Press, 1986), 205.

68. Raymond, *A Passion for Friends*, 206.

69. Garrison, *Dewey and Eros*, 51.

70. Garrison, *Dewey and Eros*, 52.

71. Bunch, "Not By Degrees," 248.

72. Michel Foucault, "An Interview by Stephen Riggins," in *Ethics: Subjectivity and Truth*, ed. Paul Rabinow (New York: New Press, 1997), 152.

Annotated Bibliography

Sources Containing Autobiographical Interviews and Accounts of Lesbian and Gay Educational Experiences

Casper, Virginia, and Steven B. Schultz. *Gay Parents/Straight Schools: Building Communication and Trust.* New York: Teachers College Press, 1999.

Casper and Schultz conducted scores of interviews with teachers, same-sex parents, and children of same-sex parents in New York City and several suburbs in Connecticut and New Jersey to build their database for this work. Likening parent–teacher participation in the education of children to a complicated dance, Casper and Schultz underscore the need for trust on both sides. However, the authors are also cognizant of the fact that, as with any human alliance, trust takes time and commitment to cultivate.

For gay parents, schools embody the socializing heterosexual world. Such parents feel anxious as they advocate for their children, fearing that a teacher's homophobia may spill over into how their children are treated. From the vantage point of educators, the increasing visibility of gay-headed families inserts homosexuality smack into the historically protected world of young children. Most teachers have questions that need answers, traditional practices to contravene, ideas and fears of their own to confront.

The authors contend that emphasis on "readiness," as defined by traditional developmental models, often prompts teachers to avoid discussion of lesbian and gay issues. Casper and Schultz suggest that this "readiness rubric" has eclipsed the simple notion that children don't have to understand a concept in its entirety to wrestle with it, just as Vygotsky suggested. The authors highlight strategies that parents, children, and teachers in this study have conceived to deal most effectively with these challenges.

Harbeck, Karen M., ed. *Coming Out of the Classroom Closet: Gay and Lesbian Students, Teachers, and Curricula.* New York: Harrington Park Press, 1991.

The essays in this volume explore conflicts in the educational system around homosexuality. Because most gay and lesbian educators and students remain invisible because of their internalized oppression or their very real fears of hostility, this book's stated purpose is empowerment of gay and lesbian students and educators. The essays cover a wide range of information, from the detrimental psychological and social effects of gay and lesbian invisibility and internalized homophobia to an in-depth analysis of James Sears's substantive empirical research on homophobia in preservice teachers. Other quantitative and qualitative research in the book substantiates entrenched homophobic stances on several "liberal" college campuses and glimpses how homosexuality is portrayed in health and sexuality textbooks.

Several essays in the collection suggest that gays and lesbians may actually have greater social support and legal protections than they perceive. The authors state that the refusal to be "out," triggered by intense internalized oppression, may play a major role in limiting the freedoms of gay and lesbian students and teachers. The research highlights stories of negative attitudes and incidents of discrimination. There are also reviews of case law on gay and lesbian teachers' dismissals and credential revocations, as well as recent changes in employment codes that support equal employment provisions.

Howard, Kim, and Annie Stevens, eds. *Out and about Campus: Personal Accounts by Lesbian, Gay, Bisexual, and Transgendered College Students.* Los Angeles: Alyson Books, 2000.

Personal accounts of gay and lesbian college students are collected in this book. Many students who question their sexuality or gender identity do so for the first time in college; but even for those who know going into college that they are LGBT, those years may be the first time they have had the chance to meet others like themselves or the opportunity to search out meaningful resources. A couple of these narratives take place on women's college campuses and recall joyous self-discovery. Most, however, voice the difficulties of learning to cope with gay and lesbian identities while living in a hostile environment filled with the violence, hate, and disdain from sorority and fraternity members, roommates, dorm members, teachers, and administrators. Throughout the accounts there is the pervasive presence of homophobia, gay bashing, and fear of violence. Stories tell of roommates who fled or enlisted peer, and sometimes administrative, support to engage in censure, harassment, and (too frequently) violence. Many of those whose narratives are told here have been embittered by the struggle of just trying to live and study on campus.

Jennings, Kevin, ed. *One Teacher in Ten: Gay and Lesbian Educators Tell Their Stories.* Los Angeles: Alyson Books, 1994.

This book is a collection of autobiographical essays written by gay and lesbian teachers that describes the current environment for gay and lesbian teachers and students. The majority of these teachers live on the East or West Coast, but a few are from the central United States. The narratives frequently recall the teachers' own difficult school days. Often it is the memory of those past incidents that has prompted these teachers to face the education system again, as teachers. Most of the teachers in these essays have chosen to be "out" at school, realizing that their potential as role models would be practically nonexistent from the closet.

Some of the stories, especially many of those hailing from the central part of the United States, underline the pain of trying to come out in conservative school districts with homophobic faculty and administration. In several of these stories the harassment and discrimination were so severe that teachers ultimately resigned, changed professions, or were dismissed by the school districts. The majority of the stories, however, underscore victories that resulted from the decision to be honest with colleagues, administrators, or students. The not-so-subtle theme running through these collections is that coming out is a difficult process and one that may not always be possible because of the local political and legal climate. Being out, however, is clearly the text's recommendation for the best way to have a happy life and a fulfilling teaching career.

Khayatt, Madiha Didi. *Lesbian Teachers: An Invisible Presence.* New York: State University of New York Press, 1992.

Khayatt's sociological study of lesbian teachers is both philosophically and historically sound. Khayatt's research is based on in-depth interviews with lesbian teachers in Canada. Her work has a very interesting slant because *all* of the teachers interviewed in Khayatt's research were closeted. In fact, Khayatt's purpose for this inquiry was to gain insight into the ways in which closeted lesbian teachers deal with the disjuncture in their lives and the coping strategies they have used for survival in a homophobic school system where there are few protections for lesbian teachers.

Khayatt draws on Gramsci's analysis of hegemonic classes, which asserts that the so-called democratic access of education to all classes is deceptive. Education, according to Gramsci, does not transcend class. Using Dorothy Smith, Gramsci, and several feminist theorists, Khayatt concludes that education may also fail to transcend nondominant forms of sexual identity. Khayatt maintains that the school system, as the established transmitter of dominant ideology, not only embraces patriarchal values overtly through curriculum requirements, but further implements male privilege and compels heterosexuality covertly by offering the behavior of those allowed to teach and administer as examples of what is acceptable. Since lesbians have been socially constructed as deviant, they thwart the established hegemonic social order. Therefore, while the stigma of being lesbian has dissipated somewhat in society, it has not done so at the same rate in all institutions. The conservative nature of hegemonic forces at work in the school system promotes a particular resistance by administrators to hire gay and lesbian teachers. The general fear seems to be that if young people come into contact with a gay or lesbian teacher, youth may take the teacher's life as an example of a legitimate sexual option.

Khayatt's study provides a great deal of autobiographical material about how these lesbian teachers in her study came to identify themselves as lesbians and how they deal with the day-in and day-out issues in school. She contemplates with her interviewees the difficulties of the ever-shifting tactics needed for living as honestly as possible while disclosing only enough of their lives as can be presumably tolerated by those with whom they associate at the school. Begrudging the secrecy in their lives, they believe that hiding keeps them from interacting as openly and effectively with students and colleagues as they would like. Khayatt concludes that these women will be safe as long as they do not present their lives as a valid alternative, an analysis supported by historical evidence that demonstrates that as long as lesbians are hidden, "integrated," silent, and invisible, they are allowed to exist.

Kissen, Rita M. *The Last Closet: The Real Lives of Lesbian and Gay Teachers*. Portsmouth, N.H.: Heinemann, 1996.

Using the stories of lesbian and gay teachers as the biographical material for this book, Kissen weaves together two major competing themes: a desire for authenticity and the need for safety. Unlike Khayatt, Jennings, or Woog, Kissen conducted this research from the relative privilege of heterosexuality and the security of a college teaching position. Dismissing contemporary philosophical and psychological arguments about sexual identity altogether, Kissen claims that in the day-to-day lives of gay teachers, it does not matter much whether homosexuality is an identity, a set of behaviors, an essential inborn characteristic, or a chosen "lifestyle." What does matter is that vast numbers of dedicated teachers do not feel safe in school, for reasons that have nothing to do with their merit as educators.

Kissen's reports of the dangers for teachers, real and perceived, seem far more difficult to surmount than the presentations by Jennings and Woog. Much of this difference may result from the different geographical locations of Kissen's interviewees. Whereas the majority of the essays in the books by Woog and Jennings were written by teachers living and working in large cities, Kissen primarily interviewed teachers from smaller, more conservative communities in less populated areas of the country.

Letts, William J., IV, and James T. Sears, eds. *Queering Elementary Education: Advancing the Dialogue about Sexualities and Schooling*. Lanham, Md.: Rowman & Littlefield, 1999.

This group of essays questions how teachers can challenge widely held assumptions about childhood, sexuality, and pedagogy in elementary education. The task for "queer" educators—a term they use for teachers whether gay or straight—is to create classrooms that challenge categorical thinking, promote interpersonal intelligence, and foster critical consciousness. Regardless of the Internet and Ellen, Sears argues that not much has changed in schools since his own days of playground torments and classroom disregard. Thus, he challenges educators to care enough to trust the human capacity for understanding and their own educative abilities to foster insight into the human condition. "Queering" education, he argues, means bracketing activities in which we routinely equate sexual identities with sexual acts, privilege heterosexuality, and presume sexual destinies. "Queer" teachers, then, are those who develop curricula and pedagogy that afford every child dignity rooted in self-worth and esteem for others.

Today the hidden and not-so-hidden costs of homophobia and heterosexism are no longer being borne solely by well-meaning educators or harassed children. School districts confront multimillion-dollar lawsuits. For example, Jamie Nabozny, a Wisconsin middle-school student, was repeatedly kicked unconscious and urinated on, while also suffering many lesser torments. The principal lamely warned him to expect such treatment if he chose to be openly gay. A jury found this principal and two other administrators guilty of violating Nabozny's rights; the family received an out-of-court settlement worth $900,000.

Sears maintains that it is important to discuss homosexuality in elementary school because it is already present in children's lives. Given the amount of gender and sexual information that comes from the media, public spaces, and peer groups, elementary educators could not keep children from learning about homosexuality if they wanted to. Whether children learn about homosexuality from teachers or peers will heavily influence how much of that information is inaccurate and bigoted. Several contributors to this volume worry about the unstated assumption in schools that says that teachers should treat all children as if they will become heterosexual. The likelihood is that at least one child in each of those classes will grow up to be gay or lesbian. Further, there is probably at least one child in every class that has a homosexual family member. Sometimes children have been told not to discuss this situation at school, fearing that he or she will be laughed at or harassed by peers or the teacher. This situation creates a difficult burden for a child to bear. All children need the freedom to feel that they can discuss their families in the classroom without fear or embarrassment.

Educators know that what is *not* taught in school also teaches—the omissions, gaps, and silences take their toll. Psychologists and critical theorists have shown the negative impact of children's not seeing themselves represented in the curriculum. These essays are dedicated to exploring ways in which gay and lesbian themes can enter into classroom talk—from literature to music, social studies to drama. One question repeatedly asked by the various authors is why so many teachers "wait" for gay and lesbian issues to come up, rather than create situations for open discussion. There is a general consensus among these essayists that such hesitancy is due to the teachers' limited knowledge and lack of comfort on the topic of sexual diversity, a situation clearly begging the attention of teacher educators.

McNaron, Toni A. H. *Poisoned Ivy: Lesbian and Gay Academics Confronting Homophobia.* Philadelphia: Temple University Press, 1997.

This book is based on qualitative research, interviews with over three hundred college teachers with at least fifteen years experience, and it examines the extent of change for lesbian and gay faculty on college campuses. While McNaron believed that many fully closeted faculty would respond to her request for information, she found a resolute lack of interest in airing grievances, even anonymously. McNaron states that she was astonished at the lack of concrete changes in attitudes and policies. She found that even most faculty members who are out to friends and colleagues are not out to students and in classes. Further, while many colleges had added the term *sexual orientation* to nondiscrimination policies, most had failed to back up that admonition with actions.

Happily, there were a few campuses in her study that appeared to be genuinely lesbian- and gay-friendly; but in the majority of the cases, faculty, staff, and students continued to experience hostility, ignorance, trivialization, and hateful prejudice, all of which reinforce an atmosphere of fear in which the need for invisibility lingers. Faculty members wrote about the research in which they wanted to engage but decided to abandon after a department chair offered "advice" or when tenure committees trivialized those research interests. These academicians were bitter and resentful toward the institutions that failed them.

The narratives throughout the book are clear: most faculty will not risk coming out unless and until their presidents, deans, chairs, and colleagues show them through direct word and deed that these actions will be not only tolerated but valued. McNaron makes the point that despite the handful of lesbian and gay academic researchers who have been able to base their careers on their sexuality, they are not representative of the overwhelming majority of gay and lesbian faculty members, whose lives are far from idyllic, even far from equal to their colleagues' situations.

Sears, James T., and Walter L. Williams, eds. *Overcoming Heterosexism and Homophobia: Strategies That Work.* New York: Columbia University Press, 1997.

Sears and Williams question the lesbian and gay movement's riveted focus on politics. They claim that a political approach cannot be effective without addressing prejudicial attitudes and institutionalized discrimination in the general population. Williams cites research that demonstrates that the most effective way to change homophobic attitudes is through one-to-one personal contacts of individuals with whom others share an ongoing association. Such repeated one-to-one discussion is shown to be more effective than all the parades, protests, political lobbying, workshops, and educational lectures put together. The editors further support a top-down antibias approach for hierarchical institutions such as corporations. Cutting down on prejudicial behaviors, from joking to violence, leads to a gradual decline in prejudicial attitudes as well.

Survey results cited in this book reveal that people who exhibit the most negative responses to homosexuals are those that believe that homosexuality is learned. There are also significant relationships among demographic variables, such as gender, race, degree of religiosity, age, and geographic residence; personal beliefs and traits, such as sexual conservatism, racism, sexism, and authoritarianism; and heterosexism/homophobia. A reasonable generalization based on the research is that those harboring negative attitudes about homosexuality are more likely to live in the Midwest or the South or to have grown up in rural areas or small towns, as compared with those less likely to harbor such attitudes. Most research studies have also demonstrated that adult males often harbor more intense homophobic attitudes or feelings than do females, are more concerned about male homosexuality than lesbianism, and are more disturbed by lesbianism than are heterosexual females.

These essays evidence beliefs that heterosexism and homophobia, despite their tenacity and widespread presence, can be reduced through purposive intervention affecting values, beliefs, and opinions in a variety of settings. Several essays focus on how various gay and lesbian groups have worked with Asian Americans, Latino/a immigrants, and African American communities to reduce bias in both groups simultaneously. Other essays suggest creative approaches for specific lessons that have been used to reduce homophobia and heterosexism.

Woog, Dan. *School's Out: The Impact of Gay and Lesbian Issues on America's Schools.* Los Angeles: Alyson Publication, 1995.

Lesbian and gay teachers are the primary subjects of this set of biographical essays. The narratives are overwhelmingly from the East and West coasts, but there are a few from the Great Plains and Midwest. Woog clearly advocates coming out as the best strategy for a successful and satisfying teaching career, but he is also cognizant of the fact that the risks of coming out vary significantly between areas in large urban settings and those in small towns and rural communities.

In addition to the stories of particular teachers, Woog also highlights several important programs that have been established to provide support for lesbian and gay teachers and students.

Selected Bibliography

Books

Addams, Jane. *Twenty Years at Hull-House*. Urbana: University of Illinois Press, 1900.

Aisenberg, Nadya, and Mona Harrington. *Women of Academe: Outsiders in the Sacred Grove*. Amherst: University of Massachusetts Press, 1988.

Altman, Dennis. *Homosexual: Oppression and Liberation*. New York: Outerbridge and Dienstfrey, 1971.

Anderson, Rob, and Kenneth N. Cissna. *The Martin Buber–Carl Rogers Dialogue*. Albany: State University of New York Press, 1997.

Arendt, Hannah. *Between Past and Future: Eight Exercises in Political Thought*. 1954. Reprint, New York: Penguin Books, 1993.

Aristotle. *The Nicomachean Ethics*. Translated by Sir David Ross. Oxford: Oxford University Press, 1980.

Atwill, Janet M. *Rhetoric Reclaimed: Aristotle and the Liberal Arts Tradition*. Ithaca, N.Y.: Cornell University Press, 1998.

Beemyn, Brett, and Mickey Eliason, eds. *Queer Studies: A Lesbian, Gay, Bisexual, and Transgender Anthology*. New York: New York University Press, 1996.

Bell, Ruth, and other co-authors of *Our Bodies, Ourselves* and *Ourselves and Our Children*, with members of the Teen Book Project. *Changing Bodies, Changing Lives*. Revised and updated. New York: Vintage Books, 1988.

Bernstein, Richard J. *Beyond Objectivism and Relativism: Science, Hermeneutics, and Praxis*. Philadelphia: University of Pennsylvania Press, 1983.

Besner, Hilda F., and Charlotte I. Spungin. *Gay and Lesbian Students: Understanding Their Needs*. Philadelphia: Taylor and Francis, 1995.

———. *Training for Professionals Who Work with Gays and Lesbians in Educational and Workplace Settings*. Washington, D.C.: Taylor and Francis, 1998.

Bordo, Susan. "The Body and the Reproduction of Femininity: A Feminist Appropriation of Foucault." In *Gender/Body/Knowledge*, edited by Alison M. Jaggar and Susan R. Bordo. New Brunswick, N.J.: Rutgers University Press, 1989.

Boston Women's Health Book Collective. *The New Our Bodies, Ourselves*. New York: Simon and Schuster, 1992.

———. *Our Bodies, Ourselves*. Boston: New England Free Press, 1971; New York: Simon and Schuster, 1973.

———. *Our Bodies, Ourselves*. Revised and expanded. New York: Simon and Schuster, 1984.

———. *Our Bodies, Ourselves for the New Century*. New York: Simon and Schuster, 1998.

Boswell, John. *Christianity, Social Tolerance, and Homosexuality: Gay People in Western Europe from the Beginning of the Christian Era to the Fourteenth Century*. Chicago: University of Chicago Press, 1981.

———. *Same-Sex Unions in Premodern Europe*. New York: Vintage Books, 1995.

Buber, Martin. *Between Man and Man*. Translated by Ronald Gregor Smith. New York: MacMillan, 1965.

———. *I and Thou*. Translated by Walter Kaufman. New York: Simon and Schuster, 1970.

Bunch, Charlotte, and Sandra Pollack, eds. *Learning Our Way: Essays in Feminist Education*. Trumansburg, N.Y.: Crossing Press, 1984.

Butler, Judith. *Bodies That Matter: On the Discursive Limits of "Sex."* New York: Routledge, 1993.

———. *Excitable Speech: A Politics of the Performative*. New York: Routledge, 1997.

———. *Gender Trouble: Feminism and the Subversion of Identity*. New York: Routledge, 1990.

Card, Claudia, ed. *Feminist Ethics*. Lawrence: University Press of Kansas, 1991.

Chaska, Norma L. *The Nursing Profession: A Time to Speak*. New York: McGraw-Hill, 1983.

Cixous, Helene. *The Helene Cixous Reader*. Edited by Susan Seller. New York: Routledge, 1999.

Code, Lorraine. *What Can She Know? Feminist Theory and the Construction of Knowledge*. Ithaca, N.Y.: Cornell University Press, 1991.

Collins, Patricia Hill. *Black Feminist Thought: Knowledge, Consciousness, and the Politics of Empowerment*. New York: Routledge, 1991.

Daly, Mary. *Beyond God the Father*. 1973. Reprint, Boston: Beacon Press, 1985.

———. *Gyn/Ecology: The Metaethics of Radical Feminism*. 1978. Reprint, Boston: Beacon Press, 1990.

De Beauvoir, Simone. *The Second Sex*. Paris: Librairie Gallimard, 1949; New York: Vintage Books, 1989.

d'Emilio, John, and Estelle B. Freedman. *Intimate Matters: A History of Sexuality in America*. 2nd ed. Chicago: University of Chicago Press, 1997.

Dewey, John. *Art as Experience*. 1934. Reprint, New York: G. P. Putnam's Sons, 1980.

———. *The Child and the Curriculum*. 1902. Reprint, Chicago: University of Chicago Press, 1990.

———. *Democracy and Education*. 1916. Reprint, New York: Free Press, 1966.

———. *Experience and Education*. 1938. Reprint, New York: Touchstone, 1997.

———. *Human Nature and Conduct*. 1922. Reprint, Carbondale: Southern Illinois University Press, 1988.

———. *The School and Society*. 1900. Reprint, Chicago: University of Chicago Press, 1990.

Diamond, Irene, and Lee Quinby, eds. *Feminism and Foucault: Reflections on Resistance*. Boston: Northeastern University Press, 1988.

Diller, Ann, Barbara Houston, Kathryn Pauly Morgan, and Maryann Ayim. *The Gender Question in Education: Theory, Pedagogy, and Politics*. Boulder, Colo.: Westview Press, 1996.

Donovan, Josephine. *Feminist Theory: The Intellectual Traditions of American Feminism*. New York: Continuum Publishing, 1994.

DuBois, W. E. B. *The Souls of Black Folk*. 1903. Reprint, New York: Penguin Group, 1969.

Duberman, Martin, Martha Vicinus, and George Chauncey Jr. *Hidden from History: Reclaiming the Gay and Lesbian Past*. New York: Penguin Group, 1989.

Faderman, Lillian, ed. *Chloe plus Olivia: An Anthology of Lesbian Literature from the Seventeenth Century to the Present*. New York: Viking Press, 1994.

———. *Surpassing the Love of Men: Romantic Friendship and Love between Women from the Renaissance to the Present*. New York: Morrow, 1981.

———. *To Believe in Women: What Lesbians Have Done for America—A History*. Boston: Houghton Mifflin, 1999.

Firestone, Shulamith. *The Dialectic of Sex: The Case for Feminist Revolution*. New York: William Morrow, 1970.

Flexner, Eleanor, and Ellen Fitzpatrick. *Century of Struggle: The Woman's Rights Movement in the United States*. 1959. Reprint, Cambridge, Mass.: Belknap Press / Harvard University Press, 1996.

Foucault, Michel. *Discipline and Punish: The Birth of the Prison*. Translated by Alan Sheridan. Paris: Editions Gallimard, 1975; translation, New York: Vintage Books, 1997.

———. *Ethics: Subjectivity and Truth*. Edited by Paul Rabinow. New York: New Press, 1997.

———. *The Foucault Reader*. Edited by Paul Rabinow. New York: Pantheon Books, 1984.

———. *The History of Sexuality: An Introduction*. Vol. 1 of 3. Translated by Robert Hurley. Paris: Editions Gallimard, 1976; translation, New York: Vintage Books, 1990.

———. *The History of Sexuality: The Use of Pleasure*. Vol. 2 of 3. Translated by Robert Hurley. Paris: Editions Gallimard, 1984; translation, New York: Vintage Books, 1990.

————. *The History of Sexuality: The Care of the Self*. Vol. 3 of 3. Translated by Robert Hurley. Paris: Editions Gallimard, 1984; translation, New York: Vintage Books, 1988.

————. *Madness and Civilization: A History of Insanity in the Age of Reason*. Translated by Richard Howard. Paris: Librairie Plon, 1961; translation, New York: Vintage Books, 1988.

————. *Michel Foucault: Politics, Philosophy, and Culture*. Edited by Lawrence D. Kritzman. Translated by Alan Sheridan and others. New York: Routledge, 1990.

————. *Power/Knowledge: Selected Interviews and Other Writings, 1972–1977*. Edited and translated by Colin Gordon. New York: Pantheon Books, 1980.

Freire, Paulo. *Education for Critical Consciousness*. Translated and edited by Myra Bergman. Santiago, Chile: Institute for Agricultural Reform, 1969; translation, New York: Continuum Publishing, 1994.

————. *Pedagogy of the Oppressed*. Translated by Myra Bergman Ramos. New York: Continuum Publishing, 1993.

Friedan, Betty. *The Feminine Mystique*. New York: Dell, 1963.

Friedman, Marilyn. *What Are Friends For? Feminist Perspectives on Personal Relationships and Moral Theory*. Ithaca, N.Y.: Cornell University Press, 1993.

Frye, Marilyn. *The Politics of Reality: Essays in Feminist Theory*. Freedom, Calif.: Crossing Press, 1983.

Fuss, Diana. *Essentially Speaking: Feminism, Nature, and Difference*. New York: Routledge, 1989.

Fuss, Diana, ed. *Inside/Out: Lesbian Theories, Gay Theories*. New York: Routledge, 1991.

Gadamer, Hans-Georg. *Reason in the Age of Science*. Translated by Frederick G. Lawrence. Cambridge, Mass.: MIT Press, 1996.

Garrison, Jim. *Dewey and Eros: Wisdom and Desire in the Art of Teaching*. New York: Teachers College Press, 1997.

————, ed. *The New Scholarship on Dewey*. Boston: Kluwer, 1995.

Gramsci, Antonio. *The Antonio Gramsci Reader*. Edited by David Forgacs. Translated by Quintin Hoare and others. New York: New York University Press, 2000.

Greene, Maxine. *Landscapes of Learning*. New York: Teachers College Press, 1978.

Griffin, Gabrielle, and Sonya Andermahr, eds. *Straight Studies Modified: Lesbian Interventions in the Academy*. London: Cassell, 1997.

Grumet, Madeleine R. *Bitter Milk: Women and Teaching*. Amherst: University of Massachusetts Press, 1988.

Harris, Louis, and associates. *Hostile Hallways: The AAUW Survey on Sexual Harassment in America's Schools*. Washington, D.C.: American Association of University Women Educational Foundation, 1993.

Hekman, Susan J., ed. *Feminist Interpretations of Michel Foucault*. University Park: Pennsylvania State University Press, 1996.

Hillyer, Barbara. *Feminism and Disability*. Norman: University of Oklahoma Press, 1993.

Hoagland, Sarah Lucia. *Lesbian Ethics*. Palo Alto, Calif.: Institute of Lesbian Studies, 1988.

hooks, bell. *Teaching to Transgress: Education as the Practice of Freedom*. New York: Routledge, 1994.

Hull, Gloria T., Patricia Bell Scott, and Barbara Smith, eds. *All the Women Are White, All the Black Are Men, but Some of Us Are Brave: Black Women's Studies*. New York: Feminist Press, 1982.

Irigaray, Luce. *An Ethics of Sexual Difference*. Translated by Carolyn Burke and Gillian C. Gill. Paris: Les Editions de Minuit, 1984; translation, Ithaca, N.Y.: Cornell University Press, 1993.

———. *je, tu, nous: Toward a Culture of Difference*. Translated by Alison Martin. Paris: Editions Grasset & Fasquelle, 1990; translation, New York: Routledge, 1993.

James, William. *Pragmatism*. 1907. Reprint, New York: Dover Publications, 1995.

Jennings, Kevin, ed. *Becoming Visible: A Reader in Gay and Lesbian History for High School and College Students*. Los Angeles: Alyson Books, 1994.

Karnos, David D., and Robert G. Shoemaker, eds. *Falling in Love with Wisdom: American Philosophers Talk about their Calling*. Oxford: Oxford University Press, 1993.

Kersey, Shirley Nelson, ed. *Classics in the Education of Girls and Women*. Metuchen, N.J.: Scarecrow Press, 1981.

Klaich, Delores. *Woman plus Woman*. 1974. Reprint, Tallahassee, Fla.: Naiad Press, 1989.

Kristeva, Julia. *The Kristeva Reader*. Edited by Toril Moi. Translated by Leon S. Roudiez and others. New York: Columbia University Press, 1986.

Lasser, Carol, ed. *Educating Men and Women Together: Coeducation in a Changing World*. Urbana: University of Illinois Press, 1987.

Lorde, Audre. *Sister Outsider*. Freedom, Calif.: Crossing Press, 1988.

Maher, Frances A., and Mary Kay Thompson Tetreault. *The Feminist Classroom: An Inside Look at How Professors and Students Are Transforming Higher Education for a Diverse Society*. New York: BasicBooks, 1994.

Malinowitz, Harriet. *Textual Orientations: Lesbian and Gay Students and the Making of Discourse Communities*. Portsmouth, N.H.: Heinemann, 1995.

Marshall, James D. *Michel Foucault: Personal Autonomy and Education*. Boston: Kluwer, 1996.

Martin, Jane Roland. *Changing the Educational Landscape: Philosophy, Women, and Curriculum*. New York: Routledge, 1994.

———. *Coming of Age in Academe: Rekindling Women's Hopes and Reforming the Academy*. New York: Routledge, 2000.

———. *Reclaiming a Conversation: The Ideal of the Educated Woman*. New Haven, Conn.: Yale University Press, 1985.

———. *The Schoolhome: Rethinking Schools for Changing Families*. Cambridge, Mass.: Harvard University Press, 1992.

Marx, Carl, and Friedrich Engels. *The Communist Manifesto*. Edited by Samuel H. Beer. Arlington Heights, Ill.: Harlan Davidson, 1955.

Miller, Jean Baker. *Toward a New Psychology of Women*. Boston: Beacon Press, 1976.

Millett, Kate. *Sexual Politics*. Garden City, N.Y.: Doubleday, 1970.

Morgan, Robin, ed. *Sisterhood Is Powerful: An Anthology of Writings from the Women's Liberation Movement*. New York: Vintage Books, 1970.

Nasaw, David. *Schooled to Order: A Social History of Public Schooling in the United States*. Oxford: Oxford University Press, 1979.

Noddings, Nel. *Caring: A Feminine Approach to Ethics and Moral Education*. Berkeley: University of California Press, 1984.

——. *Philosophy of Education*. Boulder, Colo.: Westview Press, 1998.

Nussbaum, Martha C. *Cultivating Humanity: A Classical Defense of Reform in Liberal Education*. Cambridge, Mass.: Harvard University Press, 1997.

——. *Sex and Social Justice*. Oxford: Oxford University Press, 1999.

O'Barr, Jean, and Mary Wyer. *Engaging Feminism: Students Speak Up and Speak Out*. Charlottesville: University Press of Virginia, 1992.

Okin, Susan Moller, and respondents. *Is Multiculturalism Bad for Women?* Edited by Joshua Cohen, Matthew Howard, and Martha C. Nussbaum. Princeton, N.J.: Princeton University Press, 1999.

Okin, Susan Moller. *Justice, Gender, and the Family*. New York: BasicBooks, 1989.

Olyan, Saul M., and Martha C. Nussbaum, eds. *Sexual Orientation and Human Rights in American Religious Discourse*. New York: Oxford University Press, 1998.

Plato. *The Republic*. Edited by Allan Bloom. New York: HarperCollins, 1968.

Prado, C. G. *Starting with Foucault: An Introduction to Genealogy*. Boulder, Colo.: Westview Press, 1995.

Raymond, Janice G. *A Passion for Friends: Toward a Philosophy of Female Affection*. Boston: Beacon Press, 1986.

Rich, Adrienne. *Blood, Bread, and Poetry*. New York: W. W. Norton, 1986.

——. *Of Woman Born: Motherhood as Experience and Institution*. New York: W. W. Norton, 1986.

——. *On Lies, Secrets, and Silence*. New York: W. W. Norton, 1979.

Rorty, Richard. *Consequences of Pragmatism*. Minneapolis: University of Minnesota Press, 1982.

Rossi, Alice S., ed. *The Feminist Papers: From Adams to de Beauvoir*. Boston: Northeastern University Press, 1988.

Rousseau, Jean-Jacques. *Emile*. Translated by Allan Bloom. New York: Basic Books, 1979.

Sadker, Myra, and David Sadker. *Failing at Fairness: How Our Schools Cheat Girls*. New York: Simon and Schuster, 1994.

Sawicki, Jana. *Disciplining Foucault: Feminism, Power, and the Body*. New York: Routledge, 1991.

Schneir, Miriam. *Feminism in Our Time: The Essential Writings, World War II to the Present*. New York: Vintage Books, 1994.

Sedgwick, Eve Kosofsky. *Epistemology of the Closet*. Berkeley: University of California Press, 1990.

Smith, Barbara, ed. *Home Girls: A Black Feminist Anthology*. 1983. Reprint, New Brunswick, N.J.: Rutgers University Press, 2000.

Spring, Joel. *Deculturalization and the Struggle for Equality: A Brief History of the Education of Dominated Cultures in the United States*. New York: MacGraw-Hill, 1994.

Starr, Paul. *The Social Transformation of American Medicine: The Rise of a Sovereign Profession and the Making of a Vast Industry*. New York: Basic Books, 1982.

Stein, Arlene. *Sex and Sensibility: Stories of a Lesbian Generation*. Berkley: University of California Press, 1997.

Titone, Connie, and Karen E. Maloney, eds. *Thinking through Our Mothers: Women's Philosophies of Education*. Upper Saddle River, N.J.: Prentice Hall, 1999.

Tong, Rosemarie. *Feminist Thought: A Comprehensive Introduction*. Boulder, Colo.: Westview Press, 1989.

Tyack, David, and Elisabeth Hansot. *Learning Together: A History of Coeducation in American Schools*. New Haven, Conn.: Yale University Press, 1990.

Washington, Booker T. *Up from Slavery*. 1901. New York: Penguin Books, 1986.

Wear, Delese, ed. *The Center of the Web: Women and Solitude*. Albany: State University of New York Press, 1993.

Weeks, Jeffrey. *Invented Moralities: Sexual Values in an Age of Uncertainty*. New York: Columbia University Press, 1995.

——. *Sexuality and Its Discontents: Meanings, Myths, and Modern Sexualities*. New York: Routledge, 1999.

West, Cornel. *Race Matters*. New York: Vintage Books, 1993.

Wollstonecraft, Mary. *A Vindication of the Rights of Woman*. 1792. Reprint, London: Penguin Books, 1992.

Woolf, Virginia. *A Room of One's Own*. 1929. Reprint, San Diego: Harcourt Brace Jovanovich, 1981.

——. *Three Guineas*. San Diego: Harcourt Brace Jovanovich, 1938.

Young, Iris Marion. *Intersecting Voices: Dilemmas of Gender, Political Philosophy, and Policy*. Princeton, N.J.: Princeton University Press, 1997.

Articles

Beck, Clive. "Postmodernism, Pedagogy, and Philosophy of Education." *Philosophy of Education Society Yearbook 1993* (Urbana, Ill.: Philosophy of Education Society).

Birden, Susan. "Outside the Hippocratic Brotherhood: The Liberatory Education of the Boston Women's Health Book Collective." *Journal of Philosophy and History of Education* 50 (2000).

Birden, Susan, Linda L. Gaither, and Susan Laird. "The Struggle over the Text: Compulsory Heterosexuality and Educational Policy." *Educational Policy* 14, no. 5 (November 2000).

Bunch, Charlotte. "Beyond Either/Or Feminist Options." In *Building Feminist Theory: Essays from Quest*. New York: Longman, 1981.

Chase, Bob. "Keynote Address." Gay, Lesbian, and Straight Education Network National Conference, Chicago, October 7, 2000, available at http://traversearea.com/GLSEN/articles/art23.htm.

Covaleskie, John F. "Power Goes to School: Teachers, Students, and Discipline." *Philosophy of Education Society Yearbook 1993* (Urbana, Ill.: Philosophy of Education Society).

Ford, Maureen. "Dangerous Possibilities for Differently-Situated People in Foucault's Ethics." *Philosophy of Education Society Yearbook 1993* (Urbana, Ill.: Philosophy of Education Society).

———. "Willed to Choose: Educational Reform and Busno-power." *Philosophy of Education Society Yearbook 1995* (Urbana, Ill.: Philosophy of Education Society).

Freire, Paulo. "Reprint: Cultural Action for Freedom." *Harvard Educational Review* 68, no. 4 (1998).

GLSEN editorial. "Jackson Teens under Attack by Religious Extremists." GLSEN Online, November 24, 2000, at http://traversearea.com/GLSEN/articles/art35.htm.

Greene, Maxine. "The Plays and Ploys of Postmodernism." *Philosophy of Education Society Yearbook 1993* (Urbana, Ill.: Philosophy of Education Society).

Laird, Susan. "The Concept of Teaching: *Betsey Brown* vs. Philosophy of Education?" *Philosophy of Education 1988* (Urbana, Ill.: Philosophy of Education Society).

———. "The Ideal of the Educated Teacher: 'Reclaiming a Conversation' with Louisa May Alcott." *Curriculum Inquiry* 21, no. 3 (1991): 271–97.

———. "Teaching in a Different Sense: Alcott's Marmee." *Philosophy of Education 1993* (Urbana, Ill.: Philosophy of Education Society).

Leck, Glorianne. "Theory, Pedagogy, and Politics." *Philosophy of Education Society 1997* (Urbana, Ill.: Philosophy of Education Society).

Lerner, Sharon. "Christian Conservatives Take Their Antigay Campaign to the Schools," at GLSEN Online. (http://traversearea.com/GLSEN/articles/art63.htm).

Marshall, James D. "Education in the Mode of Information: Some Philosophical Considerations." *Philosophy of Education Society Yearbook 1996* (Urbana, Ill.: Philosophy of Education Society).

Mayo, Cris. "Foucauldian Cautions on the Subject and the Educative Implications of Contingent Identity." *Philosophy of Education Society Yearbook 1997* (Urbana, Ill.: Philosophy of Education Society).

McDonough, Kevin. "Overcoming Ambivalence About Foucault's Relevance for Education." *Philosophy of Education Society Yearbook 1993* (Urbana, Ill.: Philosophy of Education Society).

Nussbaum, Martha C. "The Hip Defeatism of Judith Butler." *New Republic*, February 22, 1999.

Pignatelli, Frank. "Dangers, Possibilities: Ethico-Political Choices in the Work of Michel Foucault." *Philosophy of Education Society Yearbook 1993* (Urbana, Ill.: Philosophy of Education Society).

Quon, Myron Dean. "Teachers under Fire: Educators Caught in the Cross-hairs of the Radical Right." GLSEN Online, at http://traversearea.com/GLSEN/articles/art27.htm.

Sears, James T. "Cultural Wars in a Southern Town." *Educational Policy* 14, no. 5 (November 2000).

Wilson, Robin. "Trangendered Scholars Defy Convention, Seeking to Be Heard and Seen in Academe." *Chronicle of Higher Education*. Accessed online at http://chronicle.com/colloquy/98/transgender/badkground.htm.

Index

About the Author

Susan Birden is Assistant Professor of Educational Foundations at the State University of New York College at Buffalo. Prior to completing her Ph.D. in Philosophical, Historical, and Social Foundations of Education at the University of Oklahoma, she was Director of Education for the University of Oklahoma Teaching Hospitals.